THE CATHOLIC UNIVERSITY OF AMERICA
STUDIES IN AMERICAN CHURCH HISTORY

VOL. 3

THE SOCIETY FOR THE PROPAGATION OF THE FAITH

Its Foundation, Organization and Success

(1822-1922)

AMS PRESS
NEW YORK

THE CATHOLIC UNIVERSITY OF AMERICA
STUDIES IN AMERICAN CHURCH HISTORY

Vol. III

THE SOCIETY FOR THE PROPAGATION OF THE FAITH

Its Foundation, Organization and Success

(1822-1922)

By

EDWARD JOHN HICKEY, S.T.B., M.B.A. (Harvard)

A DISSERTATION

Submitted to the Faculty of Philosophy of the Catholic
University of America in Partial Fulfilment of the
Requirements for the
Degree of Doctor of Philosophy

1922

Library of Congress Cataloging in Publication Data

Hickey, Edward John, 1893-
   The Society for the Propagation of the Faith.

   Reprint of the author's thesis, Catholic University
of America, 1922, which was issued as v. 3 of the
Catholic University of America. Studies in American
church history.
   Bibliography: p.
   1. Society for the propogation of the faith.
2. Catholic Church—Missions. I. Series: Catholic
University of America. Studies in American church
history, v. 3.
BV2155.S7H5 1974   266'.2   73-3557
ISBN 0-404-57753-9

Nihil Obstat. †*THOMAS J. SHAHAN, Censor Deputatus.*

Imprimatur. †*MICHAEL J. CURLEY, Archiepiscopus Baltimorensis.*

Baltimore, die XXVI Maii, 1922.

Reprinted from the edition of 1922, Washington D.C.
First AMS edition published, 1974
Manufactured in the United States of America

International Standard Book Number
Complete Set: 0-404-57750-4
Volume 3: 0-404-57753-9

AMS PRESS, INC.
New York, N.Y. 10003

1810499

CONTENTS

PREFACE

The American Church History Seminar at the Catholic University of America is not principally an informational course of study but a training ground in historical research by personal work on the part of the student guided by the professor. The work done comprises an introduction to the study of ecclesiastical history together with a special subject of research for each student. In this seminar the sources and materials for the study of American Church history necessarily receive special attention.

During my first year at the University, Dr. Guilday drew my attention to the study of those Foreign Mission societies which had so liberally contributed to the Church of the United States, and to their published collections of sources which were rich in historical material for our Church.

Since 1915, the Director of the Seminar has had the plan in mind of encouraging some of the students to devote themselves to a study of these published collections, and also to research-study in the archives of these Societies. His research year in the Archives of Propaganda impressed upon him the necessity of similar researches in the Archives of the Society for the Propagation of the Faith of Lyons and Paris, and in those of the Leopoldine Association of Vienna and the Ludwig-Missionsverein of Munich.

As a member of the Seminar during the scholastic year (1919-1920), and as Dr. Guilday's companion in Europe during the long vacation of 1920, I had splendid opportunities of following out his plan. Before departing, I consulted Mgr. Freri, the American Delegate of the Society for the Propagation of the Faith. I found him in cordial sympathy with the project, and he provided me with a letter to M. Alexandre Guasco, the General Secretary of the Central Council at Paris. I called upon M. Guasco in June, 1920, and was received with his customary urbanity. He permitted me to study in the office of the Central Council and facilitated my work with his direction which was of special value by virtue of his long acquaintance with the activities of the Society.

The *Annales de la Propagation de la Foi,* which have been published since the foundation of the Society in 1822, contain a very extensive collection of letters dealing with the Church in the United States. It was quite natural that these published documents should be studied first; and this study impressed upon me the fact that the unpublished material for any diocese in the United States or, indeed, for all the dioceses, was much more vast than scholars realize. At an early date I expressed this conviction to the General Secretary, but owing to various difficulties which arose I did not succeed in obtaining access to the unpublished documents until after the New Year, 1921.

Once begun on the work of sifting all this unpublished material, the subject became more difficult of treatment; for no one scholar could copy all the correspondence of the American bishops to the Society during the last hundred years. It would take an experienced secretary at least three years to copy all this material.

At first the *dossiers* containing the letters from the American dioceses were studied in alphabetical order. Later, this plan was abandoned in favor of the *dossiers* containing the letters from the fourteen American archdioceses, together with those from other dioceses evidently of considerable importance, either by virtue of their connection with the foundation of the Society or the length of years in which they had received aid from the Society, or on account of the conspicuous importance of some of their bishops.

Later, it developed that the correspondence from America before the years 1832-1838 did not exist in the Paris Archives. Hence the necessity arose of visiting Lyons with the hope of finding this material there. Owing to the danger that these archives would be confiscated by the Government at the time of the Associations Cultuelles (1906), all the documents had been packed in cases and shipped to Fribourg, Switzerland, where they still remained.

With gracious co-operation, M. Valerian Groffier, General Secretary of the Central Council of Lyons, was kind enough to go to Fribourg for the express purpose of finding this material for my thesis. The result was that I have the most important documents from 1822 to 1838, which have never been published in the *Annales*. Monseigneur Béchetoille, President of the Central Council of Lyons, gave me copies of valuable documents concerning Pauline-Marie Jaricot and the foundation of the Society.

After these letters had been procured, however, it became evident that additional material might be located in the archives of the Superior Council. These archives disappeared in the Revolution of 1830, and no trace of them remains. In order clearly to establish the relationship between the Society and the Sacred Congregation de Propaganda Fide it was necessary to visit Rome where Cardinal Van Rossum, the Prefect of the Congregation, made it possible for me to procure all the important data on this point.

From the outset, the plan had been to treat the Society's foundation, organization, administration and accomplishments in the world in an introductory chapter, and to confine to the body of the work the story of those results which could be traced to the financial aid the Society had given to the dioceses of the United States. The large number of dioceses which had received assistance from the Society and the length of years over which this assistance was distributed, together with the impossibility of transcribing all the documents regarding these dioceses rendered this plan far too extensive. Some limitation had to be devised. A geographical limitation was not satisfactory, because there could be very little connection between the story of the foundation of the Society and its results in any restricted part of the United States. A limit in time also involved a lack of proportion in the work, since there was a dearth of material for some dioceses and a large quantity for others. A suitable *terminus ad quem* might necessitate the selection of the First Plenary Council of Baltimore (1852), but this would require too lengthy a work for a doctoral dissertation. Even the arbitrary time limit of the first ten years involved many of these difficulties.

It was found necessary, before treating the results of the Society's contribution to America, to endeavor critically to clear up the mooted questions connected with the foundation of the Society. In addition to this, its end, its means, its organization, its development through the encouragement and cooperation of the Holy See and the Episcopate, its accomplishments in evangelization, in education and in works of charity, and its services to civilization and science, together with its allied activities, required a great deal of detailed exposition.

Moreover, coming as it does, in the centenary year of the Society, it was found desirable to give in these pages a general conspectus of the Society's accomplishments in the five continents of the world, and to postpone until later the story of its contribution to the American Church.

Grateful acknowledgment is due to Rev. Dr. Peter Guilday, my major professor, to whom I owe my historical training. It was only by virtue of his generous counsel, his direction and assistance, that I was enabled to complete this essay.

Special thanks are due to Monsignor Freri, whose kind encouragement and cooperation were necessary at every stage of the research and the composition.

In Paris the Central Council of the Society has for some forty years been under the direction of M. Alexandre Guasco, the General Secretary. Undoubtedly, this gentleman is better acquainted with every detail in connection with the history of this Society than any man living. After all these years of self-sacrificing service to the missionary cause, during which he has published a number of books on the subject, M. Guasco was the one person capable of directing this work. No doubt I caused a considerable amount of labor and worry to M. Guasco by my many months of work in his office. In the archives there were so many documents which had to be located and examined that a great deal of labor was involved. For all his courtesy I am deeply grateful.

Monseigneur Odelin, the President of the Central Council of Paris, as well as M. L. Geliner, M. Huffer and the Curé of St. Sulpice, who are members of this Council, are also deserving of my thanks.

A very particular expression of appreciation is due to Bishop Alfred Baudrillart, Rector of the Institut Catholique de Paris, Membre de l'Académie, who assisted me in gaining admission to the Society's archives; also to M. Louis Veuillot, who was ever ready and eager to aid me in any way in his power. The mere statement that I was living with the Veuillot family was often sufficient endorsement to obtain special consideration in my researches. M. Gaston Lacoin displayed a marked interest in the work and often aided it by his wise direction.

Professor Berger, of the École des Chartes, Membre de l'Institut, and the Secretary of the American Legation, and Mr. Hearn, head of the activities of the Knights of Columbus in France, aided me by their interest in the work.

Mlle. Violette Louzier, who for ten months labored conscientiously in the Archives of the Society in Paris and Lyons in translating and transcribing documents, is deserving of very special gratitude; her proficiency in English proved most helpful.

At Rome Monsignor O'Hern, Rector of the American College, took a cordial interest in my work. He advised me to consult Father Thomas Hughes, S. J., who has labored for some twenty years in the Roman Archives, and also to obtain an audience with Cardinal Van Rossum. The Cardinal Prefect of Propaganda listened very attentively to my request and only desired to be reassured in respect to my motive. Being satisfied with my purpose, he referred me to the Archivists of Propaganda, and I was permitted to study in the archives, although they were closed for the summer, and also to have photographed or copied any documents I might desire, after my departure. I wish to express my heartfelt gratitude to His Eminence Cardinal Van Rossum for his courtesy and kindness in thus permitting me to obtain access to much valuable source-material.

Father André assisted me in obtaining information, and Father Havey, Rector of the Sulpician Seminary at Washington, has aided me constantly by his counsel and advice.

In Louvain, Father De Ghellink, Librarian of the Jesuit House of Study, very kindly put all the books and collections in the library at my disposal. In Paris, Father Foley, C. M., arranged for me to have access to the *Annales de la Congregation de la Mission*.

I have the pleasure of adding a word here to express my sincere gratitude to the professors of the Catholic University of America for their direction in my graduate work.

CHAPTER I

THE HISTORICAL BACKGROUND

The Society for the Propagation of the Faith may be defined as an organization authorized by the Church for the purpose of maintaining and developing the Catholic Missions which have been established among non-Catholics throughout the world.

The object of the Society for the Propagation of the Faith is as old as the Church itself. In its actual form, however, the great French organization is but one hundred years old. In an account written some eighty years ago by Frederic Ozanam, who was at that time the Editor of the Society's *Annales,* we read that the beginnings of the "Oeuvre de la Propagation de la Foi" were, like so many Christian institutions, insignificant and obscure. Divine Providence, Ozanam says, often so prepares these beginnings that no one person can claim authorship and no human name receive the glory, since "He conceals and distributes their sources like those of large rivers of which it cannot be told from what stream they flow."[1] One of the chief difficulties in describing the origin of the Society for the Propagation of the Faith is the problem of ascertaining to whom, among those who had an actual share in its foundation, the major portion of the credit should be given.

---

1. *Notice sur l'Oeuvre la Propagation de la Foi,* in the *Mélanges* of FREDERIC OZANAM, t. II, pp. 23-26, Paris 1872; Cf. *Annales,* t. XLIV (1872), pp. 157-166; t. LII pp. 147-153; FRERI, *The Society for the Propagation of the Faith and the Catholic Missions.* New York, 1912, p. 5; FRERI, *The Society for the Propagation of the Faith and the Catholic Missions* in *Annals,* vol. LXXXV, March-April, 1922, p. 44. HENRION, *Histoire Générale des Missions Catholiques,* t. II, pt. ii, pp. 675, Lyons, 1850. LOUVET, *Les Missions Catholiques au XIX Siècle* p. 1a, Lyons, Paris, 1894.

As the years went by during the century of the Society's activity (1822-1922), the end and the purposes of the work naturally assumed broader and at the same time more detailed outlines. This fact makes it somewhat difficult to define in a few words the purpose of the Society. For example, in the original rules of 1822, we find the object of the Society defined as follows: "It has for its object to extend the Society of the Catholic faithful by aiding, by all the means in its power, the missionaries entrusted with spreading the light of the Faith in the foreign nations of the world."[2] In the revised rules of 1834 we read that the purpose of the Society is given as assistance by prayer and alms to Catholic missionaries entrusted with the preaching of the Gospel in the lands "beyond the seas."[3]

To reach a definition of strict accuracy special prominence must be given to the means which have been used from the beginning of the Society: namely, prayer and the offerings of the faithful in every part of the world. The definition of the Society, which finds a permanent place in its official publications, is as follows:

L'Oeuvre de la Propagation de la Foi est une oeuvre catholique ayant pour but d'aider, par la prière et les offrandes des fidèles, au maintien et au développement des missions catholiques dans les pays hérétiques, schismatiques, et infidèles.[4]

The birthday for the Society for the Propagation of the Faith was May 3, 1822. Consequently, this present year chronicles the rounding-out of a century of successful activity on the part of the Society.

---

2. *Extrait du Règlement de l'Association de la Propagation de la Foi* in the *Annales,* t. I, fasc. iii, p. 30; *ibid* t. I, fasc. VI, p. 93.

3. Supplement to *Annales, t.* VII, fasc. XXXVI, pp. 1-4.

4. Cf. *l'Oeuvre de la Propagation de la Foi; Dix Années d'Apostolat dans les Missions* (1898-1907), p. 5, Paris, 1908; *Propagation of the Faith* in the *Catholic Encyclopedia,* vol. XII, p. 461. The Society for the Propagation of the Faith is an international association for the assistance by prayers and alms-giving of Catholic missionary priests, brothers and nuns engaged in preaching the Gospel in heathen and non-Catholic countries. Cf. *Prospectus* of the Oeuvre, printed in Lyons, May, 1835, quoted by GUASCO, *L'Oeuvre de la Propagation de la Foi,* p. 15, 1911. This Society has for its object to procure for men eternal salvation, to substitute civilization for barbarism and to relieve innumerable misfortunes.

The fact that this year, 1922, is the tercentenary of the foundation of the Sacred Congregation de Propaganda Fide, brings into bold relief the splendid history of what has been done in its past by the Church for the propagation of the Gospel. It is worthy of note that very often the Sacred Congregation and the Society are confused in the minds of some historians.[5] There is without doubt an intimate relationship between these two organizations. The one which now is celebrating the three hundredth anniversary of its organization is naturally of greater importance, both because of its longer period of activity, and because it is one of the official ministries of the Church for the purpose of spreading the Faith. The principal end of the Congregation was to reconquer, by spiritual means—that is, by prayers and good works, by preaching and by catechising—the countries that had been lost to the Church through the Protestant revolt of the sixteenth century, and to organize into one compact corps the missionaries and the missionary enterprises necessary for this purpose. The Sacred Congregation had been in existence for two centuries when the Society for the Propagation of the Faith was founded; and the Holy See perceived in the French Society another, and as it has proved to be, a most important means of carrying out its great design. The Society, therefore, must not be confounded with the Sacred Congregation, although they bear similar names. To the credit of the French Society it may be said that without its assistance during the past hundred years the Sacred Congregation would have been seriously hampered in the work of directing, super-

---

5. Cf. GUILDAY, *The Sacred Congregation de Propaganda Fide* in the *Catholic Historical Review*, vol. VI, pp. 478-494, where a complete bibliography of Propaganda will be found. FRERI, *The Society, etc.*, p. 11, 1912: GUASCO, *Catholiques de France*, pp. 9-10, Lyons; GENNEVOISE, *La Propaganda* in the *Missions Catholiques*, 1874, t. VI, pp. 410-412, 427-430, 439-441, 450-452, 476, 487-488. LE ROY, *La Propaganda* in the *Missions Catholiques*, t. XXXVII, pp. 4-5, 15-17, 27-29, 44-47: HENRION, *op. cit.*, t. II, part i, pp. 245, et seq; LOUVET, *op. cit.*, pp. 22a-26a; *L'Oeuvre de la Propagation de la Foi*, pp. 106-108, Lyons, 1898.

vising and assisting the missionaries in those lands where heresy, schism and infidelity prevail.

We can well understand that many papal documents have come from Rome in praise of the French Society. It has been enriched with spiritual favors by every Pope who has reigned over the Church during the past hundred years. On December 3, 1880, for example, Pope Leo XIII signalized the activity of the Society by praising the abundant harvest it has made during its existence and the great Pope mentions in particular the cooperation between the Society and the Sacred Congregation in sustaining the work of the missionaries throughout the world. The Sacred Congregation from the beginning divided its work into two sections; one for the Missions of the Latin Rite and those of the Oriental Rites, and one for the maintenance of both. It is consequently the supreme missionary organization in the Church of God. The Society of the Propagation of the Faith has become, in the course of the past hundred years, its greatest auxiliary in this work.[6] Both have the world as their field of action; both receive monetary assistance from the faithful in all parts of the world; both assist the Missions wherever that assistance is necessary; but the Sacred Congregation, being one of the central administrative bodies of the Holy See, is the superior organization and retains the supreme administration of the missionary field. The highest honor conferred upon the Society for the Propagation of the Faith came in 1840, when Gregory XVI by the *Probe nostis* placed the Society in the rank of Universal Catholic Institutions, thus raising the Society to an eminence in the Church second only to the Sacred Congregation de Propaganda Fide.[7] As an international Catholic organization, with its home in Lyons and Paris, the Society for the Propagation of the Faith has

---

6. LEO XIII, Encyclical Letter *Sancta Dei Civitas*, of Dec. 3, 1880 in the *Annales*, t. LIII, pp. 79-94: *Missions Catholiques*, t. XII, pp. 613-618, 1880.

7. *Annales*, t. XII, pp. 603-615.

been one of the strongest bonds of union among the faithful of all nations during the century that has just passed.

To describe the activities and the accomplishments of the Society during the hundred years of its existence, the historian naturally will first seek for that history in the accounts published by the Society itself.[8] As we peruse these documents, one fact is common to them all: The work of the Society is viewed not as the result of a modern movement towards centralizing missionary endeavor, but is considered to be the culmination of all the missionary activity in the past history of the Church. For this reason those who have written concerning the Society trace its origin to the very beginning of the Church.

The work of spreading the Faith is as old as Christianity; and there is no exaggeration on the part of these writers when they find in the charge given by Christ to the Apostles: *Go ye into the whole world, and preach the Gospel to every creature*—the actual beginning of the institution known as the Society for the Propagation of the Faith. In the various *Notices* about the Society published in the *Annales*, in the official reports published at various times during the past hundred years, and in the short history of the Society by the present General Secretary, M. Alexandre Guasco, the entire history of the Propagation of the Faith from the time of Christ down to the foundation is regarded, and with historical justice, as a preparation for the Society itself.[9]

The great French Dominican, Monsabré, in a sermon preached at Lyons on March 20, 1891, in the name of the Society for the Propagation of the Faith, has given a permanent form to this idea.[10] He has divided the epoch preceding the actual foundation of the Society into three periods. The

---

8. In the final chapter of this work entitled *Critical Essay on the Sources*, these publications are described in detail.

9. GUASCO, *L'Oeuvre de la Propagation de la Foi* Paris, 1911.

10. MONSABRE, *Discours en faveur de l'Oeuvre de la Propagation de la Foi, prononcé dans l'Eglise primatiale de Lyon*, March 20, 1891, Lyons, 1891 (p. 32); Cf. LE ROY, *Discours prononcé au Congrès National de Paris*, Nov. 29, 1898, in the *Missions Catholiques*, t. XXX, supplement, pp. 1-7, 1898.

first period in the work of the Propagation of the Faith he calls the Apostolic Age. And he sees in the organization of the Church, in the growth of the priesthood and in the final triumph of the Christian Faith over the paganism of the Romano-Hellenic world the first conquest of the Faith. To this period belongs not only the work of the Apostles and Disciples who received their mission from Christ on Pentecost Sunday, but also the work of the great national missionaries, such as St. Patrick, St. Augustine of Canterbury, St. Boniface, Sts. Cyril and Methodius, and the other missionaries to the new European nations.

The second period commences with what Monsabré has called that of the official protectorate over the Missions by the Christian Governments of the middle ages. This period lasts down to the time of the French Revolution. In this second period the spiritual and temporal powers of the world coöperated in the work of establishing the Kingdom of God on earth. The rise of the monastic orders with their ever-increasing missionary activity is one of the outstanding facts in this period. It is true that the exercise of royal protection over the spread of the missionary work brought about certain difficulties between Church and State; and these conflicts have unfortunately cast too large a shadow over medieval civilization. In the earlier part of the middle ages certain inconveniences arose that hindered the success of the Missions; and no doubt a more definite means of coöperation between Church and State in the spread of Christian civilization would have been agreed upon, had not the Protestant Rebellion of the sixteenth century badly shattered the missionary work of the Church. We see one evidence of this in the foundation of the Sacred Congregation de Propaganda Fide in 1622, since its origin can be traced to a period anterior to the so called Counter-Reformation. For almost a century before the foundation of Propaganda, the Church of God had been blessed with the presence of a religious society founded for the express purpose of spreading the Faith in pagan lands. That the activities of the Society of Jesus were turned rather to the work of salvaging those parts of Christendom which had been lost to the Church in the debacle of the sixteenth century, is an added evidence to the fact of the permanency of Christian missionary ideals; and the presence, therefore, of this splendid phalanx of scholars and missionaries, directed by the Sacred Congregation, enables us to understand how, little by little, there would grow up within the Church the idea of an organization which would centralize the interest of the Catholic laity throughout the world in the work of propagating the Faith. This second period ends with the outbreak of the French Revolution.

At the close of the eighteenth century, side by side, with the cleavage from the older form of government, there went a demoralization of Christian institutions. In the suppression of the Society of Jesus, in the dispersal of the religious orders, and in the spread of revolutionary principles, the work of the Apostolate, while not abandoned, was nevertheless paralyzed for the time being. One fact was certain, namely, that the period of union and protection, in which the political powers of Europe coöperated with the Church for the spread of Christianity, was over. But the hand of God was not weakened. The Pope, ever erect, pointed out to the Apostles of the Faith the new worlds which had to be conquered and the old worlds which had to be regained to God. No longer could the Papacy depend upon the governments of Europe for its sacred work. Consequently, the cry of the Holy See went out to the people. No new note needed to be struck. The message given was one which carried the memories of the faithful back to the early ages of the Church when, side by side with the Apostles and Disciples, could be found the faithful laymen and laywomen ready and anxious to assist in the conquest for Christ." The inspiration which crystallized this sentiment created the third and present period of the ideal for which the Society for the Propagation of the Faith stands. After a century of experience, the Society can look back on the years of its ac-

---

11. MONSABRE, *ut supra,* p. 15.

tivity and can well realize that its courageous acceptance of the task of rehabilitating the Missions of the world has never once slackened in that time.

Monsignor Freri has given us a summary of these three periods, in his recent story of the Society:

> The first was the period, properly apostolic, the age of special divine manifestation in behalf of the Propagation of the Faith. During this period the apostles and their first successors preached throughout the world; their missionary needs were supplied by divine assistance, by miracles and by the responsive devotion inspired in their early converts.
>
> The second period was that of union and protectorship; that is to say, the temporal powers of the world united to establish the Kingdom of Jesus Christ. The era of bloody persecution had closed, the Church was victorious and the Caesars bowed their heads in submission to receive the yoke of the cross; emperors, kings and republics cooperated with the Church in preaching the Christian faith.
>
> The third period of the work of the Propagation of the Faith is the one in which we are living. It began with the XIX Century. The impiety of the XVIII Century had already dealt a mortal blow to a number of flourishing missions, when the terrible revolutions which marked the end of this sad epoch effected a radical change in the religious attitude even of European nations that had remained faithful to the Catholic religion.
>
> From this moment their action was distinct from that of the Church, which they henceforth considered an outside and sometimes rival power. They were no longer to be depended upon for the extension of the Kingdom of God on earth. The period of union and protectorship was over. Then Providence substituted the people for kings. Catholic missions no longer directly supported by sovereigns were maintained by the people. Rich and poor were called to the honor of supporting missionaries of the Gospel and contributing to the development of the Catholic religion in all climes.
>
> Several societies were founded during the course of the last hundred years to give form and organization to the charity of the faithful in behalf of missions, but most of them have either a limited aim or assist missionaries of a certain nationality alone. The only one truly universal, is the Society for the Propagation of the Faith, which furnishes the principal support for the Catholic Apostolate.[12]

---

12. Freri, *op. cit.*, pp. 3-4, 1912; pp. 43-44, 1922.

Few Catholics are ignorant of the history of the Church's missionary activity; and yet few know its history in any adequate way. Many think, as Bishop Le Roy has pointed out, that the world was converted at the time of Constantine; while others consider the Missions solely in the light of their political influence in the lands where they exist.[13] But the rôle of the Catholic missionaries is the continuance of the work of the Apostles, and the history of the Missions is equivalent to the external history of the Church. The Society for the Propagation of the Faith does not constitute an independent branch of this missionary activity, but it combines into one organized corporation the assistance given by the faithful for the necessary prosecution of the missionary work of the Church.

To tell the story of the foundation of the Society for the Propagation of the Faith, and to describe its accomplishments in the last hundred years is a work that must appeal not only to the historian but to all those who see in its success another proof of Christ's presence in His Church. What Guasco has done for French readers, Monsignor Freri, the National Director of the Society in the United States, has done for the English-speaking world; and with these two little volumes before us, together with the *Annales* and the numerous documents and pamphlets which it has been our pleasure to collect, the progress of the Society from 1822 to 1922 can be told in that fulness of detail which must bring delight to the thousands in this country who have assisted in promoting the work and in helping the Society to be truly universal in its support of the Catholic Apostolate.

13. Le Roy, *Discours, etc.,* p. 1.

CHAPTER II

The Foundation of the Society

Looking backward through the hundred years of the existence of the Society, we are cognizant of a singular fact that cannot help causing considerable regret to the historical student. The unusual mass of published material for the story of its activity is in reality but a portion of the documentary sources which still need to be analyzed before a complete history of the Society can be attempted. Scarcely any aspect of its work, either of a religious, scientific, or literary nature, has been neglected by the writers who have preceded us; and one has but to glance over the voluminous historical notes in the *Annales* which have now passed their ninety-fourth volume, the works of Louvet and of Henrion who have treated the story of the Catholic Missions in detail, to realize how truly magnificent a past belongs to this great French Catholic organization.[1]

But the regret remains; for the most interesting period of all is the period of the origin of the Society, and in spite of all that has been published on this subject, we are still unable to describe its beginnings with that certainty of historical fact which is demanded by modern scientific methods. The truth is, or seems to be, that the Society is the result of an amalgam of many ideas and ideals, many plans and aspirations. There were the preliminary work of Mlle. Jaricot, and the preliminary plans of Mme. Petit; and there was the successful effort at a combination of these two movements by M. Benoît Coste, who also deserves to be numbered among the founders.

Around these three names, then, in particular, must be centred the story of the Society's origin. All three of them —Jaricot, Petit and Coste, belonged to the city of Lyons.

---

1. Louvet, *op. cit.*; Henrion, *op. cit.*

And around them may be grouped the many others who must be mentioned in the story, since all furnished plans and ideas at the outset of the work. For example, the story of Mlle. Pauline-Marie Jaricot would be incomplete without the names of her brother, Philéas Jaricot, who was a student for the priesthood at St. Sulpice, in Paris, when Pauline was originating her Society, of M. l'Abbé Chaumont, Director of the Séminaire des Missions Étrangères, at Paris, a friend of Philéas Jaricot, of M. le Curé Gourdiat, of the Church of St. Polycarp, Lyons, who encouraged Pauline through her earliest difficulties with the ecclesiastical authorities, of Mlle. Sophie David, an active worker in the Society, and of M. l'Abbé Girodon, a layman at the time of the Society's foundation, upon whom Mlle. Jaricot depended for direction and assistance.

Around the romantic figure of Mme. Petit, the saddened refugiée of San Domingo, the two chief figures are the American Bishops, Flaget of Bardstown and Du Bourg of New Orleans. There are also M. l'Abbé Cholleton, Director of the Seminary of Saint Irenaeus, of Lyons, the friend of Du Bourg, the notorious Father Inglesi, whose meteoric and unsaintly career in the United States has marred his glory as a founder of the Society, and M. Didier Petit de Meurville, who called the meeting of May 3, 1822, at which the Society was founded, and whose influence in the final organization was a preponderant one.

The third figure is that of M. Benoît Coste, a silk merchant of Lyons, who saw the grave risk both Mlle. Jaricot and Mme. Petit ran in failing at the outset to make their work universal in character and in scope. To him, probably, belongs the credit for inspiring both groups with the ideal of a truly universal society for all the Missions in the world.

These, then, are the chief personages in the story of the Society's origin, and around them has centred for almost a hundred years the rather interesting controversy: *Whose was the original idea of the Society of the Propagation of the Faith as it exists today?*

There was more than one attempt at an organization similar in design to that of the Society before the birth of Pauline-Marie Jaricot at Lyons on July 22, 1799. Although Mlle. Jaricot has been given the credit for founding the Society for the Propagation of the Faith in most of the popular literature on that subject, several different attempts were made before her time to organize a confraternity for the same purpose. Henrion, in his history of the Missions, speaks of a Society founded by a Capuchin, Father Hyacinthe, in 1632, at Paris, under the title "Congregation of the Exaltation of the Holy Cross." Its purpose was the Propagation of the Faith in Protestant lands and for the promotion of the Sacrament of Confirmation among Catholic children.[2] In one of his reports on the origin of the Society written in 1842, Ozanam, who was then editor of the *Annales,* tells a story of a certain Father Paulmyer, a canon of the Cathedral of Bayeux, who wrote for Pope Alexander VII, 1663, *Mémoires touchant l'éstablissement d'une Mission dans le troisiéme monde autrement appelé la terre australe,* indicating the means of establishing an association formed on the model of the East India Company under the direction of a group of persons who knew the East and who would spread the Faith in that part of the world.[3] The essential point of his project was that everyone, rich and poor, high and low, should be asked to contribute a small amount to the work.

A still further project was proposed by the Superiors of the Seminary for Foreign Missions at Paris. This Society was founded about the middle of the seventeenth century for the purpose of training a clergy who would go directly to infidel countries for the work of the Gospel. The Seminary is not a religious order, but a society of secular priests who are sent to China, Japan and India for missionary labors. The Seminary itself is one of the best known projects of its

---

2. HENRION, *op. cit.,* t. II, part ii, p. 675.
3. OZANAM, *Notice sur L'Oeuvre de la Propagation de la Foi,* in *Mélanges,* pp. 25-26; *Annales,* t. XV, p. 170, 1843; Cf. GUASCO, *op. cit.,* p. 13.

kind and the thought of forming a society of auxiliaries who would assist it in meeting the vast expenses necessary to carry on the work was first explained as early as 1665, when the Bishop of Heliopolis petitioned Rome for the approbation of such a confraternity which was to be known as the Confraternity of the Holy Apostles.[4] The prelate does not appear to have been successful in organizing a distinct society, but on through the seventeenth and eighteenth centuries the Catholic faithful of France had been made cognizant of the work of the Seminary by means of pamphlets on the Foreign Missions.

The first Association of Prayers and Good Works for the salvation of the infidels dates, as far as can be ascertained, from the end of the eighteenth century.[5] It is known that in 1780 a brochure on this Association was being spread broadcast throughout France. The members of this Associa-

---

4. HENRION, *op. cit.*, p. 675; Cf. *Mémoire Historique sur les Constitutions de la Congrégation des Missions Etrangères*, pp. 6, 16, 17, especially 8, 117.

5. LAUNAY, *Histoire de la Société des Missions Étrangères*, t. II, pp. 500, et seq.: ''The first association of prayers and good works for the salvation of the infidels, as it was called, dates at least, as we know it, from the end of the XVIII century. We are ignorant of the precise epoch of its foundation and the name of him who had the idea of it, but we know that in 1780 a brochure was circulated which explained the end and practices of the association. This brochure existed in the archives of the Séminaire des Missions Étrangères of Paris in 1799; it was rediscovered in 1816. Here is a résumé of the rules it contained: The associates must daily recite the prayers of St. Francis Xavier: *Aeterne rerum,* and of St. Bernard: *Memorare O Piisima,* on every Friday they must offer their good works to obtain by the merits of the passion of our Saviour Jesus Christ, the conversion of the infidels. Every year at six determined masses, they must communicate, if they were poor, or have them celebrated or celebrate them themselves if they were rich. They had no formality to observe, they were not inscribed on any list and they had no offerings to contribute. The first association which consisted only in the recitation of common prayers and in zeal for the missions disappeared during the Revolution. L'Abbé Chaumont frequently published brochures containing letters of missionaries and soliciting alms. In the expose of the condition and of the needs of the missions which he published in 1816, he explained a practice which had long been employed by the 'Anabaptists' in England. They formed associations called auxiliary societies by means of which all classes of citizens, even the poorest, by laying aside a cent or two each week for this object have the satisfaction of contributing to the progress of the Gospel.''

tion met every day to recite prayers for the conversion of the infidels; they received Holy Communion six times a year, and while they had no definite offering to give as a contribution, there is no doubt that some help was given of this nature. Father Chaumont, Superior of the Seminary for Foreign Missions, published in 1816, a pamphlet describing the conditions and the needs of the Foreign Missions, and suggested that it would be a splendid practice if the Catholics would imitate certain Protestant Societies in England, the members of which put aside a penny or two every week for this object.[6] As is well known, in several of the large cities of England, such as London, Liverpool, Plymouth and Bristol, Protestant associations of this kind had been founded in the seventeenth century for the purpose of helping Protestant Missions and it was a customary thing for them to have on display in the various shops in the town small boxes for alms, such as we are quite accustomed to in our day.

In 1817 the directors of the Seminary for Foreign Missions published a pamphlet having for its title: *Association of Prayers to ask of God the conversion of infidels, the perseverance of Christians who lived in the midst of them and the prosperity of establishments destined to Propagate the Faith.*[7]

---

6. Cf. GUASCO, *op. cit.*, p. 20; *Annales*, t. I, fasc. vi, pp. 92-93; 1825; *Encyclopedia Brittanica,* vol. XVIII, pp. 586-587, London, LAUNAY, *op. cit.*, t. II, p. 500.

7. LAUNAY, *op. cit.*, t. II, pp. 500, et seq.: The practices of the association are determined with precision and clarity; in the parishes where the associates are numerous, it recommends that they choose one among them as chief who will inscribe their names and have the associates meet to recite in common the prayers indicated. These prayers for the most part are the same as those prescribed in 1780, the prayer of St. Francis Xavier: *Aeterne rerum,* that of St. Bernard to the Blessed Virgin: *Memorare O Piisima,* which could be replaced by three *Paters* and *Aves.* Every Monday the associates recite a *De Profundis* or a *Pater* and an *Ave* for the repose of the souls of the defunct associates; the priests celebrate at least one mass each year for the same intentions. The principal feasts of the association are the Epiphany, Pentecost, St. Joseph and St. Francis Xavier. The Christians are exhorted to go to confession and communion on the day of admission into the association.

The Secretary of Propaganda was willing to present personally to the Sovereign Pontiff the résumé of the supplication which the directors of the Seminary had written on this subject. * * * * By an indult of Nov.

The means employed were prayer and almsgiving. Every Monday the Associates would recite certain prayers for the repose of the souls of departed members; priests were asked to celebrate at least one Mass a year for that purpose; and the members were exhorted to go to Holy Communion the day of their entry into the Association. By an indult of November 30, 1817, Pius VII approved the Association and granted it certain indulgences. This Association was evidently an advance over that of 1780 and it soon began to gain members. At the same time Abbé Langlois, one of the Superiors of the Seminary for Foreign Missions, began to publish the news of the Foreign Missions in a small booklet. These letters appeared from 1818-1823 and were later published in book form under the title *Nouvelles Lettres Édifiantes;* the series contained many other letters of the period anterior to 1818, and caused a considerable amount of new interest in the Missions.[8]

About this time Phileas, the brother of Pauline-Marie, entered the Seminary of Saint-Sulpice in order to complete his studies for the priesthood.[9] This was probably in 1820. There had been considerable correspondence between himself and his sister on the subject of a Society which she had founded among pious servant girls who were known as the "Réparatrices du Sacré Coeur de Jésus Christ." After his en-

---

30, 1817, Pius VII approved the association, accorded to its members a plenary indulgence each year on the feasts of the Epiphany, Pentecost, St. Joseph and St. Francis Xavier and a partial indulgence of one hundred days each time they recite the prescribed prayers. An encouraging letter from Cardinal Litta in the name of Propaganda accompanied this indult.

8. LAUNAY, *ut supra.*

9. GUASCO, *op. cit.,* pp. 19-20; MAURIN, *Vie Nouvelle de Pauline-Marie Jaricot,* p. 91, Paris 1892. Phileas Jaricot was very young when he manifested his desire to be an apostle. After having passed ten months at the Séminaire de Ste-Foy-L'Argentière, he entered the Séminaire de Saint-Sulpice in 1820. From this solitude, he continued the conversations concerning the necessities of the distant missions, by letter and excited the zeal of the *Réparatrices* and consoled Pauline when her work met with opposition. He was ordained to the priesthood on Dec. 21, 1823. His health was poor and he became chaplain of the Hotel Dieu. He died at the age of thirty-three years on February 26, 1830.

trance into Saint-Sulpice he continued his interest in the work of his sister and began to secure coöperation in a plan that he had for assisting the Seminary of Foreign Missions which he was in the habit of visiting. By this time Pauline-Marie had fairly well developed her plan of a new society.

Pauline-Marie Jaricot was born at Lyons on July 22, 1799, the seventh child of Antoine Jaricot and Jeanne Lattier, his wife. . Her life has been written by Maurin, a popular edition of which appeared at Paris in 1892.[10] At the age of seventeen she began to lead a life of unusual self-sacrifice and mortification, and on Christmas Day, 1816, she took a vow of perpetual virginity. Through the Society of the Sacred Heart of Jesus she succeeded in ameliorating the moral conditions of many of the young girls of Lyons and it was with the members of this pious society that she formed her first nucleus for the Propagation of the Faith. It was in the midst of this spiritual activity that the suggestion from her brother, Phileas, reached her and she immediately began to form a society among her intimate friends, whom she divided into groups of ten and from whom she asked the small sum of a penny-a-week for the Foreign Missions.[11] The plan of this organization was sent in 1819 or 1820 by Philéas to M. l'Abbé

---

10. MAURIN, *ut supra;* GUASCO, *op. cit.,* pp. 17-20.
11. Letters from Philéas and from l'Abbé Victor Girodon agree that the idea of a cent-a-week came from the Séminaire des Missions-Étrangéres through Philéas and the brochures of the associations of prayers sent out by the Directors. Victor Girodon gathered together a number of important letters bearing upon the activities of the founders of the Society into a cahier entitled: *Fondation de l'Oeuvre de la Propagation de la Foi.* Monseigneur Béchetoille, President of the Central Council of Lyons, loaned me this cahier with the assurance that it contained true copies of the documents that had been sent to Rome for the cause of beatification of Mlle. Pauline-Marie Jaricot. Launay says: ''She had known the Séminaire des Missions Étrangères through reading the relations of missionaries, the statutes of associates of prayers and the urgent appeals addressed to the Catholics by l'Abbé Chaumont and l'Abbé Langlois. The ardent soul of Mlle. Jaricot was touched by these sad accounts and she understood that organization was lacking in the new association and she insistently asked God that she be enlightened on that point.''

Langlois of the Seminary of Foreign Missions.[12] It is this fact which has given to Mlle. Jaricot the popular title of foundress of the Society for the Propagation of the Faith. In the notebook of one of the priests of St. Polycarp at Lyons we read: "When I was an assistant at the Church of St. Polycarp at Lyons I undertook to trace the origin of the Society for the Propagation of the Faith of Christ at this time (1867-68) there were still living certain members of the first group formed by Pauline-Marie. I visited them and endeavored to gather all the traditions which they had. I am convinced that this wonderful Society had a very singular origin and that it is difficult to distinguish the traditions and the actual history."[13] One point which seems impossible to clear up is the question of the cent-a-week system. It is true that Pauline-Marie denied any connection between the Protestant method and her own, and it is quite possible that the idea arose in her own mind independently. In Maurin's Life it is related that she was seated one evening in her study endeavoring to decide upon a plan for her work. The idea of groups of ten arose quite unconsciously in her mind and after reflection she realized that the groups of ten persons might be extended to groups of a hundred and to groups of a thousand, who would all send their funds to a common center.[14] She traced this plan on a piece of paper and then talked it over with one of the priests of Lyons. Pauline-Marie communicated this idea to Philéas, who placed it before the Seminary of Foreign Missions, and it was immediately commended by them as an excellent system. Pauline's brother-in-law was manager of a silk factory at Saint-Vallier and she proposed to the workmen in the factory and in the little town itself that they form them-

---

12. Cf. Victor Girodon, cahier on the *Fondation de l'Oeuvre de la Propagation de la Foi*. One letter of Alphonse Girodon dated 1880 claims Phileas was the intermediary between Pauline and the Séminaire des Missions Étrangères in 1819. Other letters in the same cahier such as that of Mlle. Sophie David state it was 1820. The earliest letter from Phileas written in Paris is dated April 15, 1820.

13. *Traditions concernant le question* in the cahier of Victor Girodon, *op. cit.*

14. Maurin, *op. cit.*, p. 94; Masson, *Pauline-Marie Jaricot*, p. 32, Lyons 1899; Guasco, *op. cit.*, p. 20.

selves into groups of ten for the purpose of assisting the Foreign Missions. This was probably in 1820. The difficulty of regulating the organization among the working people at this distance from her home led her to ask a young man in the employ of her brother-in-law to guide the Society. This young man, Victor Girodon, later entered the Seminary and became a priest.[15]   Around his name must be centered much of the early history of the Society. It was Girodon who was present at the meetings in May, 1822, at Lyons, when the present Society for the Propagation of the Faith was founded and he represented Pauline-Marie and her work.

We have now to chronicle a distinctly separate organization which was assuming different shape about this time, also in Lyons, some years before the birth of Pauline-Marie. Didier Petit de Meurville lost his father and maternal uncle in the general massacre of the whites by the negroes during the revolution of San Domingo in 1794. Mme. Petit, his mother, left San Domingo with her two children and came to Baltimore. She had lost her fortune and being obliged to earn her own living, opened a school for young girls in that city. She became acquainted with Father Louis Du Bourg, who was born in San Domingo in 1766. He entered the Seminary of

---

15. MAURIN, *op. cit.*, p. 108; GUASCO, *op. cit.*, p. 21; VICTOR GIRODON, in the cahier has given these details in letters from Philéas to Pauline, dated April 15, 1820; and from Girodon to Terret: ''My uncle (Victor Girodon) entered with ardor into the new association, he brought to it that spirit of exactitude and continued effort which solidly establishes and maintains. She (Mlle. Jaricot) had the plans and the initiative; it remained for him to put them into execution and to develop them. He continued the relations with Philéas, obtained more frequent and more important communications, and even some printed notices which he circulated among his groups of ten.'' The membership soon rose to one thousand which though a considerable number was not likely to increase owing to the narrow scope of the influence of the first associates. The first offerings amounted to 1,439 francs which were sent to the Séminaire des Missions Étrangères in 1820 and 1821. ''Ecclesiastical authority was indeed far from being favorable to it (the work of Mlle. Jaricot) and often the voice of the pastors was raised from the pulpit of the Chartreux at St. Nizier, against this new, almost unknown work which had not been approved by superiors, and which tended to replace works that were far more ancient and of proven utility.'' L'Abbé Gourdiat encouraged Pauline and he centralized the collections and delivered them to the Séminaire des Missions Étrangères at Paris.

Saint-Sulpice at Paris and was ordained there in 1788, and was Superior of the Seminary of Issy when the French Revolution drove him from France. The year of the massacre in San Domingo he came to Baltimore, where he was welcomed by Bishop Carroll.[16] It was not long before Mme. Petit sought him out and no doubt during the years he spent in Baltimore he proved himself a worthy director of the Petit family.[17] A most careful search has failed to reveal the correspondence which probably passed between Mme. Petit and Father Du Bourg after her return to France.[18] In 1803 Mme. Petit's family encouraged her to return to Lyons and she crossed the Atlantic in the summer of that year with the party of Sulpicians who had been recalled to France by Superior-General

16. MIGNE, *Encyclopédie Théologique, Dictionnaire des Missions Catholiques*, t. 1, pp. 441-446; *The Metropolitan Catholic Almanac and Laity's Directory for the Year of Our Lord* 1839, pp. 50-68.

17. CLARKE, in his *Lives of the Deceased Bishops of the Catholic Church in the United States*, Vol. 1, pp. 204-238. New York, 1888, says: "Baltimore received her share of these afflicted fugitives and extended a generous welcome to them. Mr. Du Bourg, himself a native of St. Domingo, felt the warmest sympathy for his scattered countrymen, and, though greatly occupied with his cares and duties at St. Mary's College, he devoted himself to their relief. Homeless and penniless, they were provided with shelter and support, and their spiritual wants especially received from him the most generous and heroic attention. To the more humble and afflicted colored people he especially devoted himself, and with the aid of the Rev. John Tessier, who had been Superior of St. Mary's Seminary, he gathered them together in a congregation, and assembled them regularly for divine service in the lower chapel of St. Mary's.

The most brilliant and fruitful service rendered by Bishop Du Bourg to the Church, not only in America, but throughout the most remote and unenlightened portions of the world, was the leading part he took in the foundation of the illustrious "Association for the Propagation of the Faith." It has been well said that "the establishment which Mr. Du Bourg, while on his return to Louisiana from Italy, made at Lyons, is of itself enough to immortalize his name. He there formed in 1815, the Association for the Propagation of the Faith."

18. FOIK, *Catholic Archives of America*, in the *Catholic Historical Review*, vol. I, p. 64, 1915, says: "Another case where priceless documents went to decay occurred in New Orleans. When the Federal troops threatened to destroy that city most of the papers of Bishop Penalver, Bishop Du Bourg and others were concealed in a fireplace and bricked up. After General Butler had been in possession of New Orleans for some time the wall was removed, and then it was found that no one had thought to close the chimney at the top; the rain had poured down and the papers were a mass of pulp."

Father Emery.[19]   Mme. Petit never forgot the generous hospitality of the country which had received her after her terrible trials in San Domingo.   She kept up a correspondence with many of the missionaries of the United States and in particular with Father Flaget, who was to become Bishop of Bardstown, Kentucky, in 1808, and with Father Du Bourg who was consecrated Bishop of New Orleans at Rome in 1815.[20]

Before returning to the United States after his consecration, Bishop Du Bourg came to Lyons to renew his acquaintance with his friends and in particular with Mme. Petit, whose splendid character and profound Christian piety had always appealed to him.   His diocese, as he explained to Mme. Petit, was larger than France, extending from the Gulf of Mexico to the Canadian Border.   Help was needed badly if the Church in that vast region was to be given a proper start. He asked her, therefore, to found a charitable association for the spiritual needs of Louisiana and suggested that she

---

19. Cf. TESSIER, *Diary.*
20. OZANAM, *Notice, etc., op. cit.,* p. 28; *L'Oeuvre de la Propagation de la Foi,* p. 11, 1898; *ibid.,* pp. 11-12, 1908; FRERI, *op. cit.,* p. 5, 1912; *ibid.,* in *Annals,* vol. LXXXV, pp. 44-45, 1922; GUASCO, *op. cit.,* pp. 15-16, 1911; *Compte Rendu de* 1871, in *Annales,* t. XLIV, 1872, pp. 158-159, *Origines de l'Oeuvre de la Propagation de la Foi,* in the *Annales,* t. L, pp. 345-346; *Notice sur la Fondation de l'Oeuvre de la Propagation de la Foi,* in the *Annales,* t. LII, pp. 148-149, HENRION, *op. cit.,* t. II, part ii, pp. 675-676; LOUVET, *op. cit.,* p. 2a. The following is an excerpt from a letter of Mgr. Du Bourg to the Cardinal Prefect of Propaganda, from the *Catholic Historical Review,* vol. IV, p. 68:

Paris, Mar. 29, 1817.
If meanwhile I went to Paris, I take God to witness, it was in no way for the purpose of winning the good graces of the Royal family, or for any human advantage, but solely for the spiritual benefit of my poor Diocese. Indeed, I went not only to Paris, but also to Belgium to secure everywhere I could both active laborers and help of every kind, and thank God my efforts were not fruitless.

For besides the thirteen men already arrived in my Diocese (among whom are Fathers De Andreis, Rosat and Acquaroni, of the Roman House of the Mission. Flaveau Rossi and Aloysius Bighi, of the Roman College) twenty and more ecclesiastics are ready to sail with me, with whose help we will be able to provide in some way for the foundation of the Seminary and the personnel of the missions. Moreover with regard to the expense, His Most Christian Majesty will furnish a ship, the Princess and some good Christians, money and a supply of sacred utensils—a very nice liberality in the present straightened circumstances.

form a group of ladies and gentlemen who would guarantee
a stipulated amount regularly for the maintenance of his
mission. Mme. Petit had already sent many articles for missionary purposes to Baltimore and she entered into the idea
of the bishop with her wonted enthusiasm. Among those
whom she had interested was M. Benoît Coste, a merchant of
Lyons.[21] She appealed to all her friends, who were among the
wealthy and noble class of the city. Very little is known
about the success of her labors, but it is certain that her organization, which seems to have been without a name, was
partially successful.[22] M. Coste had endeavored to influence
her in the idea of a truly catholic society that is the foundation of a society which would embrace the entire world and
would assist the Missions in all parts of Christendom. Father
Cholleton, the Superior of the Seminary at Lyons, an intimate
friend of Bishop Du Bourg, was called into counsel but found
the very idea of one large society too vast an undertaking.[23]

---

21. *Notice sur la Fondation de l'Oeuvre de la Propagation de la
Foi*, in the *Annales*, t. L, p. 151.

22. Mme. Petit endeavored to establish a permanent organization
with a fixed annual contribution of one or two francs per year. Through
her social position and the personal influence she exercised Mme. Petit
was enabled to give more and more efficacious aid to the Bishops of
New Orleans and Bardstown. This aid chiefly comprised sacred vessels,
ornaments and the product of collections. Mlle. Jaricot made her
collections among the working class whereas Mme. Petit collected from
the well-to-do class.

23. GUASCO, *op. cit.*, p. 17, 1911. While Bishop Du Bourg
remained in Lyons, he lived at the Seminary of St. Irenaeus, of which
l'Abbé Cholleton was the Director. Bishop DuBourg gave two ordina-
tions, blessed the statue of St. Irenaeus, and gave confirmation in several
places. At the time of his death, several notices gave him the credit
for the foundation of the Society. The *Annales* (t. VII, p. 101), states:
"We simply remark that Mgr. Du Bourg is by no means the founder
of the Association for the Propagation of the Faith. The interest which
his mission inspired had no doubt great influence upon those who did
establish the Society; hence it was founded in part for him, but not
at all by him." The *Dictionnaire de Théologie Catholique*, in an article
by l'Abbé GABRIEL ANDRE, *Amérique (Etats Unis d')* Catholicisme,
p. 1056, states: "To Mgr. Du Bourg is indirectly due the establishment
of the Propagation of the Faith. The plan which he formed on his
visit to Lyons on his return from Rome in 1815, of an association of
women to provide for the needs of his vast diocese, was the occasion of
the Society" L'Abbe Cholleton was made honorary Vicar-General of
New Orleans by Bishop Du Bourg. Many interesting letters concerning

The very grandeur of such a design seems to have frightened Mme. Petit, but Coste continued repeating his own interpretation of the work and the result was that the two groups at Lyons, finding that their designs were similar, became known to each other.

Towards the end of the year 1822 Father Inglesi, the Vicar-General of Bishop Du Bourg of New Orleans, came to France on a mission from his superior.[24] After a few days in Paris he traveled to Lyons to visit Mme. Petit and take up with her the project of organizing a more compact society for the purpose of assisting the Missions of his diocese. By his own distinguished manners and the charm of his personality the young Italian priest very quickly gained the sympathy of all. In the name of Bishop Du Bourg he entered the higher circles of society of Paris and even won the good will of Louis XVIII and his court. The three days which he passed at Lyons were spent in discussing the plans with Mme. Petit and her son, and after his return from the Congress of Leybach (April, 1822), he went to Lyons to complete the plans for his organization. M. Didier Petit, the son of Mme. Petit, called together a few of his friends to discuss the project of Father Inglesi.[25] Among these was Benoît Coste, who had already been assisting Pauline-Marie Jaricot in her work of gathering funds for the Foreign Missions. He gave the meetings of May 3, 1822, its distinctly universal phase, he himself had for many years aided in organizing a society for the American Missions, but he was emphatic in his decision

---

the founders are to be found in VICTOR GIRODON, cahier sur *La Fondation,* etc.

24. OZANAM, op. cit. p. 29; OZANAM, *Compte Rendu de* 1871 in *Annales,* t. XLIV, 1872, p. 160; *Origines,* etc. in *Annales,* t. L, p. 317, *L'Oeuvre,* ibid. p. 13, 1898; ibid. p. 13, 1908; FRERI, op. cit. p. 6, 1912; ibid. in *Annals,* Vol. LXXXV, p. 46, 1922, GUASCO, op. cit. p. 22, 1911; *Annales,* t. LII, p. 150. Important Propaganda documents in the possession of Dr. Guilday were received too late for use in the text.

25. *Annales,* t. LII, p. 149, ''Beginning at this moment, M. Didier Petit, who for a long time had identified himself with the thought, the work, and the pious desires of his mother, took a more active part, if not a preponderant part, in the grand work which Providence prepared.

not to swerve from his ideas which would assist the Catholic Missions of the entire world.[26]

The first meeting was called on May 3, 1822, and there were assembled the following persons: de Verne, Benoît Coste, Count d'Herculais, de Villiers, Magneunin, Didier Petit, Auguste Bonnet, Antoine Perisse, Terret, Victor Girodon and Father Cholleton.

The *Veni Creator* was said and Father Inglesi explained the object of his mission and gave a detailed description of the Louisiana Missions. He proposed to establish at Lyons an association which would assist in a permanent manner all the Catholic Missions of the world and in particular those of his own diocese. This resolution was adopted unanimously on that day. It took for its title, the *Association de la Propagation de la Foi dans les Deux-Mondes,* thus the new Society was at last begun. Further objections were raised by Girodon, who was present as the representative of Miss Jaricot, but before the meeting adjourned all difficulties were settled and the principle of universality which distinguished it from every preceding tentative, was made a permanent feature in the work. Girodon had explained the method employed by Pauline-Marie in her work, that of groups of ten and of a one-cent-a-week from each person and this system was immediately adopted by the new Society. A Central Council was formed at Lyons with the following officers: de Verne, President; Coste, Vice-President; Petit, Secretary; de Herculais, Treas-

---

26. Ozanam, *Notice,* etc. in the *Annales,* t. LII, pp. 150-151, says: "On Thursday, May 2, 1822, M. Petit set out to seek the most important men and those best known for the exercise of good works. He had already been assured of the adherence of some of them when he met on the street, one of his friends, M. Benoît Coste, he briefly explained to him the project and invited him to the meeting on the next day. 'Willingly' replied M. Coste, 'if it is to form a more general work, one extended to the whole world.' 'Yes,' replied M. Petit with feeling, as if struck by a ray of light, 'Yes, it is much better still, I adopt your idea; it is grander, it must be pleasing to all.' "

urer; de Verne, de Villiers and Terret, Councillors.[27] Shortly afterwards, Didier Petit went to Paris and established there a local and a Superior Council in order to have a representation at the capital. The result was that the two councils of Lyons and of Paris worked side by side from the beginning as they have done down to the present. Other meetings were held on May 8 and May 21. On May 25, 1822, a union was officially established between the work of Pauline-Marie and the new Society.[28]

Such is the story of the organization of the Society taken from an unpublished letter written by Girodon to Terret, the president of the General Council of Lyons. Victor Girodon became a priest and until his death proved to be a valuable aid to Pauline-Marie in her work. This account is corroborated by a letter written February 10, 1862, by Paul Girodon, nephew of l'Abbé Girodon, who has included in his account passages from the letter of his uncle.[29] By this time (1862) the controversy had arisen on the subject of the foundation of this Society. The question had been raised whether the credit for the organization of the Society should be given to Pauline-Marie or to Bishop Du Bourg and Mme. Petit, or to Benoît Coste, and much discussion ensued regarding the part the three groups had taken in the Society's organization. Whether either of the two organized movements, that of Du Bourg-Petit or of Missions Étrangères-Jaricot, would have succeeded alone is difficult to answer; but there is no doubt that the idea of universality and unity introduced in the meeting by Benoît Coste made a paramount change in the organization during the month of May, 1822. The question was raised whether the idea of a cent-a-week was original with Pauline-Marie. She herself, as has been

27. Ozanam, *Notice, etc.*, in the *Annales*, t. LII, pp. 151-152, *Compte Rendu de 1871* in the *Annales*, t. XLIV, pp. 160-161, *Annales*, t. L, pp. 317-318, Ozanam, *Mélanges*, pp. 30-31; *L'Oeuvre, etc.*, p. 13, 1898; ibid. p. 13, 1908; Freri, *op. cit.*, p. 7, 1912; ibid. in *Annals*, p. 46, 1922, Guasco, *op. cit.*, p. 22, 1911.

28. Guasco, *op. cit.*, p. 24.

29. This letter is in the cahier of Victor Girodon, *La Fondation, etc.*

already stated, repudiated any connection between her own plans and those of the Protestant Missionary activity. It is not possible to settle the problem of who was responsible for the amalgamation of the two movements or of the division of the associates into groups of ten. At a distance of a hundred years, it would seem, however, that one without the other would not have succeeded so well as has the Society. In the first year contributions were divided among the American Missions and the Seminary for Foreign Missions. From that time down to the close of the century the Church in the United States has been aided to an incredible extent by the Society.

CHAPTER III

THE ORGANIZATION OF THE SOCIETY

(May 3-25, 1822)

The two distinct movements towards the ideal embodied in the Rule of the Society were finally combined in a series of meetings, held in Lyons, during the month of May, 1822. "In the designs of Providence who seemed henceforth to conduct the government of the Society without the aid of man," writes Ozanam, "the first meeting was held, without premeditation, on Friday, May the third, the feast of the finding of the Holy Cross."[1]

A provisional bureau was formed; and M. de Verna was delegated to draw up a Rule. For this purpose there was named a committee composed of Messrs. Terret, Petit and de Villiers, while M. Terret was charged with the work of settling the method for collecting funds. M. Terret then interviewed his employee M. Girodon, and through him asked to be acquainted with the intentions of Mlle. Jaricot.[2] After some hesitancy, inspired solely by her desire for good, Mlle. Jaricot and her collaborators adhered to the projects of this first meeting. A second meeting, more numerous than that of May the third, took place on the eighth; a third assembly was held on the twenty-first: and finally in a meeting held the twenty-fifth of May, 1822, the First Rule was adopted. The Bureau was constituted in definitive manner with M. de

1. OZANAM, *Origines, etc.*, in the *Annales*, t. L, p. 317, 1878; *Compte Rendu de 1871*, in the *Annales*, t. XLIV, p. 161, 1872; OZANAM, *Mélanges*, t. 11, p. 30, 1872; *L'Oeuvre de la Propagation de la Foi*, p. 14, 1898, *ibid.*, p. 13, 1908; FRERI, *op. cit.*, p. 7, 1912; *ibid.*, in the *Annals*, vol. LXXXV, p. 46, 1922; HENRION, *Histoire, etc.*, t. II, part ii, p. 676; LOUVET, *op. cit.*, p. 2a.

2. OZANAM, *Mélanges*, t. II, p. 30, 1872; *Compte Rendu de 1871*, in the *Annales*, t. XLIV, p. 161, 1872; *Notice, etc.*, in the *Annales*, t. LII p. 152; *L'Oeuvre, etc.*, p. 13, 1898; *ibid.*, p. 13, 1908; FRERI, *op. cit.*, p. 7, 1912; *ibid.*, in *Annals*, vol. LXXXV, p. 46, 1922; GUASCO, *op. cit.*, p. 24, 1911.

Verna as President, M. Benoît Coste as Vice-President, M. de Herculais as Treasurer, and M. Petit as Secretary. The Society was now formed, and approbation of episcopal authority was immediately obtained. A diocesan committee, composed of seven members was then constituted.

In one of the earliest numbers of the *Annales,* this original Rule is given as follows:

ESTABLISHMENT AND OBJECT OF THE ASSOCIATION.

Art. I.   There is founded in France a pious association, taking the title of Association for the Propagation of the Faith.

Art. II.   It has for its object to extend the society of the Catholic faithful by aiding with all the means in its power, the Missionaries charged to spread the lights of the faith among the foreign nations of both hemispheres.

Art. III.   It is composed of all the faithful of both sexes, whose Christian conduct is calculated to call down upon this enterprise the benediction of God.

DIVISION AND ADMINISTRATION OF THE ASSOCIATION.

Art. IV.   The Association is divided in divisions, in centuries, in sections.

Art. V.   Ten members form a section, ten sections a century, ten centuries a division.

Art. VI.   Each division, each century, each section, has a chief.

Art. VII.   The chiefs of division of a diocese share the right of the council of administration of the Association in the diocese. They correspond on one side with the council, on the other with chiefs of their centuries.

Art. VIII.   The chiefs of the century are named by the chief of their division. They correspond on one side with the chief, on the other with the chiefs of their sections.

Art. IX.   The chiefs of section are named by the chief of their century and correspond with him. Each of them is charged to provide for the replacement of members who cease to take part in their section.

Art. X.   Each chief of division, of century, or of section keeps an exact list of the ten persons who depend upon his administration. He communicates it to his superior chiefs every time they demand it.

Art. XI.   In no case can the divisions, centuries or sections meet in assembly.

MEANS OF THE ASSOCIATION.

Art. XII.   The principal means upon which the Association founds its hope of attaining the object which it proposes for itself are prayer and alms.

Art. XIII.   To call down the graces of God upon the Association and upon the Missions each associate is invited to say every day an Our Father and a Hail Mary. It is sufficient for that to apply to this intention and once for all, the Our Father and the Hail Mary of his morning or night prayer; he will join to it this invocation: St. Francis Xavier, pray for us.

Art. XIV.   The Association chooses as more particular epochs of prayer and of thanksgiving, the feast of the Finding of the Holy Cross, day on which the Association was founded at Lyons, May 3rd of the year 1822, and the feast of St. Francis Xavier, whom it recognizes as its patron (3 December); there shall be celebrated on these days a mass for the success of the work, in all the cities where the councils are established.

Art. XV.   Each Associate gives in alms for the Missions, one cent each week.

Art. XVI.   The chiefs of sections collect the contributions of the members of their section, and place the product, the first Sunday of each month, in the hands of their chief of century: each chief of section answers for ten contributions.

Art. XVII.   The chiefs of the century send into the hands of their chief of division in the month, the sums which they have received from the chiefs of their sections.

Art. XVIII.   The chiefs of division render an account at the earliest meeting of the council of which they form a part.

Art. XIX.   The Superior Council of the Association distributes the funds: it makes distribution according to the needs of the different Missions.

Art. XX.   The Association publishes a general bulletin of news which comes to it from the Missions.[3]

-----

3. *Association de la Propagation de la Foi,* in the *Annales,* t. I, fasc. iii, pp. 30-32; *Extrait du Règlement,* in the *Annales,* t. I, fasc. vi, pp. 93-96.

In the month of July, 1822, this First Rule of the Society for the Propagation of the Faith, was communicated to Bishop Du Bourg. The prelate replied by a letter dated Washington, January 29, 1823:

Gentlemen:

It is quite late for me to testify to the admiration and the gratitude which were excited within me by reading the plan for the Association for the Propagation of the Faith, which your zeal for the Missions, and for my mission has inspired in you, and of which you have been kind enough to send me a copy. The reason of this delay will be very plain to you when you know that my successive changes have prevented me from reaching home earlier. The plan of your Association, Gentlemen, praises your discernment as much as your piety. This ruling body, so fitted to facilitate collections, to bring back all to unity in the distribution of funds between the Missions of the Orient and that of Louisiana and that of Kentucky—all looks to me to be perfectly conceived. I do not doubt that He who inspired in you the courage to undertake it and the wisdom to outline the plan of conducting it will also give you constancy enough to put it into execution. There will be difficulties of detail, a diversified correspondence to keep up, which might fatigue men less constant in their good, or animated by less pure views, but the remembrance of how much difficulty and pain it cost Jesus Christ for the redemption of our souls, the happiness of concurring with Him and His envoys, in the salvation of so many other whom the absence of pecuniary assistance would leave eternally deprived of this happiness, are motives whose strength will not be weakened in hearts where Faith rules.[4]

The Apostle of Kentucky, Bishop Flaget, to whom his venerable colleague of New Orleans had sent a copy of the Rule, after familiarizing himself with it, wrote in turn to Lyons:

All these papers, as you can imagine, were received with joy and read and reread with great avidity. I admired the wisdom of the Rule, its simplicity, and the incalculable good which will result from it. It seems to me that all Christian kings and the Sovereign Pontiff himself, should be the first to encourage it. Those who have concurred in the formation of this vast plan to propagate our holy religion merit all our gratitude.[5]

---

4. GUASCO, *op. cit.*, p. 41, 1911.
5. GUASCO, *op. cit.*, p. 42, 1911.

Acting upon the advice of the American prelates, as well as by the experience the leaders of the Society had gained in these early years, a revision of the Rules was made, the Second Rule was published in April, 1834.

REVISED RULES

The members of the two Councils of Paris and of Lyons, having believed it to be fitting to revise the Constitutional (constitutif) Rule of the Society for the Propagation of the Faith which is nothing other than a concurrence of alms and of prayers in favor of the Catholic Missionaries who carry the torch of faith into the countries across the sea,

Adopt in the following terms the rule which constitutes it:

ARTICLE ONE

The Society of piety and of charity called the Propagation of the Faith has for its unique object to aid by its prayers and its alms the Catholic Missionaries charged with the preaching of the Gospel in the countries across the sea.

ARTICLE TWO

To call down graces from on high upon the men who devote themselves to the foreign Missions, upon their work and upon the Society which must contribute to their success, one (each member) will recite every day an Our Father and a Hail Mary; it will suffice to apply to this intention, and once for all, the Our Father and the Hail Mary of the morning or the night prayers. One will join to this each time the invocation: St. Francis Xavier, pray for us.

ARTICLE THREE

The alms or subscription is one cent a week.

ARTICLE FOUR

The total of the subscriptions is placed in the hands of the two cashiers residing one at Paris and the other at Lyons.

ARTICLE FIVE

The Councils, of which there are only two, one at Paris and the other at Lyons, are each composed of eight members and of a cashier who has a deliberative voice.

Each Council is self-recruiting by voice of election; it chooses its President and its cashier and comes to an understanding with the other Council concerning the division (repartition) of the funds between the different missions.

ARTICLE SIX

The functions of the President endure five years, those of the cashier only cease by death, revocation or resignation.

Each member of the Council is named for seven years at the end of which the replacement takes place without there being here any matter of dispute.

With regard to the members actually in service lot will indicate each year, during seven years, the one among them who should cease to participate in the Council.

All these functions are essentially gratuitous.

ARTICLE SEVEN

The faithful who contribute to this good work and who are not members of the two Councils, are and remain entirely foreign to the administration.

They are simply subscribers.

This disposition applies to persons who receive alms.

Moreover, there do not exist among the subscribers, even among those of the same city, of the same parish, or who place their contribution with the same person, any other bonds than the union of their prayers and of their alms.

The Society has no place for any meeting, either general or particular, even among the subscribers who reside in the same parish or who pay to the same person.

ARTICLE EIGHT

The two Councils, in order to facilitate their collections, will, conjointly with the Council to which they are attached, designate in each diocese a subscriber who there collects the sums given.

All persons, who at the present time are willing to take the pains to collect the alms, are requested to continue, as in the past, their careful attention in this collection.

ARTICLE NINE

The news received from the Mission is published under the direction of the two Councils, in a publication (recueil) destined to continue the *Lettres Edifiantes,* under the title of the *Annales de la*

Propagation de la Foi. This publication, moreover, includes every year the statement of the alms collected by dioceses and their distribution to the different Missions.

Subscribers are enabled to read the *Annales* gratuitously.

ARTICLE TEN

Subscribers are invited to assist at mass the day of the feast of the Finding of the Holy Cross, the anniversary of the foundation of the Society in the City of Lyons in 1822, and the day of the feast of St. Francis Xavier, the Apostle of India.

ARTICLE ELEVEN

All the ancient rules and prospectuses of the Society for the Propagation of the Faith are and remain abrogated.[6]

The Rule itself evidences the fact that the Society has for its end the extension of the flock of the faithful by all means in its power, particularly by aiding missionaries charged with spreading the light of the Gospel among the foreign nations of both hemispheres. This aid took the form of prayers and offerings from the faithful. The motive behind the activity of the Society is to procure for men eternal salvation, to substitute civilization for barbarism and to relieve innumerable misfortunes.[7] The Society for the Propagation of the Faith takes no part, however, in selecting these missionaries, or in appointing them to their fields. It does not train them for their duties, and it does not concern itself with the spiritual administration of the Missions. These functions are all performed by the usual Church authorities.[8] The Society engaged itself solely, from the beginning, in the collection and distribution of temporal resources of charity in the service of the Apostolate. It proposed to facilitate the departure of the missionaries by paying their passage, the expense of which reached an enormous figure, especially for long voyages. Each Associate undertook to say for the inten-

---

6. *Supplément* to the *Annales*, April, 1834, t. VII, fasc. XXXVI, pp. 1-4.

7. *Prospectus* printed in Lyons, May, 1835, quoted in GUASCO, *op. cit.*, p. 15, 1911.

8. FRERI, *op. cit.*, p. 12, 1812; *ibid.*, in the *Annals*, vol. LXXXV, p. 51, 1922.

tion of the Mission an *Our Father* and *Hail Mary* with the
invocation: *St. Francis Xavier pray for us,* each day: and to
contribute a penny a week for the Missions. The bases, therefore, of the Society were and are prayer for each day and a
cent each week. No limits were placed upon its field; for the
Society for the Propagation of the Faith has always been
ready, to the full extent of its powers, to assist all the Catholic
Missions in whatever part of the world they may be situated or
to whatever nationality the missionaries evangelizing them
may belong.[9] However, as soon as the Missions are in the
least degree able to help themselves, the Society gradually
withdraws its aid, because the demands are many and the
resources inadequate. It is not the aim of the Society to help
those countries which are generally known as Catholic countries, however great their needs may be: for that reason
France, Italy, Austria, Spain, etc., have never received any
help from it.[10] Only the requests of bishops, vicars apostolic
and superiors of religious in charge of Missions are considered
by the Councils, and such petitions, whether acted upon favor-
ably or unfavorably, must be renewed every year. Founded
by the laity, the administration of the Society for the Propagation of the Faith is almost entirely in their hands, few
priests have taken an active part in its councils.[11] This fact is
important, for it shows that the Society, wholly spiritual in its
end, without any other object than the salvation of souls and
the transmission of the Gospel to entire nations among whom
the torch of faith has never yet shone, an institution solemnly
approved by the Supreme Chief of the Church, and making
the name of France cherished in every part of the world has
been from the beginning a distinctly lay organization.[12]

M. Alexandre Guasco, the General Secretary of the Central
Council, calls the Society a work of faith, of zeal, of charity

9. FRERI, *op. cit.,* p. 15, 1912; *ibid.,* in the *Annals,* vol. LXXXV,
p. 56, 1922.

10. FRERI, *ut supra.*

11. FRERI, *op. cit.,* p. 14, 1912; *ibid.,* in the *Annals,* vol. LXXXV,
p. 54, 1922.

12. *Annales,* t. II, p. 81.

and of patriotism. "How much good of all kinds," he says, "has befallen us through the work of our missionaries, who with our help have gone forth to carry far the name of our country, have won sympathy for it and have contributed to assure it material riches." [13]

In an article written for *L'Écho de Paris*, Baudrillart throws considerable light upon the patriotic attitude of the French missionary.[14] "From the Propagation of the Faith," he says, "comes in the greater part the material and financial resources of the Catholic Missions for the entire world, and these resources, collected throughout all the universe, are united and divided by the Councils of Paris and of Lyons. It follows that all the missionaries, of whatever nationality they may be, and in whatever country they may labor, depend in an appreciable measure upon this French centre. Another consequence is that not only French interests engaged in Catholic Missions are particularly safeguarded, but the French missionaries are subsidized by the Catholics of foreign nationality.

"It is not possible to separate the missionary and his nationality and to prevent the latter from profiting from the labor of the former, it follows that even today the French interests evidently engaged in the Catholic Missions are sustained to an important extent by the money of foreign Catholics. For if France furnishes two-thirds of the personnel it contributes only a third of the pecuniary subsidies."

The Society for the Propagation of the Faith met with difficulties at the very beginning. The first of these is the scandal caused by Father Inglesi. Father Inglesi, Honorary Vicar-General of New Orleans, whose visit to Lyons had been the occasion of the foundation of the Society, now proved to be the source of one of its gravest dangers. An enlightening note on Father Inglesi's misappropriation of some of the early funds of the Society entrusted to his care is found in a letter from Bishop Plessis of Quebec, dated October 25, 1824,

---

13. GUASCO, *op. cit.*, p. 15, 1911.
14. BAUDRILLART, in the *Echo de Paris*, Feb. 14, 1921.

written to Archbishop Maréchal: "Bishop Du Bourg has not written me since I enlightened him concerning Inglesi who grossly deceived him. It is said, and I am extremely grieved to hear it, that the prelate has done evil in his temporal affairs and finds himself embarrassed with large debts contracted by his establishment at St. Louis, Missouri."[15] Unfortunately, there had been placed in his hands at Lyons and elsewhere considerable alms of which he never rendered account. A letter from Monsignor Du Bourg unveiled his artifice and his improbity. None of the money which had been confided to him could be obtained, and it was necessary to keep silent concerning these unworthy and false representatives, in order not to compromise a work happily established and one which was of such great assistance for the distant Missions. The directors of the Society thereafter employed the wisest measures to shield the fund from all cupidity. Inglesi did not profit long by his iniquity, for at the close of a few months, although he was in the full vigor of age and health, he was called to render an account of his stewardship before the just Judge.[16] Opposition arose also from a place the least suspected—the Chamber of Deputies at Paris. The Society was attacked as a secret organization managed by the Jesuits.[17] An answer was promptly made to this attack, and Parisian Catholics were encouraged by the brilliant defence by Monseigneur Frayssinous, Minister of Ecclesiastical Affairs in the realm.[18] **1810499**

"Certainly it was a most Christian, most noble, and most wise political thought," he said, which Louis XIV conceived in founding at Paris itself a house for the Missions-Étrangères. This institution was destined to carry to the very furthermost parts of the Orient the glory of the French name, as well as the light of the Gospel. "This house still exists;

15. This letter was located in the archives of the Séminaire de Saint-Sulpice, Paris.
16. CARDINAL VILLECOURT, quoted in MAURIN, *op. cit.*, p. 112, Paris, 1892.
17. LAUNAY, *Histoire Générale de la Société des Missions Étrangères* t. II, p. 518; GUASCO, *op. cit.*, p. 48, 1911.
18. GUASCO, *op. cit.*, pp. 48-49, 1911.

it has survived our religious and political storms; not, however, without having suffered most serious results from them.
It no longer has the same subsidy nor the same resources. It
is a matter of common knowledge that zeal for the Propagation of the Faith has at all times been one of the characteristics
of the Christian Church. It is by this zeal that the Gospel
must successively make the conquest of the world, the Faith
must triumph over idolatry and everywhere the Kingdom
of Christ must be established. It is this same zeal which took
possession of some ecclesiastics and pious laymen of Lyons.
They saw that the Foreign Missions were menaced with deca-
dence. They conceived the idea of forming an Association to
support the Missions and procure assistance for them. This
Association took the name of the Propagation of the Faith.
There is nothing mysterious in this name. It is not new. At
Rome there is the Sacred Congregation de Propaganda Fide,
at the head of which is a member of the Sacred College. The
authors of the project, he continues, had sent their prospectus
into the different dioceses and addressed it to almost all our
bishops. Many of them have adopted this work. It was very
necessary to organize the Association and to make a unit of
it, to find means of collecting the alms of the faithful and
having them reach their destination.''[19] Frayssinous pointed
out that it was not a question of a contribution but of a
perfectly voluntary offering. The mites of the poor as well
as the gold of the rich were given. Nothing could be more
in conformity with the spirit of Christianity, since similar
collections were made at its very origin to relieve the poor
of Jerusalem. In this there was nothing secret, nothing
political. Every year the results of the collections were being
published and up to that time the largest amount raised by
the whole of France was only 80,000 francs. The use of this
money was made known and even the correspondence maintained with the missionaries in the two hemispheres was
published. Sums have been sent to the Orient to assist
Christians and to provide the necessary establishments: they

19. *Annales*, t. III, pp. 103-105, 1828.

have been sent to North and South America, into the provinces of Kentucky and into Louisiana, over which, as he emphasized, a French bishop, Mgr. Du Bourg, a man of very rare mind and capacity, presided. In all of this, there was nothing extraordinary, and so, the Chamber had no reason for becoming alarmed. No one could say that this Association was a state within the State.

The Society was also attacked in the press in 1826, and it is to this attack also that Frayssinous replied on May 25 of this same year in his address to the Chamber, from which we have quoted. In 1836 those who took offence at the progress of the Society went so far as to pretend that the larger part of the sums collected from the faithful of France for the Propagation of the Faith and for the defense of the Church, sums which were necessary for persecuted Catholics and for other pious objects, went almost exclusively to pay the expenses of the Infant of Portugal. Frayssinous replied that in Portugal the accusation of making a collection for Don Miguel had been taken up, and that it was fully answered by the publicity given the disbursements in the *Annales*. The *Ami de la Religion* replied to these absurd attacks in taking as a basic principle for its response the fact that the disbursements had been published every year. Moreover, in the midst of political agitation the Society was for a long time proscribed in a Catholic country, Spain.[20]

The publicity to the allocations which the administrators of the Society had given from the very beginning, has been, during the term of its long existence, a safeguard of the Society for the Propagation of the Faith as far as Government, subscribers and beneficiaries are concerned. The calumnies have passed, and if, in remote instances, up to our epoch, articles have appeared which were based on misinformation, there has been neither an echo nor any consequence to it. In spite of these and other attacks raised against the Society, its progress was phenomenal from the very beginning. "In proportion as it is added to the number of its years,"

---

20. GUASCO, *op. cit.*, p. 50, 1911.

said the official statement of 1841, published in the *Annales* of 1842, "our Society was blessed by Heaven and multiplied its progress. It is a river which continues to become larger as it recedes from its source. And just as the last total collection far exceeded the preceding ones, so also day by day the final statement gives way before a higher amount." [21]   The formal approval given to the Central Councils by the Holy See, the constant encouragement of the episcopate of the world, the gratitude of missionaries, and the efforts of the most illustrious among men to support and spread it by their words and their writings permitted the Society for the Propagation of the Faith to establish itself firmly during the first twenty years of its existence.

As Leo XIII pointed out in his Encyclical *Sancta Dei civitas* of December 3, 1880, the success of the Society for the Propagation of the Faith inspired many others in different countries to organize similar institutions. [22]   In France, for example, there were founded shortly after the beginning of the Lyons Society, two others with similar ends: there were the *Association of the Holy Childhood,* and the *Schools of the Orient.* At Vienna the *Leopoldine Association* was founded in 1828-29 with the same purpose; and at Munich, the *Ludwig-Missionsverein* was started in 1838. "At the same time," wrote Leo XIII, "due to the emulation of piety, two other societies were formed, one called the *Holy Childhood of Jesus* and the other the *Schools of the Orient.* The former proposes to save and to lead to Christian habits unfortunate children whom their parents, driven by sloth or by misery, inhumanely leave unprotected, especially in the regions of China where this barbarous custom still prevails. These infants are saved by the charity of the faithful and at times redeemed by being washed in the waters of Christian regeneration.

---

21. *Compte Rendu de 1841*, in the *Annales*, t. p. 1842.
22. LEO XIII, Encyclical Letter *Sancta Dei Civitas*, in the *Annales*, t. LIII, pp. 79-94; *Missions Catholiques*, t. XII, pp. 613-618, 1880.

These Societies came to the aid of the older Society, the Propagation of the Faith, and were united to it by a cordial agreement; they have the same end, and likewise rely on the alms and prayers of Christian people. All three have for their object to bring by the diffusion of the light of the Gospel, the largest possible number of those outside of the Church to know God and to adore Him, and Him whom He has sent, Jesus Christ.

The *Association of the Holy Childhood* is a children's association for the benefit of Foreign Missions. Some twenty years after the foundation of the Society for the Propagation of the Faith (1843), Bishop Charles de Forbin-Janson, of Nancy, established the Society of the Holy Childhood (*Association de la Sainte Enfance*), for the twofold purpose of rallying around the Infant Jesus little children from their tenderest years, and of encouraging them by the practice of charity to co-operate in saving from death and sin the many thousands of children in pagan countries who are neglected by their parents and cast away unbaptized. The further object of the association is to procure baptism for those abandoned little ones, and, should they live, to make of them craftsmen, teachers, doctors or priests, who in turn will spread the blessings of the Christian religion amongst their countrymen. Children become members of the association immediately after baptism, and may continue in membership for the remainder of their lives, but at the age of twenty-one, in order to share in the indulgences, it is necessary to become also a member of the Association for the Propagation of the Faith. The monthly contribution is one cent, or a yearly contribution of twelve cents, and the members recite daily one *Hail Mary* with the addition, *Holy Virgin Mary, pray for us and for the poor pagan children.* Until the children are able to do this themselves their relatives do it for them. The affairs of the Holy Childhood are managed by an international council at Paris, France, consisting of fifteen priests and as many laymen, with a general director as the presiding officer. It is estimated that at the present time there are enrolled in the Association about seven million Catholic children. Fully thirty-two millions of dollars are the result of their generosity, and about eighteen millions of pagan children have thus been saved to the Church.[23]

The *Society of the Schools of the Orient* was founded in 1855-56 to assist the schools, orphanages, asylums of the countries of the East. During later years, as a consequence of the special preoccupations of Pope Leo XIII, its object has been made more precise. It labors to maintain and propagate the union of the churches by the education of the new generation and especially by the formation of a good clergy in the different oriental rites. Its budget has rather great and irregular fluctuations due, no doubt, to the fact that it is not so well known as the preceding societies. The total of its ordinary subscriptions from 1855 to 1899 has been 10,650,000 fr. of which 9,890,000 fr. were furnished by France. It is also helped by the French Government.

The *Apostolic Society* under the patronage of the Holy Women of the Gospel was founded in 1838 at Orleans by Mlle. Duchesne, who consecrated her life to it. Its purpose is to furnish vestments and altar linens to the Missions. At the end of thirty years the Society had been established in thirty-two cities.

The *Leopoldine Association* is the direct result of a cry for urgent help from Father Frederic Rese, then Vicar-General of Cincinnati and later first Bishop of Detroit. In 1828, he went to Europe to solicit priests as well as funds for the Ohio Missions, a territory as large as France, and in which only sixteen priests were ministering to 40,000 Catholics. The Prince-Archbishop of Vienna, Leopold-Maxmilian became enthusiastic over the project of organizing a special society for the support of American Missions and to this end obtained an audience for Father Rese with the Emperor Francis I.

---

23. WILLMS, *Holy Childhood*, in the *Catholic Encyclopedia*, vol. VII, pp. 399-400; Cf. LOUVET, *op. cit.*, pp. 12a-16a; PIOLET, *Nos Missions et Nos Missionaires*, p. 15.

By a bull *Quamquam plura sint* dated January 30, 1829, Pope Leo XII sanctioned the proposed society, and it was officially established on May 13, 1829, in the Archbishop's palace at Vienna. In his address before the select assembly, Father Rese said: ''The Catholics of North America, especially of Ohio, Michigan and the Northwest, appeal to you through me, that you might become their helping angels.'' The Society was christened *Leopoldinen-Stiftung* to commemorate the beautiful life of the Archduchess Leopoldina, daughter of Francis I, who died in America as Empress of Brazil, having been the wife of Emperor Pedro I of Brazil. The objects of the society, as briefly stated in its statutes, are: The promotion of greater efficiency in the Catholic Missions of America, and the participation and the edification of the faithful in extending the Church of Jesus Christ unto the remotest regions of the earth. The means selected to attain these ends were, as with the Lyons Society, prayer and almsdeeds. Every member obliges himself to recite daily one *Our Father* and the *Angelus,* with the added petition: *St. Leopold, pray for us.*

To collect funds the Lyons method was followed. Circles of ten members were formed in all the parishes throughout the Empire and the promoter of each circle would deliver the collected moneys to the respective pastor, who in turn would send them to the local dean and the latter would deliver these funds to the Ordinary every three months. The Bishops would then send their reports to the Central Bureau at Vienna. The total receipts of the first year amounted to 49,823 fl. Every year the entire Austrian clergy was requested to appeal to their congregations on the Feast of St. Leopold for contributions toward the support of American Missions. It has been carefully estimated that within the first decade of its existence (1829-1839), this society had contributed to the American Missions the sum of $220,000. Let us not forget that the bulk of these contributions came from the laboring classes and from servant girls, although the nobility also contributed generously. In addi-

tion to the actual funds, the *Leopoldine Association* sent many
religious articles every few months, such as books, chalices,
copes, vestments, rosaries, oil stocks, paintings, bells, censors,
altar linens, crucifixes, etc., to the Missions in America.[24]

The *Ludwig-Missionsverein* was begun in the year 1828,
when the Reverend Frederic Rese, Vicar-General of Cincinnati, went to Munich to ask help for the Mission work in the
United States. With the sanction of King Louis I of Bavaria,
voluntary offerings for the assistance of American and of
Asiatic Missions were collected. But the contributions were
confined chiefly to the clergy of the eight dioceses of Bavaria.
The money, up to the year 1838, approximately 15,000 fl.
(25,800 marks), was deposited with the Archbishop of
Munich-Freising, and thence sent direct to Vicar-General
Rese in Cincinnati. During this time the knowledge of the
work being done by the Society for the Propagation of the
Faith, was being spread among the laity of Bavaria by the
German edition of the *Annales*. Since the organizing of
societies and the gathering of money was at that time for-
bidden in Bavaria, Father Stumpf, of the Cathedral, was
asked by his superiors to account for his activity in behalf
of the Society of Lyons. Meantime, Rese had returned to
Munich, and this time with a plan for the unification of the
various organizations existing in Bavaria and dedicated to the
extension of the Catholic Faith by assisting Foreign Missions.
In this way, he hoped to increase the contributions. To put
his plan into execution, he addressed a petition to King Louis
I on April 22, 1838, asking that the Mission society already
existing in a large part of Bavaria be reorganized into a
general society extending over the whole of Bavaria, which
would then be constituted as a self-sufficient and independent
Bavarian society under royal protection, but at the same time
empowered to establish relations with the Holy See, with the
Leopoldinen-Stiftung in Austria and with every other German

---

24. Epstein, *The Leopoldine Association, etc.,* in the *Illinois
Catholic Historical Review,* vol. III, no. i, pp. 88-92, July, 1920; Cf.
De Meaux, *L'Église Catholique et la Liberté aux États-Unis,* pp.
244-245, Paris, 1893.

society of a similar kind. Both petition and statutes were first officially submitted to the Archbishop of Munich-Freising for his approval. They were given with the highest recommendation. Two months later (July 17), royal sanction was granted. The statutes of the new society were sanctioned on December 12, 1838, by the King. The means chosen were the same as those of the Society for the Propagation of the Faith, and the same process of collection was adhered to; of these funds, two-thirds of the contributions were assigned to the needs of the Missions in Asia and in North America, and one-third for the Fathers in charge of the Holy Sepulchre, at Jerusalem.[25]

Rapid as has been the growth of the offerings to the Society for the Propagation of the Faith, it has been below that of similar Protestant Societies. These Protestant Societies had, it is true, begun earlier; but even today, the abundance of offerings in the Catholic Societies cannot be compared to the liberality of our separated brethren.

All the great sects of Protestantism have their missionaries and their budget. They consider that the propagation of the Christian Faith is an absolute duty for every Christian, and their catechisms, so light in doctrine, have a lesson destined to explain this obligation of conscience. Moreover, the *Society for the Propagation of the Gospel of London (S. P. G.)*, prints and furnishes freely, all the books necessary for the Missions. In the month of February, 1836, the *Asiatic Journal of London* published in the statement of the sums received during the course of the year 1836 by the Bible societies and the committees of different Protestant Missions. The receipts amounted to about 20,000,000 francs or 778,035

25. SCHABERT, *The Ludwig-Missionsverein*, in the *Catholic Historical Review*, p. 23, April, 1922. In July, 1920, I visited Germany and attempted to go to Munich in order to carry on a research in the archives of this Society, and to procure their collection of *Annalen* but since diplomatic negotiations had not been reestablished with the Central Powers, certain parts of Germany were closed to strangers, and no passport visa would be given for Munich. Dr. Schabert whom I met at Louvain volunteered to make a special trip to Munich where he procured all its publications for the Catholic University and from his research, procured the material for this article.

pounds sterling, to which were added the subscriptions opened in all the colonies under the British Government. The *Annales de la Propagation de la Foi* make the observation on this point, that if one adds to this what was collected in the United Kingdom and its possessions, and the collections of the other Protestant countries, there would be no exaggeration in declaring that the total sum collected for the support of the Protestant Missions far surpasses 30,000,000 francs per year. The resources placed at the disposal of Protestant action has left an ever-increasing record.

According to an article which appeared in the *Ami du Clergé*, of Oct. 26, 1899, the faithful of the Anglican Church, outside of the gifts offered by the different associations, gave as subscriptions for the Foreign Missions a sum corresponding to 23,245,675 francs. In addition to the societies supporting the personnel there are those which distribute books and Bibles like the *British and Foreign Bible Society,* which in one year from March 31, 1896, to March 31, 1897, spent a sum equivalent to 5,092,025 francs. Let us also cite the *Society for Promoting Christian Knowledge,* the *Church of England Zenana Missionary Society,* established in 1880 for the special purpose of evangelizing Indian women, the *Missionary Leaves Association,* the *Junior Clergy Association.* The total of the generosities of English Protestants for their missions is estimated as high as 50,000,000 francs. The United States had in 1900 at least 28 associations for the Protestant Missions of different denominations.[26]

If to all this we add what the associations of Norway, Germany, and other places received for the Lutheran missions, we reach a truly colossal figure for the total budget of all the Protestant sects. The budget to the Protestant Foreign Missions is very difficult to establish, for these Missions depend upon a large number of societies whose data is almost impossible to centralize. It is conceded however, that it surpasses 100,000,000 perhaps 150,000,000 francs, a figure ten or twelve times more than all the assistance granted to our

26. GUASCO, *op. cit.,* p. 52, 1911.

Catholic missionaries, incomparably more numerous and more important. Only the devotion and the indefatigable charity of our missionaries maintain the equilibrium, but one is certainly forced to admit that our generosity towards our foreign missionaries is nothing in comparison to that of the Protestants. The truth is that the Catholics, save in a few French dioceses, give relatively little for their Foreign Missions; that the Missions are not sufficiently well known or appreciated; that it would be fortunate to see the Propagation of the Faith in particular established in all the dioceses of the world, for which an official act of the Sovereign Pontiff is necessary.

CHAPTER IV

The Administration of the Society

The earliest efforts for aiding the Foreign Missions by means of prayer and alms have been described in a preceding chapter. The *Société des Missions Étrangères* carried on a campaign, restricted at the outset to the fostering of the practice of offering those indulgenced prayers for the Mission which had fallen into desuetude since the Revolution, and later, through its leaflets, emphasized the wisdom of the idea of the English Methodists, who were in the habit of contributing a penny a week for the support of their Missions. We are not certain what methods were employed by Mme. Petit in Lyons in collecting money and furnishings for the Dioceses of Bardstown and New Orleans. The decimal system so skilfully applied by Mlle. Jaricot in organizing those who contributed a cent-a-week, into groups of ten, into groups of one hundred, and into groups of one thousand, with a person at the head of each of these groups, was incorporated into the Society for the Propagation of the Faith immediately after its foundation in 1822. Thus the person at the head of each group of ten received the contributions from all the members in his group and remitted to the head of the group of one hundred members the money he had received. This head of the group of one hundred forwarded the funds he received to the head of the group of a thousand members.

The meeting of May 3, 1822, provided a slightly different form of organization by bringing together all the alms in the hands of the Central Council. The Central Council of Lyons was organized on the day of the foundation and it was soon felt necessary to enlist the interest and coöperation of influential personages at Paris. In June, 1822, M. Didier Petit went to Paris for the purpose of forming a Superior Council of the Society. In a special meeting, at which were present the Cardinal Prince de Croy, Grand Chaplain of France,

Abbé Perault, the Prince of Polignac, the Marquis de Rivière, the Count de Senst-Pilsach, the Duke of Rohan and M. de Haller, Didier Petit explained the end and the means of the new institution. These gentlemen accepted the idea submitted to them, promising to devote themselves to the Society. They met on the 27th of the following July at the home of the Grand Chaplain of France, at the chateau of the Tuileries, and created the Central Council of the North, with the special council for the Diocese of Paris.[1] This Superior Council ceased to exist after the Revolution of 1830; the two Central Councils of Lyons and of Paris agreed that there was no longer need to reëstablish it.

The Sacred Congregation de Propaganda Fide in a letter of February 25, 1841, expresses its desire that the Superior Council of the whole Society be reëstablished with the intention of placing Cardinal De Bonald at its head. The reason given for this was that the two Councils of Lyons and Paris may not be in conflict; that greater unity may be attained and somewhat greater deference may be shown to Propaganda on whom all Missions depend. Cardinal De Bonald was preferred not because he was Archbishop but because of his high office as a Cardinal, and it was recalled that the former President of the Superior Council had been Cardinal Prince de Croy, Grand Chaplain of France. Since the Society had become universal, its control should be entrusted to a Cardinal of the Church. It appears also that there had been some opposition made by the Council of Paris to the subsidies for the Missions of Europe, and a certain amount of parsimony was displayed notwithstanding the wishes of the Holy See.[2] With the disappearance of the Superior Council at Paris that part of the Rule which provided that the Superior Council of the Association was to distribute the funds according to the needs of the different Missions was no longer operative. Article 4 of the Revised Rules of 1834 provided that

---

1. GUASCO, *op. cit.*, p. 25, 1911.
2. *Propaganda transcripts, Documento XXXIII bis, Lettera della S. C.*, Vol. 325, Fol. 146v, *Monsignor Garibaldi Nunzio Apostolico,* Parigi, 25 Febraro, 1841.

the total of the subscriptions be placed in the hands of the
two cashiers residing one at Paris and one at Lyons.[3]   A
provision for forwarding the alms from the members to the
Councils is made in Article 8: "The two Councils, in order
to facilitate their collections, conjointly with the Council to
which they are attached, will designate in each diocese a
subscriber who collects there the sums donated."

The present custom of collecting and assembling the contributions is explained in a communication to me from M.
Guasco, the General Secretary, in which he states: "In the extract of the rules of the Association for the Propagation of the
Faith the paragraph entitled *Division of the Association*
where there is question of divisions, of centuries, of sections
and of divisions, long ago fell into desuetude.   There, is no
longer a question today of any division except the groups
of ten.   Today the chiefs of the groups of ten remit the
receipts into the hands of the Parish Director, who is the
Pastor or the Assistant delegated by the Pastor to look after
the Society."[4]   The promoter's duties are to organize a band
of ten to collect the offerings, and to circulate among them
the *Annals* of the Propagation of the Faith, which is published
every two months.   The offerings are then turned over by the
promoter to the parochial director, where the Society is established in the parish.   Otherwise they are sent to the General
Director.   Membership certificates are provided to new members, and cards record the collections.   In some parishes of
the United States the Society has been connected with some
other Society already existing; in others, it has an organization of its own; in those parishes where a branch of the
Society is not established, members may join by saying the
required prayers and forwarding their offerings to general
headquarters.   Besides those who contribute only sixty cents
a year, there are two other classes: The special members are
those who contribute the sum of six dollars a year representing the amount collected in a band of ten, and life members

---

3. Cf. *Chapter III*, p. 30.
4. GUASCO, letter dated August 29, 1921.

who contribute at one time a sum of money not less than forty dollars to the Society. Both special members and life members received a copy of the *Annals* every two months. Sums of money intended by the donors for particular Missions or missionaries are received and sent at once to their destination.[5] There is naturally a tendency to control their distribution.

In the United States the Society is legally incorporated and hence is empowered to receive bequests. Monsignor Freri writes: "The Propagation of the Faith, having lost many bequests through the opposition of natural heirs, the adverse decision of courts, the lack of care on the part of the executors, has established a Conditional Gift Fund in America to which several thousands of dollars have already been contributed by persons who had intended to leave legacies for the Missions. The Society receives gifts, large or small, at the same time entering into a written agreement with the donor not to spend these gifts but to invest them in well-determined and absolutely safe securities, and to pay to the donors, so long as they shall live, a yearly amount equivalent to a fair rate of interest. After the donor's death the money is placed in the general fund to be distributed among the Missions. If the money left in care of the Propagation of the Faith is intended for other purposes besides its own work, the Society assumes the responsibility of seeing that the intentions of the donors are implicitly followed and the various bequests distributed as directed. Mass intentions will be forwarded to needy missionary priests immediately after the death of the benefactor and acquitted at once, thus obviating the long delays which necessarily accompany the execution of a will."[6]

The present delegate, Right Rev. Joseph Freri, was appointed by the Cardinal Secretary of State in the year 1903. The delegates preceding him were Fathers Magnien and Granjon. They were appointed in the year 1897.[7] Father Granjon was named Bishop of Tucson in Arizona in the year

---

5. FRERI, *op. cit.*, in the *Annals*, vol. LXXXV, p. 52, 1922.
6. Ut supra.
7. Ut supra.

1900 and Father Freri was appointed assistant to Father Magnien. Later, when Father Magnien died, Father Freri was appointed sole delegate. In 1889, Fathers Terrien and Gallien were given the mission to organize the Society in America. They did much to promote the Society also in Mexico. The National delegates of the Society transmit the total collections to the Central Councils in Lyons and in Paris. The Society is not incorporated in France and hence, theoretically, there is no such Society in the eyes of the French Government; but in practice this government is quite friendly to the Society and even during the darkest day of the past war did not prevent the Society from distributing its regular allocations.[8]

Before speaking of the procedure of these two bodies it would be well to give a list of the men who have presided over them since the foundation of the Society. The President of the Central Council of Lyons at the time of the foundation was M. de Verna. A complete list of the Presidents is as follows:

DE VERNA, Victor, President from May 3, 1822, to June 17, 1841.

DE JESSE, Antoine, President from June 17, 1841, to December 16, 1854.

TERRET, André, President from December, 1854, to July 16, 1859.

DE PRANDIERES, Louis Martial, President from June 26, 1859, to July 17, 1868.

DES GARETS, Francisque, born 1897, President from December 3, 1868, to November 25, 1898.

DE PRANDIERES, Martial, President from December 2, 1898, to May 31, 1906.

TERRET, Joseph, President from June 3, 1906, to December 7, 1906.

---

8. The stringent French laws governing associations make it impossible to have this Society incorporated.

SAINT-OLIVE, Henri, President from December 7, 1906, to October 27, 1920.

BECHETOILLE, Emmanuel (Mgr.) V. G., Lyons, President from October 27, 1920.

The Count des Garets who was President of the Council for thirty years and formed part of it during forty years, had handed in his resignation at the end of the year 1898 on account of his advanced age. The unanimous vote of his colleagues bestowed upon him the title of honorary president and retained him in the Council. He died on February 28, 1900, at the age of 93 years.

The first President of the Central Council of Paris was the Count de Sanst-Pilsach. The list of all the Presidents of this Council is:

DE SENST-PILSACH, Count,	President from	1822 to 1826
DE BERTIER, Count Ferdinand,	" "	1826 to 1833
ABBE MATHIEU,	" "	1833 to 1833
ABBE SALANDRE,	" "	1833 to 1839
DE LA BOUILLERIE, Alphonse,	" "	1839 to 1847
BERARD DES GLAJEUX,	" "	1847 to 1865
GAUDRY,	" "	1865 to 1873
COLIN DE VERDIERE, Leon	" "	1873 to 1885
HAMEL, Charles	" "	1885 to 1916
DE LA ZAILLE,	" "	1916 to 1920
ODELIN, Mgr. H., V. G., Paris	" "	Oct. 1920

Father Mathieu became Bishop of Langres, and later Cardinal Archbishop of Besançon. M. A. Guasco, born in 1854, has been General Secretary of the Central Council of the Oeuvre de la Propagation at Paris since August, 1883.[9]

The names of the present members of the two Central Councils are not given in any of the Society's publications.

The two Central Councils are the administrators of the Society. These Councils do not in any way interfere with the

---

9. These lists of Presidents were compiled by M. Groffier, General Secretary of the Central Council of Lyons, Cf. GUASCO, *op. cit.*, p. 39.

interior administration of the Missions, their function being
limited to centralizing the offerings which pass successively
before arriving in their hands through the chiefs of ten to
the parish directors and from these latter to the directors
of the diocesan committees.   When, at the end of January, the yearly offerings from the entire world have been
collected, and the accounts have been closed, then commences
for the two Central Councils the work of the distribution of
the total.   The Society does not deal in investments and has
no permanent fund.   To its great credit it can be said that
with conscientious attention and with impartiality all the
reports of the chiefs of the Missions, prefects and vicars-
apostolic, are read, compared and studied.   The information
concerning the Missions which the Councils procure from the
reports which the missionary bishops address to them each
year, permit them to apportion, in the most equitable manner
and with a perfect knowledge of the needs of each Mission,
all these gifts and alms from whatsoever source.   The Central
Council of Lyons takes the initiative in dividing the budget.
The Council of Paris, in its turn, resumes the task and with the
same solicitude, approves, modifies, increases and diminishes
the allocations.   It is only when the two Councils are entirely
in accord and after the consideration of the desires of the
Pope and the data submitted by the Congregation de Propaganda Fide, that the assistance decided upon is sent to each
Mission.   The result is indicated in detail in the *Annales* of
November in a statement published in nearly 375,000 copies.[10]
These allotments are made in accordance with the extent and
the necessities of each Mission concerning the special gifts
destined for a certain missionary or a certain unforeseen need
of a given Mission, the Councils accept them with courtesy
and transmit them with fidelity.   ''The distribution of funds,''
writes Monsignor Freri, ''is made at regular intervals by the
Councils, upon the comparative examination of the petitions
of the chiefs of Missions received every year.   The division

10. *Organization de l'Oeuvre de la Propagation de la Foi,* in the
Annales, t. LXXXII, pp. 7-10.

is made by the common consent of the two Councils, and once the list of allocations has been decided upon, it is sent to the Sacred Congregation of Propaganda for revision, adjustment and approbation. When it is returned from Rome, payments are made.'' [11]

At the monthly meetings, which are private, at which the ''répartition'' is to be made each director is provided with a small booklet on the first page of which is entered the year and the amount which had been distributed the previous year and the amount which is to be distributed in the present year and the difference between the two. The director's name is also inscribed on this page. Then follow in order, the names of all the Missions assisted by the Society, grouped under the headings of the five continents: Europe, Asia, Africa, America and Oceania. Then follows one chapter in which the names of the Grand Congregations devoted to the Missions are arranged. Opposite the name of each Mission is found six blank columns in which are to be inscribed the first, second and third decisions of both councils should these be found necessary. In the seventh column the allocation of the preceding year is inscribed in red and a space is reserved for the observations which the director may care to make. The last page of this booklet contains a recapitulation showing the total sum to be distributed according to the first, second and third decisions of the two councils for each of the five continents and the Grand Congregations and the grand total. Beside these figures are entered in red the corresponding totals for the preceding year. [12]

In spite of all this elaborate mechanism, the truth must be confessed that the greatest confusion reigns in the minds of the clergy and laity throughout the world on the methods used by the Society. The existence of two independent bodies, equally potent, and in some mysterious way equally subordinate to an unseen center, is bound to create confusion. Whether

---

11. FRERI, *op. cit.*, in the *Annals*, vol. LXXXV, p. 55, 1922.
12. Cf. *Appendix* of this work wherein a *Repartition cahier* has been reproduced.

Paris is subordinate to Lyons, Lyons to Paris, or whether the world is divided arbitrarily between the two Central Councils; or whether one can consider the Sacred Congregation de Propaganda Fide as the overruling director of the two Councils—are questions that no amount of research has cleared up. As we shall see, later, this confusion of authority—objectively, at least, has done harm to the Society in such business-like countries as England and America. Moreover, the Rule is antiquated and has fallen into disuse. No new Rule has been made since 1834, and this Rule antedates the present system of organization. As Freri has said:

> It is quite natural that an institution one hundred years old should be in need of some changes and reforms and we know that the Holy See has been contemplating them for some time. The 'Osservatore Romano' (the official organ of the Vatican) published on January 18, 1921, an article on the 'Propagation of the Faith' in which it was stated that the authorities of the Church had decided to transfer to Rome the Councils of Lyons-Paris and place them under the jurisdiction of the S. C. of Propaganda and the direction of an international committee. This will probably lead to a reorganization of the Society, but at this writing we have no knowledge as to the lines on which it will be made.[13]

Secrecy prevails over everything, and at Paris even the names of the members of the Councils were refused me.

Many Catholics, therefore, even among those whose social position and religious sentiments place them at the head of works of Catholic benevolence are ignorant as well of the organization as of the mode of operation of the Society for the Propagation of the Faith. This ignorance is due, in large part, to the traditions of the Central Councils' Directors, who have always concealed their labors under the veil of anonymity. The two Councils are self-recruiting and the functions of their members are entirely gratuitous. They are composed of ecclesiastics and laymen commendable by their social positions, the functions which they perform, their experience in business, their talent and their piety.[14]   Since

---

13. FRERI, *op. cit.*, in the *Annals*, vol. LXXXV, p. 14, 1922.
14. *Organization de l'Oeuvre, etc.* in the *Annales*, t. LXXXII, p. 7.

laymen were in the majority at the foundation meeting of the Society in 1822, the administration has remained almost entirely in their hands. Hence only a few priests have taken an active part in its deliberations.[15]

Recently, however, the Holy See expressed the desire to have ecclesiastics placed at the head of the two Councils, and as a result of this Mgr. Béchetoille, Vicar-General of the Diocese of Lyons, has been named President of the Central Council of Lyons, and Mgr. Odelin, Vicar-General of the Diocese of Paris, has been named to head the Central Council of Paris. Another recent innovation in the government of the Society was introduced by Pope Benedict XV when he created a Central Council at Rome, which he placed under the direct dependence of the Sacred Congregation de Propaganda Fide for all the dioceses of Italy and charged to procure a greater development of the Society in that country.[16] Just what will be the relations between this Council and those of Lyons and of Paris remains to be seen. It is problematical whether an international Council will be created at Rome or elsewhere and whether the ancient French Councils will become simple intermediaries between the faithful and this international Council or whether the former will conserve their present character. There is also a possibility that the Congregation of Propaganda may take over the effective direction of the Society.[17]

For the purposes of daily correspondence the two Central Councils have in some unknown way divided the Missions of the world between them. The dioceses and Missions in America have been under the jurisdiction of the Paris

---

15. FRERI, *op. cit.*, p. 14, 1912.

16. *Osservatore Romano*, January 21, 1921.

17. GUASOO, *L'Oeuvre de la Propagation de la Foi, Un Siècle d'Histoire*, in the *Correspondant*, t. 284, September 25, 1921; Cf. FRERI, *op. cit.*, in the *Annals*, vol. LXXXV, p. 55, 1922: "The Osservatore Romano . . . stated that the authorities of the Church had decided to transfer to Rome the Councils of Lyons and Paris and place them under the jurisdiction of the S. C. of Propaganda and the direction of an international committee. This will probably lead to a reorganization of the Society but at this writing we have no knowledge as to the lines on which it will be made."

Council. The Missions of the various religious orders have been somewhat arbitrarily divided between the two councils. The money contributed to the Society is sent by each delegate or by a diocesan director to the Central Council of Lyons or of Paris by means of bank drafts and it is distributed to the Mission fields by the same means. At times the insistence by the Central Councils that all mass stipends, particular gifts, as well as collections which are later to be distributed to the Missions of the same country in which they were donated, conform to this set method has resulted in certain delays and in losses incurred by the transfer and retransfer of these funds.

There is no doubt that as early as 1840, and earlier, the American bishops were not altogether pleased with the cumbersome methods of the Society. In that year we find Father Hercule Brassac submitting to the American hierarchy a prospectus for a general Agency to be established in Paris for the transactions of all ecclesiastical affairs with the Society for the Propagation of the Faith. This prospectus was as follows:

The need of an Ecclesiastical Agency established in Paris and devoted entirely to the interests of the episcopate and the clergy of the United States has been felt for a long time and yet an establishment of this kind is still wanting.

The undersigned, after having consulted persons of experience, has decided to attempt the enterprise, provided that his plan obtains the approval and encouragement of the archbishops and bishops of the United States, as it has already received it from Bishops Rosati, Portier and Miles. Here is what he has the honor of proposing:

I. The undersigned will act as representative before the Council of the Association for the Propagation of the Faith for the Right Reverend American prelates, who will thus authorize him for the purpose, to explain the needs of the dioceses, to defend their interests, to solicit assistance, to receive the sums allowed and send them to their destination by the surest means and with the shortest delay.

Nearly all the different Missions of the world have with the Association a representative in the Superiors of the Seminary of the Foreign Missions, of the Lazarists, the Jesuits, and the House of Picpus, etc. Those of the United States are almost the only ones which are not officially represented and from this may come the difference in the allocations. In as much as the directors of the Association have no other information about the missions than the letters of the Bishops, which are often read a long time before the sessions where the allowances are made, the demand made and the considerations to support them are likely to be forgotten, while a few remarks made verbally at that very moment might exert a very happy influence.

The funds allowed to the dioceses of the United States often remain a considerable time in the treasury of the Association. The time necessary to notify the interested parties of these allocations, the sending thereof or possibly the negotiation as to the manner and terms of payments which often follow long after the time when the matter has been presented, cause delays that could to a great extent be avoided by the proposed Agency.

II. Priests in Europe often obtain from their bishops an *exeat* gladly given in order to get rid of them; they arrive in America and the Ordinaries of the place where they present themselves for the missions, have no means of assuring themselves at once of their past conduct and their capabilities. Others again, led undoubtedly by good motives, but having had none to judge their vocations other than persons ignorant of the customs and ways of the United States, find themselves disappointed and unable to do much good. The undersigned will take it upon himself to obtain all possible information about the candidates who present themselves for America. He will try to learn of their character, their talents and their aptitude. As he knows a great number of the Dioceses of France, Belgium and even Germany and Italy, and as he moreover exercised the holy ministry in the United States for nearly twenty years, he would be better able than many others to judge, with less chances of being mistaken, -those who would be fitted for this kind of a mission. He could also provide for their embarkation according to the orders of the bishops.

III. In compliance with the wishes of prelates to obtain the establishment of religious orders of women, the undersigned will attempt to procure them and to attend to everything necessary for their voyage.

IV. The undersigned would also take care of the buying of books, ornaments, sacred vessels, paintings, engravings and lithographs and church furniture, also subscriptions to papers and magazines, and in general, of everything that would be recommended to him. He would give his personal attention to these matters, profiting by the assistance of merchants and manufacturers; he would spare no pains in obtaining the most advantageous terms at all times.

V. The undersigned promises to the archbishops and bishops that he will justify their confidence by constant zeal and absolute discretion in the matters entrusted to him.

VI. The undersigned would ask of each of the bishops and archbishops who would honor him with their confidence the sum of $50.00

(250 francs) as compensation for his services and would pledge himself not to charge any further commissions for the business he would have to do; at least where he would not himself be obliged to pay interest in procuring the drafts for the transmission of moneys.

VII. In cases where the undersigned would be obliged to advance moneys, he would charge at the rate of 5 per cent interest annually and 1 per cent commission on the sum advanced.

VIII. The undersigned will also charge himself to fill the orders given him by colleges, convents, religious institutions and the clergy at large for a reasonable commission according to the importance of the demand; but those orders must be sent to him through the hands of the bishops, or otherwise the money must be sent in advance by draft or otherwise.

IX. The undersigned will give to the archbishops and bishops who desire it, a guarantee for the faithful administration of their funds.

The undersigned feels it his duty to impress upon the archbishops and bishops of the United States that his enterprise is not a money speculation, but simply a work which he believes to be most advantageous for the country that he considers as a second Fatherland.

Bishops Rosati, Portier and Miles have authorized the undersigned to make known to their venerable brothers of the United States the approbation and encouragement which they have given to his project, and to give their names as his reference. He takes the liberty to add the names of Bishop Purcell of Cincinnati, of Mr. Jeanjean of New Orleans, of Madame Gallitzin, Superioress of the Sacred Heart of the United States. The agency will open on January 1, 1841.

Correspondence with the undersigned may be in French or in English. The following form signed and sealed will be a sufficient proxy to authorize the undersigned to act with full power. ''I, the, undersigned, Archbishop (or Bishop) of N. N. in the United States of America, recognize and authorize Monsieur l'Abbé Brassac, formerly missionary in America, as my agent with the Association for the Propagation of the Faith established in Europe, and I ask all persons whom it may concern to honor him in this quality with their confidence.''

I have the honor to remain, most respectfully of Your Grace, the most humble and devoted servant.

H. Brassac,
V. G. of Cincinnati and Nashville

Paris,
Rue Cassette 28.

P. S.—There will always be with this agent an apartment for the Archbishops and Bishops during their stay at Paris.[18]

---

18. Messmer, *The Rev. Hercule Brassac, European Vicar-General of the American Bishops, 1839-1861,* in the *Catholic Historical Review,* vol. III, pp. 413-415.

How many bishops joined this *Agence,* it is impossible to state.

The main item in the operating expenses of the Society is that for the printing, publishing and distributing the *Annales*. The other publications of the Society are sold for a modest price which generally covers their expense and at times leaves a small surplus which is also devoted to the Missions. The salaries of the employees, as well as rent, taxes, heat, light and insurance, and the expenses of correspondence constitute the other chief items of expense.

The receipts of the Association for the year 1842 amounted to 3,233,486 fr. which is upwards of $600,000. The Missions of the United States received of this sum, $126,000. The whole sum distributed throughout the world is about $550,000. The expenses of the administration which include those incurred not only in France, but in other countries, are composed of the salaries of persons employed, postage of letters in the correspondence which is kept up, as well as the various dioceses of Europe, as with the missions of the whole world, rent, stationery, etc., and amount to about $6,500. The Society publishes, every two months, a pamphlet containing intelligence of the different missions, consisting principally of letters from clergymen who are stationed in those various points. These pamphlets are called *Annals of the Association,* &c., and the printing of them amounts annually to $45,000. One hundred and fifty thousand copies of the Annals are now printed; namely 77,000 French; 21,000 German; 15,000 English; 2,000 Spanish; for South America; 3,500 Flemish; 28,000 Italian; 2,000 Portugese; and 1,500 Dutch; this number published six times a year, gives a total of nine hundred thousand copies. The number published in the course of the last year has been somewhat less, on the average, than this; but there must be added besides, the printing of the *Glance,* Prospectus, collector's sheet, &c., in all languages as well as the re-printing of several of the old numbers. In the expenses of publication must be also included paper, printing, stitching of the numbers, editing, translating into foreign languages, &c.[19]

One of the traditional methods of keeping the attention, the interest and the zeal of the faithful alive to the missionary work in which the Society is engaged has been the annual discourse delivered by one of the foremost pulpit orators of

---

19. *Association for the Propagation of the Faith* in the *United States Catholic Magazine,* Vol. III, pp. 124-128. Baltimore, 1844.

France on the subject of the Propagation of the Faith. This discourse generally took place on the third of May or the third of December, the two principal feast days of the Society, in the primatial church of Lyons in the presence of the Archbishop. Among the most prominent of these orators has been Father Monsabré, O. P., Father Didon, O. P., Mgr. Touchet, Bishop of Orleans, Father Janvier, O. P., and Mgr. Le Roy. They have all been printed and are on sale in Lyons for about ten cents apiece, the whole collection amounting to about two dollars.

At an early date the public character of the Society which had been assured by the rescript of Pius VII in 1823 which was its canonical institution and the progress which it made each day prevailed upon the Superior Council of the Association at Paris to give its publicity all the extension necessary for the national development of the work. There remains, however, in the administration of the Society the two defects: an absence of hierarchical organization between the Councils, and the prevalance of secrecy in the meetings, monthly and annual. For the latter, the French attitude towards such activity as that embraced by the Society must be understood; for the combination of patriotism and religious zeal has never been broken since the proud old days when the *Gesta Dei per Francos* was the boast of the people of France.

CHAPTER V

ECCLESIASTICAL AND LAY COOPERATION

In the year 1817 the Holy See gave its approbation to the *Association of Prayers* which was being reëstablished by the *Séminaire des Mission-Étrangères* of Paris and enriched it with certain indulgences.[1] After the foundation of the Society for the Propagation of the Faith it was necessary to obtain ecclesiastical approbation; hence in the beginning of the year 1823, M. de Villiers, a member of the Central Council of Lyons, went to Rome and was received by the Sovereign Pontiff, Pius VII, in private audience.[2] In this audience, of March 5, 1823, the Association for the Propagation of the Faith requested the Holy Father to grant to each of its members certain indulgences applicable to the souls in Purgatory.[3] In an audience granted to the Cardinal Secretary of State on March 15, 1823, Pius VII accorded to the Association the indulgences asked.[4] Pius VII died in 1823 and was succeeded by Pope Leo XII. Shortly after his elevation to the Papacy, the Central Council of Lyons, through the agency of one of its members, rendered its homage to the Pope; and on May 11, 1824, Leo XII granted to those Associates of the Society, who were infirm, the privilege of gaining the indulgences granted by his predecessor without the obligation of visiting the parish church.[5] Nor was Pius VIII forgetful of the

---

1. Cf. LAUNAY, *op. cit.*, t. II, pp. 500, et seq.; Cf. Note 7, at the end of Chapter II of this work.
2. *Association de la Propagation de la Foi*, in the *Annales*, t. I, fasc. iii, pp. 6-7.
3. Ut supra, pp. 6-8; Cf. *Propaganda Transcripts, Documento I, L'Associazione della Propagazione della Fede domanda l'approvazione a S. S. Pio VII*, Roma, 5 Mars, 1823.
4. Ut supra, pp. 9-11; Cf. ibid. *Documento II, Sua Santita Pio VII nell 'Udienza concessa al Card. Segretario di Stato, il 15 marzo 1823 accorda all'Associazione l'approvazione delle grazie domandate.*
5. *Annales*, t. I, fasc. v, pp. 8-10; *Extrait du Règlement de l'Association de la Propagation de la Foi*, in the *Annales*, t. I, fasc. vi, p. 96; *Propaganda Transcripts, Documento IV, Leone XII accorda agli associati infermi della pia Opera di poter lucrare le indulgenze con-

Society. The rescript of September 18, 1829, granted to the associates the privilege of gaining the indulgences by visiting any church whatsoever instead of the parish church or the oratory of the Association.[6] Gregory XVI, who had been prefect of the Sacred Congregation de Propaganda Fide, bestowed special benevolence upon the Society which had become such a powerful auxiliary of this important Roman Congregation. In a rescript dated September 25, 1831, he granted to those Associates, who are not French, the privilege of belonging to the Association and of gaining the indulgences accorded to the same.[7] These privileges were extended in perpetuity to those Associates outside of France. Moreover, on November 15, 1835, Gregory XVI, granted that the indulgences accorded to the members of the Society on the Feast of the Finding of the Holy Cross and on that of St. Francis Xavier might be gained either on their octave or on the day fixed for the celebration of the feast by the Ordinary.[8] On July 22, 1836, he also granted a plenary indulgence on Feasts of the Annunciation and Assumption.[9] Gregory XVI, issued on March 22, 1839, a brief whereby the Feast of the Martyr Esuperius was to be instituted in the metropolis of Lyons and whereby divers indulgences are accorded to the Associates of

---

cesse dal suo predecessore, senza l'obbligo di visitare la chiesa par-rocchiale. Die undecima maii, 1824.

6. *Annales*, t. IV, p. 259; *ibid.*, t. VIII, p. 408; *Propaganda Transcripts, Documento VII, Pio VIII accorda ai fedeli associati in-fermi di poter visitare una chiesa parrocchiale o oratorio dell'Asso-ciazione.* (18 Settembre, 1829) Rome.

7. *Annales*, t. V, p. 294; *Propaganda Transcripts, Documento IX:* 25 Settembre, 1831. *Il Sommo Pontefice Gregorio XVI, su domanda del Presidente dell'Associazione della Prop. della Fede di Lione, concede ai non Francesi di poter far parte dell'Associazione, e di lucrare le indulgenze accordate alla medesima.*

8. *Annales*, t. VIII, p. 407; *Propaganda Transcripts, Documento XVI: Gregorio XVI concede che le indulgenze agli ascritti della pia Opera per le feste dell'Invenzione e S. Francesco si possano lucrare o nella loro ottavo, o il giorno in cui la festa e fissata dal proprio Or-dinario.* 15 Novembris, 1835.

9. *Annales*, t. IX, p. 112; *Propaganda Transcripts, Documento XXVI, Gregorio XVI concede agli ascritti della Pia. Opera di poter lucrare l'indulgenza plenaria, applicabile ai defunti, nei giorni dell'An-nunziata e dell'Assunta.* Die 22 Julii, 1836.

the pious Society for the Propagation of the Faith.[10] In his Encyclical of August 13, 1840, Gregory XVI recommended the pious Society to all the patriarchs, archbishops and bishops, of the whole Catholic world. The opening words from the Encyclical, which we have already cited, are:

Probe nostis, Venerabiles Fratres, quantis undique calamitatibus tristissimo hoc tempore urgeatur et quam miserandum in modum Catholica vexetur Ecclesia: nec ignoratis quanta omnis generis errorum colluvione, effrenataque errorum audacia Religio Sancta oppugnetur, et quali astutia quibusque fraudibus haeretici, atque increduli homines connitantur fidelium corda mentesque pervertere. Nostis uno verbo, nullum prope esse laboris ac moliminum genus, quod ad inconcussum Sanctae Civitatis aedificium ex iuris, si fieri posset, sedibus evellendum non insumatur. . . . Quid denique, nisi magna cum laude dicendum, de celebri illa societate quae non solum in catholicis regionibus, sed etiam in Catholicorum et infidelium terris, nova semper obtinet incrementa; quaeque fidelibus omnibus cuiuscumque conditionis facilem viam modumque aperit, ut de apostolicis missionibus bene mereantur, ac de spiritualibus illarum bonis participes et ipsi fiant? Iam intelligitis, sermonem hic esse de notissima societate sub titulo Propagationis Fidei. Communicatis modo vobiscum, Venerabiles Fratres, et angoribus, quibus ab iacturas conficimur, et consolationibus quibus sustentamur ob catholicae Religionis triumphos, restat nunc ut pariter vobis communicemus sollicitudinem quae Nos urget pro maiori Societatum tam bene in Religione merentium prosperitate.[11]

His successor, Pius IX, in a rescript dated October 17, 1847, freely confirmed the spiritual graces granted to the Society by his predecessors.[12] On May 2, 1850, Pius IX, thanked the Councils of Lyons and Paris for the congratulations extended to him on the occasion of his return to Rome.[13]

10. *Annales*, t. XI, pp. 168-182; *ibid.*, pp. 459-462: *Propaganda Transcripts, Documento XXXI; Breve col quale s'istituisce la festa del martire S. Esuperio nella metropoli di Lione e si accordano diverse indulgenze agli associati della pia Opera della Fede.* Roma, *22 marzo, 1839. Gregorius PP. XVI, ad perpetuam rei memoriam.*

11. *Annales*, t. XII, pp. 603-615; *Propaganda Transcripts, Documento XXXIII, Enciclica con la quale Gregorio XVI, raccomanda l'Opera a tutto l'Orbe cattolico.* 13 Agosto, 1840. "*Probe nostis.*"

12. *Annales*, t. XXII, p. 320; *Propaganda Transcripts, Documento XXXVII, Pio IX conferma ampiamente alla Pia Opera le grazie spirituali accordate dai suoi predecessori.* Die 17 Octobris, 1847.

13. *Annales*, t. XXII, no. 328 bis, pp. i-viii; *Propaganda Transcripts, Documento XLVII; Pio IX ringrizia i Consigli di Lione e Parigi per le congratulazione inviategli in occasione de suo ritorno a Roma.* 22 Maii, 1850.

His rescript of August 5, 1851, decreed that the spiritual graces conceded by his predecessors might be gained by the members regardless of the sum contributed by them each month.[14] In the brief of December 31, 1853, Pius IX, accorded to the priests who are the collectors of the hundred groups of ten the favor of a privileged altar five times a week.[15] The rescript of April 17, 1855, accords to the children who are members of the pious work and who have not yet made their First Communion the privilege of gaining the indulgences by simply going to confession.[16] New indulgences were accorded in the rescript of March 7, 1862.[17] The rescript of January 26, 1865, granted to priests who each year collected (or themselves give 260 *lire* or who are members of a committee or council of the Society), the faculty of imparting to rosaries the indulgence of St. Bridget, the ordinary indulgence for crosses and medals, and the plenary indulgence and papal benediction in the hour of death.[18] On December 31, 1871, his rescript conceded other privileges to priests who are either collectors for the Society, are zealous in its behalf, or who are members of it.[19] On June 5, 1872, another rescript

---

14. *Annales*, t. XXIV, pp. 81-88; *Propaganda Transcripts, Documento XLVIII, Pio IX stabilisce che le grazie spirituali concesse dai suoi predecessori si possono lucrare dagli ascritti qualunque sia la somma da essi mensilmente elargita.* Die 5 Augusti, 1851.

15. *Annales*, t. XXVI, pp. 325-326; *Propaganda Transcripts, Documento L, Pio IX accorda ai sacerdoti ascritti alla Pia Opera il favore dell'altare privilegiato.* Die 31 Decembris, 1853.

16. *Annales*, t. XXVII, pp. 256-257; *Propaganda Transcripts, Documento LI, Pio IX accorda ai fanciulli ascritti alla Pia Opera di poter lucrare le indulgenze con l'accostarsi semplicemente al sacramento della confessione.* 17 Aprile, 1855.

17. *Annales*, t. XXXV, pp. 5-7; LOUVET, *op. cit.*, p. 11a.

18. *Annales*, t. XXXVIII, p. 253; *Propaganda Transcripts, Documento LII: Pio IX accorda ai sacerdoti che avranno raccolto ogni anno, o dato del loro, la somma di L. 260, ovvero che facciano parte di un Consiglio o di un Comitato dell'Opera, la facoltà di annettere o dare: alle corone le indulgenze dette di S. Brigida: alle croci e medaglie le indulgenze ordinarie; l'indulgenza plenaria e la benedizione papale in articulo mortis.* Die Ianuarii, 1865.

19. *Annales*, t. XLIV, pp. 79-83; *Propaganda Transcripts, Documento LIV, Pio IX concede altri privilegi ai sacerdoti o collettori o zelatori o ascritti alla Pia Opera.* Die 31 Decembris, 1871.

granted the concession of a plenary indulgence to the Associates on the occasion of the Society's fiftieth anniversary.[20]
The first rescript of Leo XIII, dated June 16, 1878, amplified the powers and faculties accorded to the priests who are collectors of the Society.[21] His Encyclical Letter of December 3, 1880, *Sancta Dei Civitas* recommended to the bishops of the Christian world the Institutes of the Propagation of the Faith, of the Holy Childhood of Jesus Christ, and of the Schools of the Orient. An extract from this memorable Encyclical follows:

> Eminet autem inter ceteras pia consociatio ante annos fere sexaginta Lugduni in Galliis coalita, quae a *propagatione fidei* nomen accepit. Haec primum illuc spectavit ut quibusdam in America missionibus opem ferret: mox tamquam granum sinapis in arborem ingentem excrevit cuius rami late frondescunt, adeoque ad missiones omnes, quae ubique terrarum sunt, actuosam beneficentiam porrigit. Praeclarum hoc institutum celeriter Ecclesiae pastoribus probatum fuit et luculentis laudam testimoniis honestatum. Romani illud Pontifices Pius VII, Leo XII, Pius VIII, Decessores Nostri et commendarunt vehementer et Indulgentiarum donis ditaverunt. Ac multo etiam studiosus fovit et plane caritate paterna complexus est Gregorius XVI. . . . Eodem tempore aemulatio pietatis effecit ut binae aliae societatis coalescerent quarum altera a *Sacra Iesu Christi infantia* altera a *Scholis Orientis* nuncupata est. . . . Itaque cum tria sodalitis tam certa Pontificum Maximorum gratia floruerint, cumque opus singula suum studio concordi urgere numquam desierint, uberes edidere salutis fructus, Congregatione Nostri de Propaganda Fide haud mediocre attulere subsidium et levamen ad sustinenda missionum onera, atque ita vigere visa sunt ut laetam quoque spem facerent in posterum segetis amplioris.[22]

On December 6, 1883, Leo XIII, expressed his appreciation of *Les Missions Catholiques*.[23] His rescript of May 25, 1885,

---

20. *Annales*, t. XLIV, pp. 315-317; *Propaganda Transcripts, Documento LV: Pio IX ringrizia i Consigli di Lione e Parigi per i voti da loro espressi in occasione dell'80mo genetliaco e del 50mo della fondazione della pia Opera.* 5 Giugno, 1872.

21. *Annales*, t. LI, p. 5.

22. *Annales*, t. LIII, p. 79; *Propaganda Transcripts, Documento LVI: Epistola Encyclica de institutis a propagatione Fidei a Sacra Iesu Christi infantia et a scholis orientis provehendis; Sancta Dei Civitas.* Leo PP. XIII, Die III Decembris, 1880.

23. *Annales*, t. LVI, p. 63.

accorded new indulgences to the Associates.[24]   On August 4, 1889, Leo XIII, extended new indulgences to all priests who are members of the Society or zealous in its behalf or who have paid in whatever money has been collected by them.[25] Another Encyclical Letter of Leo XIII, in favor of the Society was written on December 25, 1894, the *Christi Nomen*. We translate the following passage of this letter:

> For this reason we have never ceased to favor, to multiply the holy missions which spread the lights of the Christian faith among the people lost in the darkness and the Societies which sustain them by the subsidies collected from the faithful. . . . A Society which has loaned to the missions of the entire world such an efficacious aid and promises for the future still more abundant assistance. And with the blessing of God our words obtained a happy result; the generosities of the faithful respond to the urgent and zealous appeal of the bishops and the well-meriting Society has made notable progress in these latter years. But now more urgent needs lay claim to an increase of zeal and generosity on the part of Catholics, and on your part, Venerable Brothers, to all your intelligent activity. . . .   With what singular care, we are thinking of the Orient and of its illustrious and venerable churches, Our Apostolic letters concerning the necessity of conserving and of defending the discipline of the Orientals, have made you understand it. . . . But to the help from on high, human means must be added and we must neglect nothing in what depends on us to seek out and to indicate all the measures suitable for obtaining the coveted result.
>
> To bring back to the unique Church all those Orientals whatsoever, which are separated from it, you see Venerable Brothers, there is need at the outset of recruiting a numerous clergy from among themselves, a clergy commendable by its doctrine and its piety, and capable of inspiring in the others the desire of union; then, to multiply as far as possible, these institutions in which the knowledge and discipline shall be taught in bringing them into harmony with the particular genius of the nation. It is also very opportune to open everywhere that it will be advantageous, special houses for the education of the clerical

---

24. *Annales*, t. LVII, pp. 265, 345; *Propaganda Transcripts, Documento LVIII: Leone XIII concede altre indulgenze agli ascritti*, Die 24 Maii, 1885.

25. *Annales*, LXI, p. 414; *Propaganda Transcripts, Documento LIX: Leone XIII estende a tutti i sacerdoti ascritti alla Pia Opera le indulgenze accordate dai suoi predecessori ai sacerdoti membri di un Consiglio o zelatori, qualunque sia la somma da essi raccolta, o versata.* 4 Augusti, 1889.

youth, colleges in proportion to the importance of the population, in order that each rite may be practised with dignity, and that the diffusion of their best books initiate all the faithful into the knowledge of their national religion. The realization of these and of other similar projects, you readily understand will necessitate great expenses, and you also understand that the Oriental Churches are unable to suffice by themselves, for such numerous and such heavy charges, and it is not possible for us, in the midst of these difficult times through which we are passing, to contribute ourselves, in the measure we desire. It remains for us therefore, to request, within the bounds of moderation, the largest part of the subsidies necessary, from the Society whose praise we have sounded, and whose object is in perfect conformity with that which we have at heart. . . . It is just to also recommend the similar and so useful *Society of the Schools of the Orient,* whose directors are equally engaged in applying to the same object, the largest possible portion of the alms which they collect. . . . Make then, every effort, Venerable Brothers, in order that the *Association for the Propagation of the Faith* make the largest possible development among you.[26]

On December 12, 1903, Pius X in a brief filled with praise, expressed his joy at seeing the periodical, *Les Missions Catholiques,* translated into various languages.[27] In a brief of March 25, 1904, Pius X highly praised the Society and its patron. A portion of this brief is as follows:

In the first rank, by its utility and its action, is placed this Society, so worthy of sovereign praise, which has received the illustrious name of *The Propagaton of the Faith.* It seems to have been born and made its appearance in the midst of men by an inspiration wholly divine; for it is in conformity with the plan of the Providence of God that the faithful people of the Church who have not received the mission of preaching the Gospel of Christ, nevertheless aid by their assistance and subsidies, the heralds of the Gospel. That is why the love of Christ the Redeemer moved the hearts of excellent men, inspired them

---

26. *Annales,* t. LXVII, p. 84; *Propaganda Transcripts, Documento LX: Enciclica di Leone XIII in favore della Pia Opera. "Christi Nomen."* Die XXV Decembris anno MDCCCXCIV. Pontifical Rescript according indulgences to the priests who are collectors for the Society is published in the *Annales,* t. LXVIII, p. 468. The response of Leo XIII to the doubt submitted to him by the Sacred Congregation of Indulgences is given in the *Annales,* t. LXXXI, p. 384.

27. *Annales,* t. LXXVI, fasc. 453, supplement; *Missions Catholiques,* t. XXXV, pp. 613-614; *Propaganda Transcripts, Documento LXI: Pio X si rallegra con la Pia Opera per la pubblicazione del periodico Les Missions Catholiques, tradotte in parecchie lingue.* Die XII Decembris, MCMIII.

to unite in an Association the faithful of all the peoples and of all the nations; to have them contribute of their goods to the holy expeditions of the missionaries; to come to the assistance of the dispensers of holy things, in associating their prayer and thus to obtain the object of all their desires the progress of the kingdom of God upon earth. Everyone knows that such an association has grandly merited from the propagation of the Christian faith. If the resources permit the envoys of the Catholic doctrine to reach the most distant and the most barbarous countries and to bring to them the benefits of our holy religion and of our civilization, it is to the generosity of this noble Association that it must be attributed. . . . Wherefore, in virtue of our Apostolic authority and by the present letters solely for this motive we absolve and declare absolved from all excommunication, suspension, interdict, and other sentences, censures and ecclesiastical poena, if by chance they have been incurred, all and each of them in favor of whom the said letters are given; and in order, to the exterior support furnished to the Association, may be equally added the protection and the grace from on high we choose for it and give St. Francis Xavier as its Heavenly Patron and we desire that to this Saint there be accorded all the honors due to Heavenly Patrons; moreover, that the extension of his culte and that an increase of liturgical honors may still more increase his glory we elevate his Feast to the rite of a double-major, conformably to the rubrics, for the universal church. And, doubtless, the generous efforts of Catholics, even if they be isolated cases of individual liberalities, contribute much to this result; but nothing would be more profitable than the organization of groups of ten among the Catholics according to the very wise rule; for the less cohesion the efforts have the less is the effect produced, and on the contrary, united and prescribed efforts are most powerful. To act individually, we say, is to do well; but to act altogether is to do as one should.[28]

On February 1, 1908, Pius X conceded other privileges to priests who are members of the pious Society.[29]

Benedict XV, in a brief of January 6, 1916, renewed the benevolence of his predecessors towards the Society:

Truly with the blessing of God your solicitude and your zeal have produced abundant fruits as the subscriptions attest which you have obtained from the faithful and the enterprises of Apostolic labors which

28. *Annales*, t. LXXVI, fasc. 455, supplement; *Propaganda Transcripts, Documento LXII: Breve di Pio X in favore della pia Opera.* Die XXV Martii, MCMIV.

29. *Annales*, t. LXXX, fasc. 478, supplement; *Propaganda Transcripts. Documento LXIV: Pio X concede privilegi ai sacerdoti ascritti alla pia Opera.* Die I Februarii, MDCCCVIII.

they have permitted to multiply, but alas at the very moment that we would wish that the charity of Catholics become more generous for this Society we have seen a distressing group of circumstances which your piety rightly deplores for the same reason as ours, reduce at once the number of sacred ministers and the subsidies which are necessary for the missions of the Church.[30]

On November 28, 1919, Benedict XV recommended the Society in his Encyclical *Maximum Illud.*[31] Since the one hundredth anniversary of the foundation of the Society for the Propagation of the Faith occurs on May 3rd of this year (1922), the Catholic world anticipates some new favors and commendations from His Holiness, Pius XI.

Besides all these evidences of Papal sympathy and support, hundreds of bishops throughout the world have raised their voices in the favor of this Society and have called the attention of their clergy to it. One year after his acceptance of the Presidency of the Superior Council, on August 18, 1823, the Grand Chaplain of France, Mgr. de Croy wrote to all the bishops of France to recommend the Society to them, for it had already stood the test and obtained the benediction of Rome."[32] The bishops hastened to promise their support to the infant institution, formed committees and wrote pastoral letters. From all parts there also arrived expressions of thanks and testimonies of gratitude to a Society which had already rendered such signal services and which was destined, with the advance of years, to render still greater services. The Cardinal Prince de Croy believed he ought to join his felicitations to all those which were extended to the Society and on the fifth of November, 1824, he wrote to M. de Verna, President of the Central Council of Lyons:

> Since I have had the honor to preside over the Association for the Propagation of the Faith, you as well as the members of the Central Council over which you preside have given me the proof of your zeal for the success of this splendid work. It is with very sweet satisfaction

---

30. *Annales,* t. LXXXVIII, fasc. 525, supplement; *Propaganda Transcripts, Documento LXV : Benedetto XV rinnova alla pia Opera la benevolenza dei suoi predecessori.* Die VI Ianuarii, MCMXVI.

31. FRERI, *op. cit.,* in the *Annals,* vol. LXXXV, p. 62, 1922.

32. *Annales,* t. I, fasc. iii, pp. 12-14; GUASCO, *op. cit.,* p. 47.

that I have seen both what true Christians can do and what they are doing, animated like yourself by the desire of extending the knowledge of our holy religion and to concur in the salvation of souls. Kindly accept, and make known to the members of the different Councils, and to all those that are associated with us for this same end, the assurance of how much I am touched by their generous efforts and by the success with which God has deigned to crown these efforts in the Society of France.[33]

From a large number of bishops, who followed the example of the Vicar of Christ, recommendations have been given in favor of this Society. From the time of its foundation in 1822 until 1894, the Society for the Propagation of the Faith had been recommended to the faithful by 620 pastoral letters which may be grouped as follows: France and Colonies, 297 pastorals; Italy, 208; America, 42; Belgium, 12; England and Ireland, 11; Germany, 11; Switzerland, 9; Asia, 3; Spain, 3; Australia, 2.[34]

The proposition in favor of the Society for the Propagation of the Faith presented to the Congregation of Eminent and Reverend Fathers of the Vatican Council instituted to receive the propositions of the Fathers, by the Most Reverend Patriarchs, Archbishops and Bishops placed in charge of the government of the Missions, in January, 1870, was the most important episcopal endorsement the Society ever received. A translation of it is therefore given in full:

Venerable Fathers:

Among the different pious societies which due to the approbation of the Holy See and the favor of the bishops, sustain our missions by the prayers and alms of the faithful, that which bears the name of Society for the Propagation of the Faith undoubtedly ranks first.

It is from it indeed, that nearly all of us, without any exception of nation or of person, receive the food and clothing, that with which the Apostle St. Paul declares evangelic workers should be content; it is by its help that the Catholic institutions are established and developed, the Catholic institutions and the works of mercy which so eloquently announce the Lord Jesus to the eyes of the peoples who know Him not, and who are plunged in error; these works and these institutions

---

33. *Annales*, t. I, fasc. v, pp. 29-30; *ibid.*, t. II, p. 55.
34. LOUVET, *op. cit.*, p. 11a.

are so many striking signs by which we are recognized as the veritable disciples of the true God, in spite of all indignity.

Profiting therefore by the happy and holy occasion which unites us all, from the most distant regions of the world, at the feet of the Supreme Pastor, we have the unanimous desire of manifesting the immense gratitude which fills our hearts for this pious Society, the nurse and almost the mother of all the missions. We have at heart to recommend it to the venerable prelates who sit in the holy council and particularly, to the chief of all the prelates and of all the church, to the Sovereign Pontiff Pius IX, whose paternal benevolence we have already so often experienced.

This paternal benevolence and your own, Venerable Fathers, appears today to be much more necessary for the development of this Society since now for many years, the alms it receives for the Propagation of the Faith, instead of increasing as heretofore, remain stationary, or even as has happened this year, run the risk of diminishing.

There results from this, on the one hand, that the Society for the Propagation of the Faith, finds it impossible to suitably sustain all the missions whose number has increased; while on the other hand, the ministers in the regions committed to our care, lavish immense sums, whose amount increases each year, to pervert souls, or rather to buy them by a sacrilegious bargain.

An extreme danger menaces our missions and to avoid it, it is necessary to inspire in the faithful, new ardor in order that recalling their ancient energy, this grand society may always make new progress.

And we are confident that a single word from the Holy See and the Ecumenical Council will produce a result which is so desirable and so advantageous for the propagation of the Christian name in the whole world.

Relying on these sacred motives, Venerable Fathers, we humbly request that among the decrees relating to the Catholic missions which must be presented to the holy Ecumenical Council of the Vatican, one be added by which the Church accords to the Society for the Propagation of the Faith a solemn consecration and a new recommendation.

We cannot doubt that such a decision would be suitable to animate the zeal of the so Catholic directors of this pious Society, and to inspire in the faithful a sustained zeal in the places where it has seemed to languish.

That is then, Venerable Fathers, the favor which we humbly ask of you as well as of the Ecumenical Council, glorying in styling ourselves.

Your very humble and very devoted servants and brothers,

(Then follow the signatures of one hundred and fifty-one missionary bishops.)[35]

---

35. In the *Annales*, t. XLII, pp. 159-161.

The bishops of the Catholic nations of the Old and the New World have on several occasions given to the Society of the Propagation of the Faith marks of their high sympathy and generous coöperation by means of these pastoral letters which they have issued, which, when they were received by the Central Councils, had the effect of both a recompense and an encouragement.[36]   One might say that the bishops of all the Sees of France have successively recommended the great Society to the Faithful with high commendation.   On the occasion of the solemn Triduum celebrated at Lyons in honor of the Blessed Perboyre and Chanel, their Eminences, the Cardinals of Lyons and Paris, made an urgent appeal in favor of the Society of the Propagation of the Faith.[37]   At the time of the appearance of the Encyclical *Christi Nomen*, a large number of pastoral letters gave echo to the word of the Venerable Chief of the Church.[38]   The *Annales* have published excerpts from the sermons of His Eminence the Cardinal Archbishop of Rheims, and of the Archbishops of Aix, of Albi, of Sorrento; the Bishop of Carcassonne, of Valence, of Vannes, of Versailles, of Saint Flour, of Montpelier, of Oran, and of Auckland.   The pastoral letter of the Bishop of Nevers of December 25, 1890; of the Archbishop of Mexico of February 12, 1890; of the Bishop of Puebla of August 8, 1890; of Leon and of Vera-Cruz, in 1891; of Syracuse in 1895, of la Platta in 1898, of San-Juan-de Cuyo (Argentine Republic) in 1900, of Ancud (Chile) in 1903, were also cited.[39]

The long list of testimonials given in favor of the Society for the Propagation of the Faith, can hardly be exhausted. In the words of a venerable South American prelate, the Society for the Propagation of the Faith was the "marvel of the XIX century, the most eminent which the religion of Jesus Christ has inspired in recent times."   It is a work eminently Catholic, and it has often been so qualified by the

---

36. *Proposition en faveur de la Propagation de la Foi, presentée aux PP. du Concile du Vatican par cent cinquante-un évêques missionnaires*, in the *Annales*, t. XLII, pp. 159-161.
37. *Annales*, t. LXII, p. 7.
38. *Annales*, t. LXVII, pp. 229, et seq.
39. *L'Oeuvre*, etc., p. 33, 1908.

Chief Pastors. Not only from Missions but from all parts of the Christian world, from France, Ireland, Belgium, Italy, Spain, Germany, the United States, Mexico, the Argentine Republic and other South American republics, the Central Councils have been continually rewarded by the most gratifying letters. In the eloquent words of the illustrious prelate, Bishop Freppel, it may be said:

"May God's Kingdom come! May it come for those infidel peoples still living in darkness and in the shadow of death! May it come for those idolatrous races who know not Jesus Christ, who are deprived of the light and the consolations of the Faith; who have not, like us, those divine remedies against sin that the Church offers to her children! May it come also for those countries in the East which are being moved at this moment by the life-giving spirit of God; may it come also for those perishing branches which for centuries have been detached by schism from the trunk of Catholic unity! And, finally, may it come for our separated brethren in both the old and new world who have retained but a few shreds of doctrine and some semblance of Christian life! *Adveniat regnum tuum!* Then, when that glorious day shall have dawned upon the world, that day of spiritual birth for some and of resurrection for others, if we would wish to know the source of these divine blessings, we shall find, I say, as the principal instrument in God's right hand, the society for the Propagation of the Faith. This kingdom of God on earth will be its terrestrial crown, whilst awaiting the time when it shall please God to grant its active and zealous members their eternal reward."[40]

Reference has already been made to the letters of Bishops Du Bourg and Flaget, commenting upon the Rules of the Association shortly after its foundation. The optimistic attitude they assumed towards the Society proved fully justified, especially in reference to the Church in the United States, which is evidenced by the letters written to the Society and in favor of the Society by the provincial and national Councils. The first Provincial Council of Baltimore, on the eve of its conclusion, addressed a joint letter of thanks to the Councils of the Society of the Propagation of the Faith which follows:

---

40. Freri, *op. cit.*, in the *Annals*, vol. LXXXV, p. 64, 1922.

We eagerly seize the favorable occasion in which we are united in national council to testify to His Eminence the President of the Society of the Propagation of the Faith, to the Councils which direct it, and to all the members of which it is composed, our lively and sincere gratitude for the extraordinary favors which most of us have received from this zealous and generous association. Even those among the bishops who have not yet participated in its benevolence, convinced that all the amounts distributed into the hands of their confreres have served to form establishments extremely advantageous to the progress of our holy religion, rejoice in this before the Lord, and from the depths of their hearts join their thanks to those of their confreres who have been more privileged; hoping that in the future donations this inexhaustible association will deign to recall their names and furnish them the same means to make religion flourish in their respective dioceses. Thus, this beautiful Church of France, but a short while ago purified by a persecution not less murderous than those which took place under the pagan emperors, today offers to the Christian world the holy and touching example of the primitive church. For, as in former times, the Christendom of Greece and that of the Holy City generously contributed to the Holy Church of the Gauls in sending their missionaries filled with the Apostolic spirit and abundant alms, eighteen centuries afterwards this France, justly grateful, distributes in her turn into the new world immense sums for the formation of new churches and sends here missionaries who endeavor to tread in the footsteps of the Apostles.

Oh, may Heaven grant that the generosity of this illustrious Church of Christ will place us in a position to be able, in our turn, to form churches which will not delay to be established from the banks of the Missouri as far as the Pacific Ocean! In this holy expectation will you not seek to encourage the faithful confided to our care to pray for their pious benefactors; whilst the bishops and the clergy of the United States make it a duty never to offer the sacrifice from our altars without thinking of all the members of the venerable Association of the Propagation of the Faith, and of the most Christian king, who encourages such holy institutions in his vast empire.

Penetrated with all these sentiments, we have the honor to be, of all the members of the Association (for the Propagation) of the Faith, the very grateful and very devoted servants, James, *Archbishop of Baltimore,* Benedict Joseph, *Bishop of Bardstown,* John, *Bishop of Charleston,* Edward, *Bishop of St. Louis,* Benedict, *Bishop of Boston,* William Mathew, *Administrator of the Diocese of Philadelphia.*[41]

41. *Annales,* t. IV, pp. 112-114.

In 1830, Bishop Du Bourg, at that time Bishop of Montauban, France, wrote a letter on the Society from which the following is cited:

Asia and Africa have their missionaries of whom we will speak in a moment and America also has hers to whom we are bound, my dearest brethren, by an affection, the cause of which you understand. There is in America a vast and flourishing country known by the name of the United States where some men, animated by invincible courage and boundless charity, labor to establish the realm of Jesus Christ and to make His Gospel prosper. The most consoling and most unexpected successes are every day attained to encourage their efforts and increase their hopes. Everywhere, at the voice of the generous Apostles, the awakened people come out of their indifference, abjure their errors, prostrate themselves before their new altars, rejoicing to be able to address to God their sentiments of gratitude for the inappreciable benefit of their vocation to the faith. In a small number of years, ten dioceses, established on most solid bases, several seminaries perfectly organized, numerous colleges confided to very learned and very respectable priests, preachers full of zeal and talent, pious and benevolent associations, convents, monasteries and an ever increasing multitude of faithful and devout Christians promise to this infant church a long and glorious prosperity.[42]

On October 26, 1833, a letter from the Fathers of the Second Council of Baltimore to the Central Councils of the Society for the Propagation of the Faith, said in part:

. . . The benevolent hand, which in your Catholic zeal, you extend over all parts of the earth has spread a holy joy both in our cities and as far as the extremity of our forests and our deserts: the religion, of which we are the interpreters owes you its vows (voeux) and its prayers, and has inspired us to offer them to you according to the ancient custom terminating the sessions of this Council. If it is consoling for us to contemplate the holy eagerness of the faithful of France to share with America the heritage of charity which they have received from Asia it will not be less consoling for you to learn that the grain which you have planted is bearing fruit; that new temples rise up each day for the worship of the true God; that in nearly all our dioceses we have established seminaries; that the colleges founded for the instruction and the religious education of the youth obtain an astonishing success; that the convents are multiplied; that the natives shall finally be assisted; that 320 laborers at present work

---

42. *Annales*, t. IV, p. 262.

in the vineyard of the Lord and that a number twice as large or even greater still would scarcely respond to the needs of our vast province. The twelfth diocese will be born without delay. Pray therefore, our, well beloved, that those who are the successors of the Apostles and who represent them in this important portion of the new world, in equaling their number walk in their footsteps, everywhere carrying before them the torch of the faith and that of Apostolic virtues; then your works shall be worthily crowned and the sowing of the grain of mustard seed which you have sprinkled with your generous contributions will become a large tree in the shadow of which other peoples will be able to take refuge.[43]

The Fathers of the Fourth Provincial Council of Baltimore wrote to the Presidents of the Councils of the South and of the North (Lyons and Paris) and to the members of the Society for the Propagation of the Faith on May 23, 1840:

By the benefit of a merciful Providence you were inspired, our dear brethren, to come to the aid of the American Church at the very epoch when, leaving a state of infancy, it sought a protecting hand to steady its tottering steps and to send it forth into the desert to seek there the abandoned sheep. A happy and noble inspiration which impelled you, in the land sprinkled by the blood of Pothin and Irenaeus, of these generous martyrs who seem to have bequeathed to you the beautiful mission of in some way rendering to the entire universe this heritage of faith which you received from Asia. Your Society, like the grain of mustard of which the Gospel speaks, has developed with that vigor of life which comes from on high; and after you have had scarcely a few years of existence you have already extended its branches of benevolence as far as the extremities of the earth and you have accompanied the priest of Jesus Christ amongst the peoples so long seated in the shadow of death. We rejoice, our dear brethren, in these superabundant benedictions which God showers upon you, for if even the glass of cold water given in the name of His Disciple is not without merit for eternal life; if God contemplates with joy the widow's mite, you who by your common offerings sustain the existence of his zealous ministers who divide the world, have you not the sacred right to the recompense of a prophet?[44]

---

43. *Annales,* t. VI, pp. 632-634; *Missions Catholiques,* t. IX, p. 523, 1877.
44. *Annales,* t. XII, pp. 409-410.

The Fathers of the Fifth Council of Baltimore on May 20, 1843, sent a letter to the Presidents, Directors and Members of the Propagation of the Faith.

No one can appreciate with more justice the benefits of this Catholic spirit and the miracles of this ardent charity which sustain as far as the extremities of the earth the torch of faith than those who, in the new world have seen at close range the progress of the grain of mustard seed which becomes a tree and furnishes shade and repose to those who have grown weary in the ways and the errors of this mortal life. Twenty-five years have scarcely passed by and already seventeen pastors are united in the Sanctuary of the Metropolis to form new flocks, to call around them other collaborators, to carry to the Holy See a testimony of their veneration and of their entire submission and to make uniform by uniting their counsels and their experiences, the ecclesiastical discipline. . . . It is God that has done all these things. . . . It is to your Society to which we in large part owe these marvels: it is to your charitable solicitude that we recommend our infant churches; you will aid us to lay these foundations (six new dioceses will soon be added to the sixteen which represent our province) which are as the ramparts of truth. We will endeavor, sirs, to respond to the appeal of your zeal and to extend the name and the influence of this precious Society before God and before men.[45]

The Fathers of the Sixth Provincial Council of Baltimore wrote the following letter to the Directors of the Society for the Propagation of the Faith:

The Fathers of the Sixth Provincial Council of Baltimore could not close their grave and laborious session without expressing their lively admiration of the marvelous success which your Society everywhere attains and without offering you the homage of their gratitude and that of all the faithful committed to their care. They have not forgotten that the needs of their infant Church gave birth to this grand Society, that it is to your industry and charity that they are indebted for the astonishing progress of the Faith in the United States, and that if their venerable metropolitan presides over the deliberations and directs the ''conseils'' of twenty-two of his brothers, it is through you that he contemplates this admirable meeting which recalls the beautiful days of the Church. Is it not touching, Gentlemen, to see assembled around the same altar, twenty-three prelates and more than fifty priests, all having but one heart and one soul, animated by the same spirit of strength and of truth, partaking of each other's

---

45. *Annales*, t. XV, pp. 361-362.

troubles and hopes, encouraging each other to combat under the old standard which the successor of Peter, after eighteen centuries, still shows to all the nations with ever-fresh vigor?   .   .   .

Our progress is sure, peaceful and full of promise, but we do not wish to hide from you, Gentlemen, that our needs multiply in proportion as we advance, that there is not a single diocese that is freed from the bonds of its infancy, and that if we rejoice in the good of which you have been the life-giving source, there remains still more to be done. In 1810, the Church of the United States, as temples, had nothing but cabins. The oldest dioceses therefore are still young, and are very far from having acquired enough strength to walk without aid. Seminaries, colleges, cathedrals, churches, religious houses, presbyteries, asylums for the orphans of both sexes, hospitals, free schools, ornaments of culte, everything, in a word, was to create. It is not yet a quarter of a century since God raised you up to become the nursing fathers of all Catholic Missions. The Kings at one time, glorified in this title and in this privilege. It has passed from their hands to those of the poor, and you are their faithful administrators. Cast your glances towards our part of the New World; count the crosses which everywhere show as the symbol of salvation. The work is solid, permanent, sheltered from the vicissitudes of all the enterprises which charity has formed in the Orient. It is not, it is true, sprinkled with the blood of martyrs, but it does not cease to be by the sweat of its indefatigable priests. We think, and our thought is not too much at hazard, that Providence is reserving for us a special mission, and that the designs of God are great and magnificent for our future existence, and since we are still only at the point of departure, that the emigration from Europe is always unceasing and more numerous, that our sheep are in general of those poor to whom the Gospel must be incessantly announced, that the Christian education of the children belongs to our position, that as resources, we only have what is sent us, we think, I say, that as pastors, we owe to our weak flocks, to expose to you their distress. Never was an epoch more important or more critical; it is that of our development, it is that in which all upright and generous spirits turn towards us, it is that of action and of combat. In continuing to sustain us you will sooner enjoy the triumph of the Catholic Faith, you will encourage us to persevere until the end, you will sow in a field which already bears fruit in abundance, and perhaps you will one day receive what you have loaned us. Witnesses of divine truth, we are also the natural witnesses, the interpreters in regard to the needs which burden us.

To respond to your appeal, Gentlemen, we recommend in the pastoral letter of the Council, to the pastors and to the faithful, the establishment of your Society in all our dioceses. We hasten to concur in your good work, to give evidence of how much we appreciate the benefits. . . .[46]

On May 14, 1849, the Fathers of the Seventh Council of Baltimore wrote to the Presidents and Directors of the Councils of the North and of the South of the Society for the Propagation of the Faith:

The future of the Church which everywhere seems to be covered with a mysterious cloud which presages the moment of combat, of trials and of triumph; this future opens before us with the hopes, the consolations and the vigor of a church still young, which grows like a new vineyard and which will soon count among its laborers six Archbishops and thirty Bishops. Besides the secular clergy, we have as collaborators nine religious bodies or pious societies, a precious portion of the militant church which edifies the pastors not less than the faithful and of which the branches multiply from day to day. Our communities of Sisters present a spectacle not less consoling. The hospitals, the asylums for the orphans, the schools for the poor, the boarding schools for the well-to-do class, establishments without number, prosper under the direction of the virgins consecrated to God. One thought always afflicts us, that of not being able to spread to all the children of the faith the benefits of a religious education. You will easily understand, sirs, the immensity of our needs and the greatness of our responsibility when you (will) learn that the European and Catholic emigration now surpasses the figure of 250,000 souls per year. The emigrants are, with few exceptions, poor and destitute of resources; they are driven to America by famines and by revolutions; they come to seek here an existence which the old world only offers precariously. For these poor, churches and pastors are needed; for their children, instruction, spiritual bread and often nourishment for the body (are needed) you will well understand, sirs, for the annual increase of Catholics alone we ought to annually procure 300 priests, build 300 churches, 300 schools. Now that is what our position is: the old dioceses which for the most part are found to be the most favored and solidly established respond but weakly to the cries and the needs of the multitude: those (dioceses) which are in their infancy and have only small, scattered and poor populations have not yet an assured existence and languish through lack of assistance. The charity of Jesus Christ urges us, sirs, to recommend to your protection and to your generous solicitude this church of which we are the pastors. . . . And to express to you this gratitude of heart for which there is no more just or more eloquent expression than that of the Apostle: We

---

46. *Annales*, t. XVIII, pp. 393-396.

have a great joy, my brethren, and a great consolation into your charity, for the hearts of the saints have been refreshed and comforted by you.[47]

A pastoral letter of the Archbishops and Bishops of the United States in First National Council assembled at Baltimore (1852), to the Clergy and Laity of their charge follows:

Our Holy Father Pius IX has recommended to our notice, as well as that of all the Bishops of the Church, the Society established at Lyons in France, for the purpose of aiding apostolic missionaries in the Propagation of the Faith. Independently of the authority which has thus spoken, our own feelings would prompt us to address you on the subject. From the time of its first establishment, almost thirty years ago, up to the present time, this association has contributed, generously and uninterruptedly, to the support of our missions. If our churches have so rapidly multiplied; if our religious and educational establishments are now comparatively numerous; if new missions and new dioceses amidst most appalling discouragements, still continue to be founded—we must, in truth, and justice, acknowledge, that in all this the Association for the Propagation of the Faith has afforded us the most generous and most enlightened cooperation. We feel the obligations which we have to an Association which is identified with the progress of religion in every part of the world: and we, therefore, exhort you Brethren, to encourage its establishment in your respective districts, agreeably to the wishes of the Sovereign Pontiff, who desires to see the whole Catholic world united in an effort to diffuse the Gospel of Christ throughout all nations. The small annual contribution made to this Association will not interfere with any effort of Christian zeal or charity; and we cherish the conviction, that its establishment will draw down from God the choicest blessings on all who unite in this truly good work.[48]

The Fathers of the First Plenary Council of Baltimore on May 20, 1852, sent the following letter to the Society:

The Fathers of the First National Council of the United States, six Archibshops and twenty-six Bishops, united by the authorization and the desires of the Venerable Successsor of St. Peter, have received the prayer which you have offered, with joy and gratitude. They have decreed by a vote of acclamation that the Society for the Propagation of the Faith shall be established in all their dioceses, even envious of marching in your footsteps, they have appreciated the simple but fecund

47. *Annales*, t. XXI, pp. 289-291.
48. *Metropolitan Catholic Almanac and Laity's Directory for the Year of Our Lord 1853*, p. 51.

manner which distinguished the administration of your Society from
all the others. How could they not have responded to tne appeal of
your zeal in seeing the great things which Providence has created about
them and of which you have been the principal instruments by the
charity of the poor? The Fathers of the Council recall the epoch when
six bishops governed the Church of the United States and today there
are as many metropolitan churches. The hierarchy is composed today
of thirty-three prelates, and soon twelve new cooperators shall be added
to this number. What a glorious future is reserved for us, I dare, or
we dare say, they already belong to us. Our work of creation progresses
in proportion' to the past, striving in speed with the movement of the
country and extending itself as far as the Pacific Ocean, we are permitted to hope and to believe that before twenty-five years at most the
American portion of the Catholic Church will have as many Episcopal
Sees as the most ancient realms of Europe. Is it not a miracle of
Providence that the rapid increase of the true church in this part of
the New World, where the prejudices of error have sunk such deep
roots, where riches and influence formed a wall of opposition, where
the greatest poverty was the least of our difficulties? But God knew
that a large part of Europe was to set forth towards North America
and that is why (voila qu'il) He renews the prodigies of the Apostolate
and of the missions. He inspired the idea of your Society and He
surrounded it with the fullness of his benediction, and presents what
is unique in the annals of the Church that is that a small number of
laymen, receiving their first mission of charity, become, under the
protection of the Holy See, the husband of a nursing mother of all the
missions of Catholicism. How can one refrain from crying out: "How
beautiful are your tabernacles, oh God of Israel" when we contemplate in one and the same sanctuary the Bishops who, although separated
by a distance of more than two thousand leagues, have at the voice
of the Holy Father, braved the distances, the fatigues, the sea and
the privations in order to consult upon the need of their infant churches.
We pray you, sirs, not to forget in the object of your prudent charity
the multiplied needs which are necessarily born in America from this
extraordinary development and to be mindful that we have to provide
for the spiritual, and often the bodily existence of 200,000 Catholics
at least who annually arrive from Europe. There is not here a single
diocese the organization of which is complete and which is capable of
responding to the demands of the faithful. New Sees cannot exist but
by your charity and among those we recommend to you in a particular
manner that of Oregon. . . .[49]

---

49. *Annales*, t. XXIV, pp. 401-403.

A letter of Archbishop Hughes, of New York, written in the name of the First Provincial Council of New York to the Members of the Councils of the Propagation of the Faith, New York, October 9, 1854, contains the following eulogy:

. . Our first duty after we have addressed the Common Father of the Faithful is to express with unanimous voice our gratitude to the Society for the Propagation of the Faith. In the vast territory which now forms the ecclesiastical province of New York there were thirty years ago only two Bishops, eleven priests and about 40,000 Catholics. Today we have an Archbishop with eight suffragans, very nearly 500 priests and about 1,000,000 Catholics. At the sight of the rapid progress of our holy religion it is impossible for us not to bring our thoughts back towards the admirable Society for the Propagation of the Faith to which we are in large part indebted for such a great benefit: it is equally impossible for us to disperse without testifying our gratitude toward you, sirs, who are its representatives and who distribute its funds with so much wisdom. These thousands of poor immigrants who annually settle in our respective dioceses and find here, thanks to your charity, priests and altars; these poor lost sheep which every year we have the consolation of bringing back into the fold of the unique Pastor; these numerous orphans tenderly brought up by our good sisters; the number still greater of young children preserved in our Catholic schools from the poison of heresy; this body of zealous missionaries which you sustain by your prayers and your alms; all our faithful in a word unite their voice to ours to testify to you their lively and very sincere gratitude. For a long time, sirs, we have desired to establish among us the Society for the Propagation of the Faith; but the circumstances under which we found ourselves did not permit us to do it in all the dioceses. The Fathers of the Council of New York have resolved to take immediate measures to propagate it in their dioceses and they are eager to communicate to you this resolution unanimously adopted in their assembly. It is unfortunately too certain that there now exists in this country some secret and powerful coalitions, whose end is none other than to abolish Catholicism in the United States. Witness the insults, the daily calumnies to which we are exposed; witness the churches which have been burnt or demolished. May it not please God that we be discouraged! Mary Immaculate is our powerful and glorious protector and the extension of Catholicism among us which is already so great a gauge of the merciful views of God towards our Church. Yes we are convinced that God desires to communicate the lights of the Faith to this people whom He has conquered by the blood of His Son; we say more: God desires to make use of our nation to bring back to the truth these distant peoples to whom it has access by the extension of its commerce. Permit us therefore, sirs, to urgently solicit a continuation of the assistance which you have accorded us, the good which these allocations will aid us to accomplish is the good which will have permanent effect. We are living in the midst of an intelligent, civilized people in a vast and fertile territory; it is therefore permissible for us to hope, following the ordinary course of Providence, that our pious institutions shall be a source of sanctification for the present generation and for those to come in the midst of a people which appears destined to play a grand role in the history of nations. It is impossible for us in a letter to expose to you the extent of our needs. If we rejoice to have been able to establish some schools and orphan asylums, our heart is wrung with sorrow in thinking that the larger part of our children remain exposed to the dangers of error, to the contagion of bad example, without a sufficient number of teachers to instruct them, of priest to sanctify them by the sacraments. Often we rejoice to learn that a new church is to be consecrated to Catholic worship, but more often still we grieve to see entire parishes without pastors to guide them, without resources to construct a modest chapel. However, our Catholic population becomes every year more numerous by immigration so that the Bishops of even the most flourishing cities often have reason to bewail not being able to finance the construction of churches in proportion to their ever increasing number. Moreover, there are in the province of New York some recently erected dioceses for which must be procured a more numerous clergy, churches, seminaries, where all, in one work, is to be created. It is therefore with a just title and I dare say, with confidence, that we pray you to continue your allocations. It remains with us to bless you with all our heart and to assure you of our gratitude and our respect.[50]

The Fathers of the Eighth Council of Baltimore, to the Councils of the Propagations of the Faith, Baltimore, May 14, 1855, wrote as follows:

. . . There remained only six Suffragan Bishops of the province of Baltimore, but the dioceses of Charleston and Savannah are represented in this Council by their worthy administrators. Several among us have made known to you in particular the needs and the progress of their respective dioceses, and have made it a pleasure and a duty to recognize the generous liberality of the Association of which you, sirs, are the administrators. Now that we are assembled, we are eager to do in common what we have already done separately: we thank you with all our hearts for the zeal which you have shown for the missions of America; we pray and we have the faithful of our dioceses pray for

---

50. *Annales*, t. XXVII, pp. 81-84.

you. Through your agency we express the sentiments of our hearts towards these generous souls who, in all the countries, are associated with the Society for the Propagation of the Faith. We declare anew our sincere desire to here cooperate as soon and as much as circumstances permit us. But sirs, permit me also to recall to you the pressing and ceaselessly recurring needs of the dioceses which are confided to us and to represent to you by a united voice that in several dioceses of this province these needs are very great. Without citing any one in particular, we are content to say that there is almost no one of them which has not a right to your charitable solicitude. But we are not ignorant of your good will towards ourselves and our missions and we do not believe it our duty to add anything to this general testimony by a report of the condition of our province. You have learned by the published papers and the private letters of Bishops the progress which Catholicism makes, the increase of the number of churches and of priests and the multiplication of the faithful still more rapid than that of the temples of religion. We rejoice in it and you, sirs, have good reason to participate in our joy, having comforted our labors and facilitated our success. May God recompense you in bestowing upon you while on earth the riches from on high and after this life the crown promised to the faithful and zealous servant.[51]

On May 20, 1855, the First Provincial Council of Cincinnati wrote the following letter to the Councils of the Society:

We are happy, in terminating our first Provincial Council to offer you the homage of our lively gratitude for the generous assistance which we have received from such an eminently Catholic Society.

We must loudly proclaim it, our young Church of America is languishing; it even suffered deplorable losses before your Association came to its assistance. Since then, a great amelioration has taken place: the lights of faith have been carried more regularly and more efficaciously to our poor natives; the number of conversions among our erring brethren has increased; our Catholics, hastening here from all parts of Europe, and scattered here and there in the midst of our forests and our cities, are no longer as heretofore, exposed unprotected to the artifices of error, or to the fatal consequences of ignorance; a more numerous clergy visits them; consoles and protects them against the snares and the persecutions of these later times. In place of the savage hut or of the rustic fireside in which we distributed the bread of the word, we have seen chapels, churches, cathedrals erected in which the Catholic is encouraged, fortified, and in which the Protestant of

51. *Annales,* t. XXVII, p. 401.

good faith is stripped of his prejudices and his hatred against the Spouse of Jesus Christ. Our seminaries, the source of ecclesiastical learning and virtue, are organized and begin to furnish us subjects, to relieve the veterans of the priesthood who have so nobly fought on the field of the Gospel. We will not attempt to tell you how great has been the number of orphans whom the Church has lost, and whom it now counts in the midst of its most violent enemies; moreover, I will not speak of that multitude of sick who have appealed in vain for the consolations of the faith at their last hour; nor of those thousands of children who from their infancy have drunk from the cup of error and of indifference in our public schools. Fifty years ago, the Church of the New World sighed and bemoaned the loss of its unfortunate children; fifty years ago, it labored to close its mortal wounds. Oh, may Heaven be blessed! Here as everywhere, the old Faith has the remedies for all ailments, the consolations for all sorrows; it has commenced to found its schools, its religious communities, its hospitals, its asylums. To the youth it gives an instructor to teach him at one time, his duties as a citizen and the route to Heaven; to the orphan and the sick, it gives a mother or a sister of charity: that is how, little by little, our Infant Church responds to its noble mission.

But who gives it strength and life, and who sustains it today in the midst of its perils and the furious strife in which it is engaged? We must publish it, Providence has raised up your Society, Gentlemen, as one of the most efficacious means to prepare and complete its triumph in this hemisphere. But it is not enough for us to recognize it, it is our duty to imitate you. That is why, at the solicitaton of the Sovereign Pontiff and to cede to the voice of conscience we are eager to establish the Society for the Propagation of the Faith; only we regret that by reason of the financial crisis and of the high cost of living which so cruelly make themselves felt here this year, the result of our effort will not respond to our expectation. We hope, however that better times will soon aid us to put a more abundant alms in the common treasury of your Society, and to offer to your wise administration, by it a feeble compensation for your long and generous benefits.[52]

The letter sent by the Fathers of the First Provincial Council of New Orleans to the Members of the Central Councils of the Propagation of the Faith, dated New Orleans, January 27, 1856, was:

---

52. *Annales*, t. XXVII, pp. 334-337.

The Fathers of the First Provincial Council of New Orleans in devoting themselves to the interests of their respective dioceses and blessing God for the graces which He has accorded to all their flocks, naturally think of the benefits which your noble and holy Society has spread over the young church of America and of which the fruits are today so visible and so remarkable. The last act of their sessions, a spontaneous act from their Catholic hearts, and one which resumes all the deliberations, has been to thank Providence for having inspired at the determined time in the faithful of Europe of which your Councils are the soul, to console, fortify and vivify by their charity the faithful of the United States. Admirable successes have crowned your first efforts and lead us to hope that you will enjoy the benedictions of a small flock which you have seen born, grow and multiply. Five bishops are grouped around their elder brother, the Bishop of New Orleans, and labor to lay the foundation of the Holy Catholic Church upon the rock. These dioceses are still young and only received a little assistance from European immigration, they still have need of the superabundant charity of your Society. You will no doubt learn with pleasure that we have established branches of the same Association in all our province, and that pastors and flock rejoice to be members of this body which so well represents the strength and the extent of the charity of our Lord Jesus Christ. Our alms shall be that of the widow of the temple. May the eye of Him which nothing escapes see it and His hand bless it.[53]

On May 8, 1858, the Fathers of the Provincial Council of Cincinnati wrote to the Associates of the Propagation of the Faith:

Gentlemen, Sensible to the pecuniary assistance accorded by the Association for the Propagation of the Faith to the different dioceses of the province of Cincinnati; and in view of the precious advantages which have resulted from this assistance, for the advancement of religion and the sanctification of a multitude of souls, who would be exposed to perish without such aid, the bishops of this province, assembled in council, cannot separate without testifying and expressing through you to all the Members of the Councils of your excellent Society, the sentiments of our gratitude.

When, looking around us, we consider the good already accomplished and for which we are in large part, indebted to the ardent zeal of the faithful who make up the important and pious Association for the Propagation of the Faith, our hearts naturally rise towards God, to ask Him to bless and propagate more every day, a Society so con-

---

53. *Annales*, t. XXVIII, pp. 257-258.

formable to the designs of His mercy, and we pray especially that His benedictions be extended to all those who direct it, who sustain it by their offerings or their alms.

This sentiment is rendered more lively by the consideration of the needs which are multiplied with the increase of the Catholic population, which is spreading into all parts of our dioceses, and also by the difficulties which the opulence of the sects which surround us and unjust legislation give rise to.

The education of our children, which they seek to snatch away from us in the schools sustained by the public funds, which expand from the enormous taxes we are forced to pay, without procuring any advantage from it, does more to expand our resources; and it is only by sacrifices, too often in excess of our strength, that we can sustain the faith and protect the morals of our children. This difficult situation will not, however, prevent us from spreading, in as much as this is in our power, in our respective dioceses, an Association of which we ought by a very just title, to appreciate the benefits, since each of us owes to it, more or less, the prosperity of that part of the vineyard of the Lord confided to his care.[54]

The Fathers of the Provincial Council of St. Louis wrote the following letter to the Directors of the Society for the Propagation of the Faith, dated St. Louis, September 12, 1858:

Assembled in Council in the Metropolis of St. Louis the different dioceses which compose this province were unwilling to disperse without testifying their gratitude to the admirable Society for the Propagation of the Faith. We experience a great consolation in having this occasion to render to you such a well merited tribute. The assistance which we have received and still receive from your charity has aided us in the most efficacious manner to build our churches, to found our establishments and to maintain them. It would be useless to enumerate that which each of our dioceses owes to the Society; still more so to repeat how many Bishops and missionaries in all parts of the world are indebted to it, the large number of churches, schools and houses of charity erected through its assistance.

''We see with joy that Providence is pleased to bless this Association, so eminently religious, and that it has made it prosper throughout so many difficulties; we keenly share the solicitude of the Holy Father in favor of the Society and what we regret is that our poverty does not permit us to increase still more the number of your subscribers. Most of our dioceses are newly erected in the least inhabited part of this

---

54. *Annales*, t. XXX, pp. 399-401.

vast continent: we have therefore to face the greatest embarassments and obstacles; but the visible benedictions which God deigns to shower upon our feeble labors and the rapid progress of our holy religion sweeten the burden of our formidable responsibility.[55]

The Archbishop and Bishops of the Province of New Orleans wrote the following letter to the President and Members of the Central Councils which was received on February 24, 1860:

The labors of the Second Provincial Council of New Orleans are at an end.

Before separating, the Fathers of the Council desired to offer the collective expression of their respect and of their profound gratitude to you, Gentlemen, to whom the dispositions of Providence have confided the high direction of one of the most astonishing Catholic societies which since the Apostolic times, Our Lord and Saviour Jesus Christ has raised up for the extension of his reign upon earth.

Accustomed, as they are, to hear the cries of distress which ceaselessly come to them from all parts of the world, your eminently Christian souls have always generously had compassion on the numerous necessities of the peoples confided to our solicitude by the Prince of pastors; your charity has always heard and welcomed our humble requests.

It is with happiness that we express our gratitude for it, Gentlemen; it is with consolation also that we recall that the first inspiration, and as the germ of the grand Society for the Propagation of the Faith, came forth, over forty years ago, from the noble heart of one of the first bishops of New Orleans. Since the day on which Monsignor Du Bourg deposed it in some pure and humble souls of our France, the little seed has once again realized the prodigious growth promised by Jesus Christ to His Church, to the Kingdom of God on earth. The tender plant has become an immense tree, in which, from one end of the earth to the other, the powerful branches protect with their shade, and nourish with their fruit the numerous and devoted laborers of the Father of the family.

The reports which you have successively received from the different dioceses of our province have sufficiently well informed you, Gentlemen, of the ever increasing prosperity of the Holy Church of Jesus Christ in this old land of Louisiana and the Floridas, for the miseries of which the voice of Monsignor Du Bourg had accents of such just and profound sorrow.

---

55. *Annales*, t. XXXI, pp. 5-6; *Annales*, t. XXXII, pp. 201-203.

In the solemn circumstances which assemble us, what we maintain and proclaim is that after God, it is to the grand Society for the Propagation of the Faith that are for the most part, due the very fruitful benedictions which have not ceased to descend upon our people.

God is faithful, Gentlemen, and so many benedictions showered from your hands upon the indigence of our missions will return a hundredfold to the members of the Society and to you, especially, Gentlemen, who bear with such generous devotion the incessant fatigues of an administration which has no other end than the end of our ministry itself.   That in all things and in all places, Jesus Christ be glorified and that His truth and His charity reign over all the earth.[56]

The Fathers of the Provincial Council of Cincinnati, on May 6, 1861, wrote the following letter to the Directors of the Society for the Propagation of the Faith:

Mr. President, The prelates of the Province of Cincinnati, assembled in Council, have been unwilling to separate without giving testimony to the Members of the Council of the Propagation of the Faith of their lively gratitude.   The benevolence manifested towards all during long years and which several (dioceses) are still today the object, could not be forgotten and they are pleased to renew to you their thanks.   The institutions and the religious edifices for which we are in large part indebted to the Association which your Councils rule over with so much zeal and wisdom, are so many monuments of generosity which will always recall to the faithful of the United States that which they owe to their brothers of Europe and which will assure to our benefactors a very dear remembrance in our prayers.

Mr. President, May God grant the sincere good wishes which we nourish for the success of a Society so useful to religion; may He bless all the Members of this pious and holy Association; may He bless especially those who so generously devote themselves to maintain and extend it.[57]

The following letter of the Bishops united in the Second Plenary Council at Baltimore to the Central Councils of the Society for the Propagation of the Faith was dated Baltimore, 1866:

The Bishops assembled in Plenary Council have a lively sense of the debt of gratitude imposed on them by the liberalities of Catholic charity concentrated in your hands. . . . We openly acknowledge that your offerings have had a considerable share in the development of our church. . . . Henceforth, the Church of the United States

56. *Annales,* t. XXXII, pp. 201-203.
57. *Annales,* t. XXXIII, pp. 337-338.

will endeavor to occupy in your reports a place more worthy of the
rank assigned to it by the extent of its territory, the abundance of its
resources and the wonderful increase given it by the Almighty.[58]

The Central Councils of the Society for the Propagation
of the Faith received the following letter from the Bishops
united at Baltimore in Provincial Council, dated Baltimore,
May 2, 1869:

The Bishops assembled for the celebration of the Tenth Provincial
Council of Baltimore believe they would fail in a very sweet duty
which is imposed upon them by gratitude joined with the desire of
seeing the realm of God extended more and more among them if they
did not profit by the favorable occasion which presents itself of
testifying to the Directors of the Society for the Propagation of the
Faith and in them to all the so numerous and so zealous members of the
Association, the sentiments which fill their hearts. The ways of God
are truly admirable: Quis cognovit sensum Domini? aut quis Consiliarius
ejus fuit (Rom. XI., 34). At an epoch when the furious Revolution
had overturned the churches, annihilated the ancient liberties of
sanctuary, despoiled the clergy, usurped the riches with which the
faith of our fathers have enriched the altars, He inspired by His all-
powerful grace, a thought of zeal and generosity in some poor, but
devout souls. And from their poverty has risen a fund almost equal
to that which impiety had seized but on which it could no longer lay
its sacrilegious hands. The mite of the widow, of the artisan, of the
peasant, of the laborer and of the servant girl has been changed into
a colossal sum which will go on as it has for nearly a half century
increasing more and more and thus more and more proving the large
number as well as the generous charity of the children of the Catholic
Church. The offering of the poor enables the missionary to penetrate
into China and into Japan, to visit the burning sands of Africa and the
frozen regions of the two poles. This offering gives us the means of
building our churches in the inaccessible forests of the New World and
if Catholicism has dug deep its roots in our country, if it has received
rapid and marvelous development we owe it in large part to the cooperation of your admirable Society. We have quite recently enlarged the
sphere of our ecclesiastical hierarchy and we hope that your ingenious
zeal will see new posts where your assistance will become the necessary
instrument of a thousand good works.[59]

---

58. *Annales*, t. XXXIX, pp. 79-81.
59. *Missions Catholiques*, t. II, pp. 169-170; *Annales*, t. XLI, pp.
251-253.

The Fathers of the Third Provincial Council of New Orleans addressed the following letter to the Members of the Central Councils of the Society of the Propagation of the Faith, dated New Orleans, January 21, 1873:

. . . Yes, in truth, it is from God that this work, unique in the history of the centuries and which in commanding the admiration of the faith offers itself in these latter times to the Holy Church as a consolation in the midst of her immense sorrows. . . . It was at this epoch . . . that under the hand of God was born in humility a Society destined to grow to the height of a power which we have not known since the Apostolic days, the Society for the Propagation of the Faith, the simplicity and the charity of which have hurled a victorious defiance down to the very depths of Satan. Who will not admire with us the so prodigious and so rapid extension given by this Society of Faith to the realm of God in the entire world? Who would not admire this net work of Apostolic ways opened by it during a half century to these thousands of evangelical workers who have illumined with the great lights of the City of God the lands which were covered by darkness, the peoples who were enveloped in the sombre night? Who would not admire this ever increasing multitude of Episcopal Sees which seat in a stable manner the Kingdom of Jesus Christ there where Satan reigned, indefinitely pushing back the boundaries of the Divine Realm? Who would not admire this number of altars which has become innumerable, erected by the great Society in all climates and concerning which is finally verified to the letter the sacred oracle which promised that from the rising of the sun to the going down thereof there shall be offered the immaculate oblation of the Lamb immolated from the foundation of the world? Who would not admire and who will count the colleges, the communities, the holy asylums of all kinds, sown by it with profusion as far as the most unknown lands and whence rise towards Heaven more praises, prayers and love than impiety was able to hurl of hatred and of malediction? Who would not admire, finally, how in our days, otherwise so evil, the map of our globe has become that of the pacific and benevolent conquest of the holy Church, conquest of blood and of sweat of Apostolic men, nourished, clad, encouraged by this truly Christian Society of the Propagation of the Faith? If, resting our gaze upon the American Union to which we belong we consider the present condition of the Church of Jesus Christ, with its seven ecclesiastical provinces, its 62 Bishops, its 5,000 priests, its 150 convents of men, its 400 communities of women, its 4,000 churches, its 90 colleges, its hospitals, its asylums for children and for the old and its numberless Christian schools and then we consider that scarcely a half a century ago this vast republic had only a few Bishops directing some hundred priests and a dozen or more religious establishments, we adore the hand of God who has done all these things and a just gratitude carries us back towards the Society of which it pleased God to make the principal instrument of His mercies. The millions of francs which it has so generously showered upon us have not done all, no doubt, and should not do all. And without this Society, however, where would we be? How many dioceses whose creation would have been impossible! How many vocations to the Apostolate would have rested useless! How many establishments, without it, either would never have existed or would have perished through lack of resources! Therefore, blessed be this Society which will remain one of the grand glories of our century as it is one of the highest manifestations of the indestructible life of the church and of the power of God for its conservation. Blessed be the faithful who have understood that the first of the alms is that which saves souls. Blessed be the generous men who for fifty years have succeeded one another in the prudent direction of the Society for the Propagation of the Faith and in the wise distribution of the treasure of Catholic charity. For us, Sirs, who owe you so much and who dare to rely upon a concurrence of your charity as much for our dioceses as for the new dioceses which we solicit the Holy See to create in our province, we exert ourselves to communicate to the people who are confided to us the sentiments which animate us and to increase, according to our strength, the prosperity of the Society.[60]

Finally, the Third Council of Baltimore held in 1884, the most important ecclesiastical assembly up to our time in the United States, recommended the Society in still stronger terms to the charity of the faithful, obeying in this the orders given to the bishops by His Holiness Leo XIII. Following the example of their predecessors, the Fathers of the Council again decreed the establishment of the Society in all dioceses in which it did not already exist. His Eminence Cardinal Gibbons, in the name of the Council, dated Baltimore, December 6, 1884, wrote to the Directors of the Society:

With admirable wisdom which he had received from Jesus Christ, the Doctor of the Gentiles, traced for us with His Apostolic hand the symbolic image of the Church. He represented it to us as the living body of which we are the members and of which the Saviour is the head. As the influence, the direction, and the empire of the head is extended over the entire body so the members united in a compact body

---

60. *Annales*, t. XLV, pp. 235-239.

transmit the influences which they receive from their Chief. That is why the Divine Saviour considered as done to Himself the good or evil which one does to His Church; that is also why, in the language of St. Paul, if one member of this mystically organized body is in suffering, all the members sympathize with him and if one member is in joy all participate in his rejoicing. This doctrine, so beautiful, so just and so edifying, you have constantly presented to the memory, Sirs, when from a prosperous and generous country you extend your inexhaustible charity to all the countries, to all the people of the Catholic world. You fly to the help of those who are in need, you furnish to those who are in distress the means of doing good, you aid to edify, you contribute to repair ruins with the intimate persuasion that Jesus Christ Himself will render account of the good which you do to the distant members of His mystic body. It is a very sweet duty which gratitude imposes upon us of publicly recognizing the signal services which the blessed Society of the Propagation of the Faith has rendered to the young Church of the United States. If the grain of mustard seed planted in the virgin soil of America has struck deep roots and has grown into a gigantic tree which extends its branches from the shores of the Atlantic Ocean as far as the coast of the Pacific Ocean, it is mainly to the assistance rendered by your admirable Society, Gentlemen, that we are indebted for this blessing. Assembled for the third time in Plenary Council, the Archbishops and Bishops of the Republic of the United States feel a justifiable joy in thinking of the cooperation which you have never ceased to extend to the Apostles of the Catholic Faith in the New World, from the year 1822 to the present day; and the sums which during that time you have allotted to the different dioceses and missions of this vast country, are a striking proof of the zeal and charity with which you never cease to aid us. In our turn, we ardently desire to contribute to the immense good which you are doing in all parts of the globe; and if up to now our most prosperous provinces have only succeeded in furnishing you a relatively modest sum it is because there are great vacant spaces among us to be filled in and pressing needs to satisfy, however the time is approaching when we will be in a position to prove to you that the Catholic people of this country do not permit themselves to be surpassed in generosity and in benevolence in the great work of the Propagation of the Faith. And while we still recommend .most earnestly to your charity of which we have received so many evidences, the poorest churches and the most desolate churches of this Republic, we dare give you the sweet hope that if Divine Providence blesses our efforts the gifts of our faithful will become at the same time a powerful means of aiding you to continue your charity and as a restitution of the benefits which your solicitude has showered upon us.[61]

61. *Annales*, t. LVII, pp. 120-122.

One of the most important ways in which the Church has coöperated with the Society during the last hundred years is the steadfast support given it by Propaganda.

All matters concerning the Missions in general fall under the jurisdiction of the Sacred Congregation de Propaganda Fide, and although the Society for the Propagation of the Faith submits the schedule of its allocations to the Congregation for approval before the money is paid out, and also considers the wishes of the Sovereign Pontiff in formulating this schedule, nevertheless Propaganda does not exercise an active rôle in the functions of the Society. The Sacred Congregation encourages, blesses and applauds the efforts of private initiative, but it refrains from distributing the free aid which Providence raises up for its envoys. The chief function which the Sacred Congregation has performed for the benefit of the Society for the Propagation of the Faith has consisted in exerting its constant and repeated efforts to maintain the unity and universality of this Society.[62] In treating this matter in chronological order it will only be necessary to mention a few of the important communications between the Society and the Sacred Congregation.

On August 28, 1827, the Sacred Congregation expressed its gratitude to the President of the Council of Lyons for having appropriated a sum of money to aid the Church of China.[63]

On February 23, 1828, a reply of the Sacred Congregation to a request from the President of the Central Council of Lyons, asking the Sacred Congregation which Missions were most in need of assistance, dwelt upon the need of Bishop John Dubois, of New York, in which it quotes this phrase from a letter of that prelate: "Quid vero dicam de gravi

---

62. LE ROY, *La Propaganda* in the *Missions Catholiques*, t. XXXVII, p. 46, 1905; FRERI, *Propagation of the Faith* in the *Catholic Encyclopedia*, vol. XII, p. 461.

63. *Propaganda Transcripts, Documento VI: La Sacra Congregazione ringrazia il presidente del consiglio di Lione per aver, secondo il voto da Iei espresso, destinata una somma a beneficio della diocesi di Scio.* Lugdunum, 28 Augusti, 1827.

aere alieno, quo Cathedralis ecclesia ipsa opprimitur, videlicet 28,000 nummis argenteis Americanis, circiter 147,000 galli- cana pecunia?'' This quotation emphasizes the debt of the New York Cathedral of $28,000 as the most urgent need of all the Missions at this time.[64]

The next communication between the Sacred Congregation and the Society is that the Cardinal Prefect Cappellari (later Gregory XVI) rejoiced in the fact that the Society had not suffered losses from the Revolution in France. This is dated November 27, 1830.[65]

On June 2, 1832, the Sacred Congregation sent the list of the new Bishops in missionary lands to the President of the Council of Lyons asking that the sums appropriated for each diocese be sent directly to them.[66] The Society on July 26, 1834, inquired from the Sacred Congregation the method to be followed in sending subsidies; in this letter it expressed some doubt concerning its relations with the bishops and religious superiors.[67] The Sacred Congregation in January, 1835, inquired from Father Michael Tecchinelli, S. J., concerning the most needy Missions which should be assisted by the money collected by the Society.[68] On February

---

64. Ut supra, *Documento V: Il Presidente del Consiglio Centrale della Francia meridionale della pia Opera domanda alla S. Congregazione quali siano le Missioni più bisognose di aiuto.* Lugdunum 23 Februarii, 1828.

65. Ut supra: *Documento VIII: Il Card. Cappellari, Prefetto della S. Congregazione di Propaganda si rallegra che pia Società non abbia sofferto danni dalle rinnovate rivoluzioni.* R. P. Pelagaud, Lugdunum in Galiis—Vol. 311, Fol. 1006—27 Novembris, 1830.

66. Ut supra, *Documento X: La S. Congregazione di Propaganda manda al presidente di Lione la nota dei nuovi Vescovi dei luoghi di Missione, ai quali dovranno direttamente essere inviate le allocazioni stabilite per le singole missioni.* 2 Iunii 1832. (Archivio della S. C. de Prop. Fide, *Lettere,* Vol. 313, Fol. 513-v.)

67. Ut supra, *Documento XI: L'Opera pia interroga la S. C. Congregazione di Propaganda circa modo da tenersi nell'inviare i sussidi.* 26 Luglio, 1834. (Vol. 315, Fol. 406-v.)

68. Ut supra, *Documento XII: La S. Congregazione di Propaganda chiede il parere del P. Michele Tecchinelli della C. di G. circa le missioni più bisognose da sussidiarso colle somme raccolte dall'Opera pia. Gennaio, 1835* (Archivio della S. C. de Prop. Fide.—Lettere della S. C., Vol. 316, Fol. 88-v.)

11, 1835, the President of the Society asked the views of Propaganda concerning the use to be made of the interest on the money of the Society and concerning the method of sending subsidies.[69] On August the 6th, 1835, the Society expressed its desire to work in concert with the Sacred Congregation in respect to the subsidies that were to be sent to the various Missions. It sent the list of the Missions that were to be helped in order that it might be approved or modified.[70] On November 28, 1835, the Sacred Congregation defended the unity of the Society against the supposed tentatives for autonomy of Switzerland in regard to paying out the sums collected. Its decision was that the intentions of the donors to apply the alms to the Foreign Missions across the sea was binding in conscience.[71]

On February 27, 1836, Gregory XVI granted the request for a part of the sums collected in Switzerland to be directly used by the respective Ordinaries for the benefit of the Missions within that region.[72] On November 22, 1836, the Sacred Congregation assured the Central Council of Lyons that the Councils of the Society to be established in Rome and in Naples would be entirely subject to the Central Council.[73]

---

69. Ut supra, *Documento XIII: Il Presidente dell'Opera pia chiede alla S. S. Congregazione di Propaganda il parere circa l'impiego fruttifero dei denari dell'Opera, e circa il modo d'inviare i sussidi.* Lione, 11 Febbraro, 1835 (Vol. 316, Fol. 105).

70. Ut supra, *Documento XIV: L'Opera Pia dichiara di voler agir di concerto con questa S. Congregazione in rapporto ai sussidi da spedirsi slle varie missioni. Manda la nota delle missioni da sussidiarsi perche la si approvi o la si modifichi.* 6 Agosto, 1835.

71. Ut supra, *Documento XV: La Sacra Congregazione difende l'unita dell'opera contro supposti tentativi di autonomia della Svizzera, per quel che riguarda la erogazione delle somme raccolte,* 28 Novembre, 1835 (Ibid., Fol. 806-v).

72. Ut supra, *Documento XVII: Gregorio XVI concede che una par parte delle somme raccolte in Svizzera siano direttamente erogate dai rispettivi Ordinari a beneficio delle missioni interne di quella regione.* 27 Febbraio, 1836 (Lettre della S. C., Vol. 317, Fol. 123).

73. Ut supra, *Documento XVIII: La Sacra Congregazione assicura il Consiglio centrale di Lione che i consigli dell'Opera pia da stabilirsi a Roma e a Napoli saranno pienamente soggetti al medesimo Consiglio centrale.* Li 22 Novembre, 1836 (Ibid., Fol. 867).

On January 24, 1837, Cardinal Brignole was nominated President of the Council of the Society that was to be established in Rome.[74]

On March 18, 1837, the Sacred Congregation of Propaganda recommended that the Archbishop favor the foundation in Naples of a Council of the Society for the Kingdom of the two Sicilies which was to be subject to the Central Council of Lyons.[75] On April 10, 1837, the Government of Naples expressed its desire that the Council of the Society established in the Kingdom of Naples, correspond, not with the Central Council of Lyons, but with the Council to be established in Rome.[76] On May 2, 1837, the permission was accorded to the Central Council of Naples to correspond directly with Propaganda as well as with the Central Council of the Society at Lyons.[77] On July 8, 1837, the Sacred Congregation indicated to the Central Council of Lyons the African Missions that were to be assisted.[78] On July 15, 1837, the Sacred Congregation warmly recommended to the Bishop of Ghent the spread of the Society in his diocese.[79] On January 30, 1838, the Sacred Congregation manifested to Cardinal Brignole the desire of the Central Council of Lyons that the Council of the Society established in Rome be made dependent

74. Ut supra, *Documento XIX: II Card. Brignole viene nominato presidente del Consiglio Dell'Opera pia da stabilirsi in Roma.* Li 24 Gennato, 1837 (Lettere della S. C., Vol. 318, Fol. 46).

75. Ut supra, *Documento XX: La S. Congregazione di Propaganda raccomanda all'Archivescovo di favorire in Napoli di un Consiglio dell-'Opera per il regno delle Due Sicile, il quale resti saggetto al Consiglio di Lione.* 18 Marzo, 1837 (Ibid., Fol. 238-v).

76. Ut supra, *Documento XXI: II Governo di Napoli desidera che il Consiglio della pia Opera da stabilirso nel Regno corrisponda non col Consiglio Centrale di Lione, ma con quello da stabilirsi in Roma.* Li 10 Aprile, 1837 (Ibid., Fol. 374-v).

77. Ut supra, *Documento XXII: Si accorda al Consiglio di Napoli di poter corrispondere direttamente con la Propaganda anziche col centro dell'Opera a Lione.* Li ii Maggio, 1837 (Ibid., Fol. 460-v).

78. Ut supra, *Documento XXIII: La S. Congregazione di Propaganda indica al Consiglio centrale di Lione le missioni di Affrica da sussidiarsi.* 8 Luglio, 1837 (Ibid., Fol. 580-v).

79. Ut supra, *Documento XXIV: La S. Congregazione raccomanda caldamente al Vescovo di Gand la diffusione della pia Opera nella sua diocesi.* 15 Iulii, 1837 (Ibid., Fol. 601).

upon Lyons.[80]   On July 26, 1838, the Sacred Congregation defended the unity of the Society which was menaced by the attempted separation of Bavaria, which would prefer to be united to the Leopoldine Society of Vienna.[81]   The ruling was that Bishop Rese's claim to an authorization of the Sacred Congregation to transfer funds of the Bavarian Society to Vienna, and hence that they would no longer be sent to France, was not valid; Rese had no authority to treat these or other questions, hence the money would have to go to Lyons.

On November 8, 1838, the Sacred Congregation expressed its desire that the dioceses of Northern Italy continue to correspond directly with the Council of Lyons.[82]   On December 13, 1838, the Sacred Congregation asked the Council of Lyons what regulations it believed to be opportune for the preservation of unity between the newly established Roman Association and the Central Council; and asked if it did not think it opportune to send the money collected in Rome directly to the missions in order to avoid unnecessary losses occasioned by the useless transfer and exchange of money.[83]   On January 22, 1839, the Sacred Congregation endeavored to prevent the organization of pious Societies different from that of the Propagation of the Faith of Lyons in Belgium,

80. Ut supra, *Documento XXV: La S. Congregazione manifesta al Card. Brignole il desiderio del Consiglio Centrale di Lione che il Consiglio dell'Opera della Propagazione della Fede eretta in Roma sia posto sotto la dipendenza del medesimo.*   Li 30 Gennaro, 1838 (Lettere della S. C., Vol. 319, Fol. 129).

81. Ut supra, *Documento XXVII: La Sacra Congregazione difende l'unita della Pia Opera della Propagazione della Fede minacciata da tentativi separastisti della Baviera che desidererebbe piuttusto di unirsi alla Societa Leopoldina di Vienna.*   Li 26 Luglio, 1838 (Lettere della S. C., Vol. 320, Fol. 724).

82. Ut supra, *Documento XXVIII: La S. Congregazione desidera che le diocesi dell'Altœ Italia continuino a corrispondere direttamente col Consiglio di Lione.*   Li 8 Novembre, 1838 (Ibid., Fol. 1301).

83. Ut supra, *Documento XXVI: La S. Congregazione domanda al Consiglio di Lione quali disposizione si credano piu opportune per condervare l'unita fra la neonata associazione romana ed il Consiglio Centrale e se non creda opportuno l'invio diretto alle missioni dei fondi raccolti in Roma, per evitare perdite d'inutili passaggi di denaro e relativi cambi.*   Li 13 Decembre, 1838 (Lettere della S. C., Vol. 320, Fol. 1379).

England and Bavaria in order that the unity and universality of the Society for the Propagation of the Faith might not be injured.[84] On February 5, 1839, after the Council of the Society established in Ghent had refused to correspond with the Council of Lyons, the Sacred Congregation wrote an urgent appeal to the Bishop of Ghent, Louis Joseph Delebecque, insisting upon the unity of the Society which His Holiness Gregory XVI had very much at heart.[85] On November 16, 1839, the King of Bavaria, after much hesitation, agreed to the union of the Bavarian Council of the Society to the Central Council of Lyons.[86]

On July 14, 1840, the Holland branch of the Society expressed its purpose to correspond directly with the Sacred Congregation.[87] On February 25, 1841, the Sacred Congregation endeavored to reestablish the Superior Council of the whole Society, by confiding its direction to Cardinal De Bonald.[88] In the letter to Mgr. Garibaldi, Apostolic Nuncio to Paris, the reasons given for reëstablishing this Superior Council were that the two Councils of Lyons and Paris might not be in conflict; that greater unity might be attained, and somewhat more deference paid to Propaganda on whom all Missions depended. The selection of Cardinal De Bonald was made in virtue of his high office, as a Cardinal, and it was recalled that the Grand Chaplain of France, Cardinal de

84. Ut supra, *Documento XXIX: La Sacra Congregazione cera d'impedire che in Belgio, Inghilterra, Baviera s'istituiscano pie opere diverse dalla Pia Opera della Propagazione della Fede di Lione che ne compremettano l'unita el'universalita.* Li 22 Gennaro, 1839. (Lettere della S. C., Vol. 321).

85. Ut supra, *Documento XXX: Il Consiglio della Opera stabilito in Gand si rifiuta di corrispondere col Consiglio di Lione.* Die 5 Februarii, 1839 (Ibid., Fol. 121).

86. Ut supra, *Documento XXXII: Il Re di Baviera, dopo molte esitazioni annuisce alla unione del Consiglio bavarese per l'Opera Pia della Propagazione della Fede al Consiglio Centrale di Lione.* Die 16 Novembris, 1839 (Ibid., Fol. 1136).

87. Ut supra, *Documento XXXIIbis: Il ramo olandese dell'Opera Pia preferisce di corrispondere direttamente con la S. Congregazione di Propaganda.* 14 Luglio, 1840 (Lettere della S. C., Vol. 324, Fol. 638-v).

88. Ut supra, *Documento XXXIIIbis: La S. Congregazione si adopera per ristabilire il Consiglio Superiore di tutta l'Opera, affidandone la disrezione al Card. De Bonald, 25 Ferraro, 1841* (Lettere della S. C., Vol. 325, Fol. 146-v).

Croy, was its former President. On November 27, 1841, the Sacred Congregation insisted that the Society as established in Holland depend upon the Central Council of Lyons.[89]

On December 11, 1841, the Sacred Congregation took up again the project of reconstructing the Superior Council of the whole Society and asked the Internuncio to remind the Directors of the deference due to His Holiness.[90] On January 22, 1842, the Sacred Congregation urged the Archbishop of Salerno to preserve the unity of the Society.[91] On January 31, 1842, the Sacred Congregation recommended to the Archbishop of Lima that the Society, instituted in his diocese to aid the Missions, be joined to the Central Council of Lyons.[92] On July 2, 1842, the Council of the Society established in South America demanded complete independence from the Council of Lyons.[93] On August 3, 1844, a decree of the King of Bavaria ordered that the Council of the work existing in his States deal directly with Rome and have no further relation with the Central Council of Lyons. Another document of the same date relates to the same question.[94] A decree of the Sacred Congregation of August 3, 1844, made the Council

89. Ut supra, *Documento XXXIV: La S. Congregazione insiste perche il Consiglio dell'Opera Pia costituitosi in Olanda entro in corrispondenza col Consiglio Centrale di Lione.* L'Aja, 27 Novembre, *1841* (Vol. 326, Fol. 1231).

90. Ut supra, *Documento XXXV: Sul progetto della ricostruzione del Consiglio Internunzio Apostolico in Parigi.* 11 Decembre, 1841 (Ibid., Fol. 1324).

91. Ut supra, *Documento XXXVIII: La Sacra Congregazione raccomanda all'Archivescovo di Salerno l'unita della Pia Opera.* 22 Gennaio, 1842 (Lettere della S. C., Vol. 327, Fol. 54-v).

92. Ut supra, *Documento XXXIX: La Sacra Congregazione raccomanda all'Archivescovo di Lima che, istituita l'Opera Pia a favore delle missioni, sia aggregata al Consiglio Centrale di Lione.* 31 Gennaro, 1842 (Ibid., Fol. 86-v).

93. Ut supra, *Documento XXXVbis: I Consigli dell'Opera Pia della Propagazione della Fede stabiliti nell'America del Sud reclamano una completa indipendenza dal centro di Lione.* 2 Luglio, 1842 (Lettere, Vol. 327, Fol. 533-v).

94. Ut supra, *Documento XL: Un decreto del re di Baviera stabilisce she il Consiglio dell'Opera Pia esistente nei suoi Stati se la intenda direttamente con Roma e non abbia piu alcuna relazione col centro di Lione.* 3 Agosto 1844 (Lettere della S. C., Vol. 331); *Documento XLI: Sul medesimo argomento.* 3 Agosto, 1844 (Ibid., Fol. 589-v).

established in Bavaria directly depend upon the Sacred Congregation.[95] On November 13, 1844, the Sacred Congregation lamented the character of complete independence from Rome of the Central Council of the Society, a character which, it felt, on account of national susceptibilities, imperilled the unity of the same.[96] On May 13, 1848, Spain sent directly to Rome the money collected in that kingdom for the Propagation of the Faith.[97] On June 7, 1848, the Sacred Congregation begged the Internuncio to Bavaria to send to Rome the remainder of the amount of the allocations made.[98] On September 20, 1848, the Sacred Congregation paid the appropriations determined upon by the Council of Lyons with the money collected by the Council of Rome.[99] On June 10, 1904, the Council of the Society in London decided to send to Lyons, in the future, only one-tenth of the collections made in England.[100]

The projected general union of the Austrian Mission Societies (the Societies of St. Peter Claver, of Mary, both of which are for Africa; the Leopoldine Society for North America; the Society of the Immaculate Conception and those of the Holy Childhood and the Propagation of the Faith)

95. Ut supra, *Documento XLII: II Consiglio della Pia Opera stabilito in Baviera, passa alle dipendenze dirette della S. Congregazione.* 3 Agosto, 1844 (Ibid., Fol. 500-v).

96. Ut supra, *Documento XLIII: La Sacra Congregazione lamenta il carattere di completa indipendenza da Roma assunti dal Consiglio Centrale dell'Opera, carattere che unito alle suscettibilita nazionali mette in periculo l'unita della medesima.* 13 Novembre, 1844 (Ibid., Fol. 819-v).

97. Ut supra, *Documento XLIV: La Spagna invia direttamente a Roma la somma raccolta per la Propagazione della Fede in quel regno.* 13 Maggio, 1848 (Vol. 337, Fol. 343).

98. Ut supra, *Documento XLV: La Sacra Congregazione prega l'Internunzio di Baviera di voler rimettere a Roma il sopravanzo delle allocazioni fatte.* 7 Guigno, 1848 (Ibid., Fol. 420-v).

99. Ut supra, *Documento XLVI: La Sacra Congregazione di Propaganda paga col denaro raccolto dal Consiglio di Roma le allocazioni stabilite dal Consiglio di Lione.* 20 Settembre, 1848 (Ibid., Fol. 694-v).

100. Ut supra, *Documento LXIII: II Consiglio dell'Opera della Propagazione della Fede in Londra decide dinon piu rimettere a Lione se non un decimo del prodotto delle collette fatte in Inghilterra.* 10 Giugno, 1904.

were all involved in this tentative.[101]   Finally, owing to the
growing demands in various parts of the world for a more
modern method of organization, a definitive basis for the
constitution of the Society of the Propagation of the Faith
in Spain is being planned,[102] and as Guasco has written:
"According to all the previsions, at the beginning of the
second century of its existence, the Society for the Propagation of the Faith is sure to suffer transformations in its
administration.   Some national councils are in process of
formation.   We have a First Pontifical Act constituting one
of these Councils; in a decree of March 1, 1921, His Holiness
Pope Benedict XV, created at Rome a Central Council placed
directly under the dependence of the Sacred Congregation de
Propaganda Fide, for all the dioceses of Italy and charged
it with the duty of procuring a fuller development of the
Society in the Peninsula (Italy).   What will be the relations
of this Council with those of Lyons and at Paris?   Will they
assist in an International Council at Rome or somewhere else
or will the ancient French Councils become simple intermediaries between the faithful and this International Council or
will they preserve their present character?   Will the Sacred
Congregation take over the effective direction of the Society?
Will the American project for independence from the Councils of Lyons and Paris succeed?   These and many other
questions regarding the Society are yet to be solved."[103]

The following indulgences have been granted to all mem-
bers of the Society for the Propagation of the Faith by the
Sovereign Pontiffs Pius VII, Leo XII, Pius VIII, Gregory
XVI, Pius IX, Leo XIII, Pius X and Benedict XV.

The Plenary and Partial Indulgences may be gained by
all those who are Ordinary or Special Members of the Asso-

---

101. Ut supra, *Documento LXVI: La progettata Unione Generale
delle Missioni Austriache.*

102. Ut supra, *Documento LXVII: Basi dedfinitive per la costitu-
zione della Propagazione della Fede nella Spagna.*

103. GUASCO, *L'Oeuvre de la Propagation de la Foi, Un Siecle d'
Histoire* in the *Correspondant,* t. 284, p. 1030, Sept. 25, 1921.

ciation. By a decree dated May 25, 1885, His Holiness, Pope Leo XIII, extended these privileges for life to those who fulfil the conditions of life membership.

To gain the Plenary Indulgences, the usual conditions of Confession, Communion, a visit to the parish church and prayers for the intentions of the Sovereign Pontiff are required. We may remark that a virtual intention suffices, and that those who go to confession once a week (*saltem semel in hebdomada*) can gain all Plenary Indulgences occurring in the interval between one Confession and another. Pope Pius X removed the condition of weekly confession in favour of those receiving Holy Communion daily or at least five or six times a week. Consequently, priests who celebrate every day may gain all these Indulgences, though they do not make weekly Confession. These Plenary Indulgences can be gained on the days mentioned once only at any hour from the First Vespers, 2 p. m., of the eve of the Feast, to sunset on the following day, or on any day of the octave, if there is an octave; should these feasts be transferred by proper authority, the Indulgences likewise accompany them and therefore, may be gained on the same conditions. Members of religious houses, convents, seminaries, colleges, etc., may visit the private chapel of the establishment instead of the parish church.

Children who have not made their first communion can gain them by performing some pious work appointed by their confessor.

I. PLENARY INDULGENCES

May 3d—Feast of the Finding of the Cross. The day on which the Association was established.

December 3d—Feast of St. Francis Xavier, the Patron of the Association.

The Epiphany, the Annunciation, the Assumption, St. Michael (September 29th).

On all Feasts of the Apostles.

Every Month—On any two days chosen by the Associates.

Once a Year—On the day of the general commemoration of the deceased Members of the Committee or the Circle to which one belongs.

On the Day of Admittance into the Association.

At the Hour of Death, by invoking, at least in the heart, the Name of Jesus.

Members gain the favour of the privileged Altar for every Mass said in the name of an Associate for a deceased Member.

II. PARTIAL INDULGENCES

Seven Years and Seven Quarantines every time an Associate performs in aid of the Association any work of devotion or charity.

Three hundred days every time an Associate assists at the "Triduum" on May 3rd and December 3rd.

One hundred days every time an Associate recites the "Our Father" and "Hail Mary," together with the invocation to St. Francis Xavier.

All these Indulgences, both Plenary and Partial, are applicable to the souls in purgatory.[104]

III. SPECIAL FAVORS GRANTED TO ECCLESIASTICAL BENEFACTORS

A—To every Priest who shall be charged in any parish or establishment to collect alms for the Society for the Propagation of the Faith, or who, either from his own resources, or otherwise, shall contribute to the funds of the Society a sum equal to the subscription of an entire band of ten:

1st. The favor of the privileged Altar three times a week.

2d. The power to apply the following Indulgences:—
To the faithful at the hour of death, a Plenary Indulgence;

---

104. *Spiritual Privileges Granted to the Association for the Propagation of the Faith*, pp. 25-27, London, 1916.

to Beads or Rosaries, Crosses, Crucifixes, Pictures, Statues and Medals, the Apostolic Indulgences; to Beads, the Brigitine Indulgences.

3d. The faculty of attaching to Crucifixes the Indulgences of the Way of the Cross.

B—(a) To every Priest who is a Diocesan Director, or a Member of a Committee, appointed to watch over the interests of the Work:

(b) To every other Priest who in the course of the year shall pay to the account of the Society a sum equal at least to the amount of one thousand subscriptions ($600.00), from whatever source derived:

1st. The same favors enjoyed by Priests in the preceding category.

2d. The favor of the privileged Altar five times a week personally. (Brief of Pius IX, December 31, 1853.)

3d. The power to bless Crosses with the Indulgences of the Way of the Cross, and, moreover, the power to invest with the Seraphic Cord and Scapular, and to impart all the Indulgences and privileges granted to such investiture by the Sovereign Pontiffs.

4th. The power to bless, and invest the faithful with, the Scapular of Mt. Carmel, the Immaculate Conception, and the Passion of Our Lord.

In case the collection of the special subscriptions should be for the moment incomplete, His Holiness prolongs the privileges of the Priest who shall have brought in the entire amount the preceding year, up to the current account. (Rescript of Leo XIII, June 16, 1878.)

C—Every Priest who shall contribute once for all out of his private resources, a sum representing the amount of one thousand subscriptions ($600.00) shall enjoy, during his life, the favors granted to the Priests who are Members of a Committee.

D—On February 1, 1908, Pope Pius X has granted to all Priests who are Diocesan or Parochial Directors, Perpetual or Special Members of the Society, the faculty of applying (unico crucis signo) the Crosier Indulgences to Rosaries (an Indulgence of 500 days for each *Our Father* and *Hail Mary*).

IV. Feast Days of the Society

In order to bring down the blessing of God on the Work and on the Missions, the Society has selected, as times of special prayer and Thanksgiving:

I. The third of May, feast of the Finding of the Holy Cross, the anniversary of the foundation of the Society in 1822.

II. The third of December, feast of St. Francis Xavier, patron of the Society.[105]

The Feast of the Second Patron of the Society, St. Exupere, was established in 1838.[106]

A Society, such as the Propagation of the Faith, founded and organized chiefly by laymen and laywomen, would naturally attract the interest and the zeal of the laity throughout the world. Hence, the historian has the pleasure of recording, side-by-side with the cooperation of the Holy See and of the Catholic Episcopate, the lay cooperation of the past hundred years.

During the period of union and protectorate when the civil power was united with the Church in its missionary endeavors and supported them with its budget, there was a strong tradition among the crowned heads of Europe which caused them to foster the Missions. But with the French Revolution all this was changed. At the time of the foundation of this Society in France, King Louis XVIII was apprised of its exis-- tence and appealed to by his Chaplain, Cardinal Prince de Croy for his permission to arouse the interest of all the Bishops

---

105. Freri, *op. cit.*, pp. 18-19, 1912; ibid., pp. 59-60 in the *Annals*, vol. LXXXV, 1922.
106. *Annales,* t. XI, pp. 168-182; 459-462.

of his realm in favor of the spread of this Society.[107] In the Cardinal's remarks to his sovereign he dwelt upon the traditions of the illustrious Kings of France such as King St. Louis and of Louis XIV, who had distinguished themselves by their efforts to promote the Missions. The good will and financial support of Louis XVIII was easily won for the Society; not only did the king contribute to the Society but he and the royal family seemed ever willing to turn an attentive ear to the requests of missionary bishops. For the United States one striking instance of this liberality is found in providing one of the ships of his royal navy, La Caravane, in which Bishop Du Bourg brought to America many missionaries and seminarians as well as many pious objects which he had collected abroad. The successor of Louis XVIII, Charles X, also manifested his good will towards the Society and wished his name to be placed at the head of the subscription list.[108] In the New Orleans Cathedral were hung six religious paintings which were gifts from the Kings of France. At the time that Mt. St. Mary's Seminary and College was destroyed by fire, a special gift of 3,000 francs from the King of France is another evidence of his interest in the Missions.[109]

The King of Sardinia also showed particular benevolence and encouragement towards this Society as did also the King of the two Sicilies.[110] But the characteristic of missionary activity during the modern period is that it is carried on not by the sovereigns or the great and powerful of the world. The new plan of supporting the Missions by frequent small donations was both devised and carried into execution chiefly through the efforts of the common people. Under these conditions all that the Society asks and expects of any government is a full measure of liberty in carrying on its work.

Perhaps the most conspicuous services rendered to the Society by prominent laymen has been in the field of the

107. *Annales,* t. I, fasc. iii, p. 11; t. I, fasc. v, pp. 5-6.
108. GUASCO, *op. cit.,* in the *Correspondant,* pp. 1010-1011: "Charles X declared himself its protector and made an offering to it."
109. *Annales,* t. I, fasc. v, p. 32.
110. *Annales,* t. I, fasc. v, pp. 30-40.

administration of the Society and the editing of its various publications. Frédéric Ozanam, the illustrious founder of the St. Vincent de Paul Society, was for some time the editor of the *Annales de la Propagation de la Foi*. A list of the names of the Directors of the two Councils of Lyons and Paris and of the editors of the *Annales* and the *Missions Catholiques* would contain a large number of names of persons prominent not only by virtue of their birth and station but also distinguished for the services they have rendered to God, to their Church, to their country and to their fellowman. One example alone will suffice to illustrate this truth. The present General Secretary of the Central Council of Paris, M. Alexandre Guasco, in the year 1883, gave up a promising career as an avocat to consecrate his life to the supervision of this Council. Through his intense application and keen discernment he has discovered the proportionate needs of each of the hundreds of Missions aided by the Society each year, and thus he has wisely directed the distribution of vast sums of money to all the Missions of the world wherever and whenever he believed it was needed most and could do the most good.

CHAPTER VI

The Growth of the Society

In his *Histoire Générale de la Société des Missions Étran-gères,* Launay, with characteristic piety, has said that societies such as the Society for the Propagation of the Faith are generally founded by the successive efforts of many minds and many hearts, their birth is difficult and slow up to the day when a ray of providential light passes over them and makes them flower and bear fruit.[1]

The Propagation of the Faith spread at first especially in France with extreme rapidity. The ecclesiastical authorities of Rome and of France published mandates in its favor, and designated priests to receive the collections. The pastors, the assistants, and the clergy made themselves its ardent supporters. The grandeur of the work was pleasing to all minds; the universality touched the hearts. The modesty of the alms permitted the poor to join their contributions to those of the rich. And so, the news of the Society's foundation came to the Missions with that of its progress and was received with gratitude.

What motives, we read in one of the early *Annales,* to redouble one's ardor and zeal in such a holy enterprise! What could be more consoling than the perspective of the immense good to be produced for the salvation of souls by prayers so short and by a contribution so modest! And what one of the faithful, in thinking of this small alms given each week, which often goes more than a thousand leagues to aid in the conversion of the soul for whom Jesus Christ died, would not feel his heart thrill and his charity be inflamed! It has pleased Providence to bless this generous Association and to multiply

---

1. Launay, *op. cit.,* t. II, p. 500.

its members for the sanctification of the Christians who compose it as well as for the conversion of those in whom it places its interests.[2]

The object of the Society could not long be confined within the boundaries of a province, as Louvet has written.[3] A few days after the first assembly, one of the members of the Central Council of Lyons set out to arouse the ever-ardent charity of the cities of the South of France. Diocesan committees were formed at Avignon, Aix, Marseilles, Nîmes, Montpelier, Grenoble. The most eminent members of the clergy joined with the most religious laymen, and the confident activity of so many good men seemed already to give promise of great success. Not long afterwards, one of the founders went to Paris; through his efforts, a Superior Council as well as a Diocesan Council were formed there, and, henceforth, the Society embraced the whole nation. In the year 1823, a delegate of the Council of Lyons, obtained papal approbation together with the indulgences which enrich the Society in perpetuity.[4] Then encouraging words came from almost all the bishops of France. Thus the new institution, strengthened by the approbation of the Holy See, sure of its support, sustained by its encouragements, crossed the frontiers of France, and began the conquest of the world. The realm of Piedmont was the first to welcome it. The King of Sardinia inscribed his own name at the head of the list of subscribers, and a committee was promptly established at Turin, which soon made its activity felt in the Dioceses of Turin, Chambéry, Annecy, Nice, Pignerol, etc.[5] Then the different countries in turn became interested in the Society. Belgium did not long delay her entrance into the work and began her magnificent annual liberalities by a donation of 497 francs in 1825. Italy began in 1827 with a contribution of 288 francs. Next came Germany with her donation of 358 francs. In the same year, Switzerland gave 896 francs. The British

2. *Annales,* t. I, fasc. pp. 3-6.
3. LOUVET, *op. cit.,* p. 2a; *Annales,* t. II, pp. 79-82.
4. *Annales,* t. I, fasc. p. 4.
5. *Annales,* t. V, p. 31.

Isles began their regular contributions in 1836. Portugal and Holland came next in 1837. In 1839, the United States, Spain and Austria sent in their first donations. In 1840, South America began its contributions.[6] By this time 300 bishops had raised their voices in its favor. Finally, as we have said, Pope Gregory XVI, by the Encyclical Letter of 1840, placed the Society in the rank of Institutions common to Christendom.[7]

It was during these latter years that the Bishop Flaget went to Europe and undertook the memorable voyage which permitted half of France to see and hear the envoy of the Sovereign Pontiff, preaching his holy crusade of prayers and alms. Flaget had passed more than forty years in the Missions; he knew the innumerable needs of the churches; he was able to appreciate the services which the Society for the Propagation of the Faith had already rendered, and the letters which the associates of the Society had received from him were all filled with testimonies of his lively gratitude. He had been in Europe for one year and his reputation had already attained great prominence. Each of his acts, each of his words, was clothed with authority. It would have been difficult to have found a preacher better fitted to recommend the society which embraced, in its solicitude, all the Missions of the two worlds. The men who, with the assent of the Sovereign Pontiff, directed his excellent Society, hastened to claim the cooperation of this venerable bishop. They profited by his stay in Rome to address a humble appeal to the Pope, and this appeal met with complete success. Gregory XVI had more than once given to the Society the most flattering marks of his paternal esteem. He understood the intentions of the Bishop of Bardstown, and Flaget himself penetrated the heart of the Pontiff, and found there the will to second his own views. Returning to France, Bishop Flaget, with the sim-

---

6. GUASCO, *op. cit.*, in the *Correspondant*, t. 284, p. 1022, Sept. 25, 1921.

7. *Annales*, t. XLIV, p. 162.

plicity of a child and his customary devotion, placed himself at the disposal of those who had claimed his services.[8]

In a first journey through France the American prelate visited twelve dioceses: Le Puy, Clermont, Moulins, Nevers, Bourges, Limoges, Tulle, Cahors, Montauban, Rodez, Albi and Saint-Flour. Then his failing health obliged him to seek repose in his own family circle. Having returned to Clermont on the 20th of March, 1838, he departed on June 6, and visited Valence, Viviers, Montpelier, Toulouse, Auch, Aire, Bayonne, Tarbes, Pamiers, Perpignan, Carcassonne, Nîmes, Avignon, Aix, Marseilles, Fréjus, Digne and Gap—eighteen dioceses in all. He returned to Lyons on October 6, and after a repose of some few days, again set out on the 29th of the same month. This time he was to visit Grenoble, Belley, Autun, Saint-Claude, Besançon, Annecy, Saint Jean de Maurienne, Turin, Asti, Alexandrie, Genoa, Savona, Albenga, Vintemille, Nice and Chambéry.

It was proposed to Bishop Flaget to visit the North of France, but, for reasons which we shall shortly explain, he was obliged to limit his journeys. After all, to travel through forty-six dioceses, notwithstanding the burden of seventy-five years, was rather a test for the strength of a venerable man. In the beginning, he visited in each of the dioceses, six, eight, ten or fifteen parishes, preaching everywhere, and complying with the desires of seminaries and religious communities to hear him, such was his zeal that his time and strength were matters of secondary importance. In most of the dioceses, especially in France, he continued to visit the principal cities and their institutions. Continually preaching and traveling, great fatigue finally overtook the good bishop; but it became sweet in his eyes when he recalled the origin of his mission, for he was working under the obedience to the Pope.

However, it is impossible to sketch in detail the great results of his journeys. Crowds gathered, wherever he went. All wished to see and to hear him. His speech, however, was

8. Desgeorge, *Mgr. Flaget, Évêque de Bardstown et Louisville,* pp. 115, et seq., Paris, 1855.

simple and familiar; but the saintly old man could not appear in a pulpit without preaching a sermon by his simple presence alone. His visits were like a continual mission. No one could estimate the services he rendered to the Society. Today his name is held in veneration by its members, as he said so often from the pulpit: "Everyone admires this mite of the poor, this cent each week, which after having received from God the power of miracles, goes across the seas to pay the ransom of captives, to furnish traveling expenses to the missionaries, to build churches, to found seminaries, and to produce other marvels which permit the infant and the aged, the infirm and the unfortunate, to believe themselves to be apostles, for all this good is the work of their faith and of their charity." At the moment when Bishop Flaget began his visitation, the Society for the Propagation of the Faith was far less known than it is today. Some, indeed, were asking if the alms which came into its treasury always went to the destination publicly announced. Others still entertained doubts whether the extent of the distress which hampered the Missions overseas, was as great as was pictured. But all these uncertainties were soon removed, and it is to Bishop Flaget's eternal credit that he helped to dispel these doubts. Everywhere the faithful became interested in a Society which had already been so fruitful and which was called to still greater things.'

Soon its work was established upon a larger and more solid basis, and every one considered it an honor to offer his humble tribute of prayers and alms to the work. In some cities its progress surpassed all hopes, to such an extent that the Bishop of Bardstown, passing through Montpelier two months after his first meeting, had the happiness of finding there a thousand more Associates.

---

9. PIOLET, *La France au Dehors, Les Missions Catholiques Françaises au XIX Siècle*, Paris, 1900. At Turin the King Charles Albert wished to receive him at his table. A letter from Ct. Vt. Gaitter, dated Paris 22 Juillet 1835, describes Flaget's audience with the King and Queen of France. This letter was found in the Archives of Saint Sulpice, Paris.

The immense good which Bishop Flaget was thus able to accomplish for the Society, as well as the religious devotion which he stimulated in Europe, was but one aspect of his saintly life.[10]

Benedict Joseph Flaget was born at St. Julien, France, November 7, 1763. He was the youngest of three sons. At the age of two, he was left an orphan, and a pious aunt took care of him and his brothers, devoting herself assiduously to bringing them up piously, bestowing on them the blessing of a Christian education. He attended the college and later the seminary at Clermont, the latter being then in charge of the Sulpicians. He joined the Congregation of St. Sulpice and after his ordination to the priesthood, he was sent to the Seminary at Nantes, and later to that at Angers, in the capacity of professor of theology. When the French Revolution broke out, it threatened to bring about the utter destruction of religion, and the clergy, both regular and secular, were openly persecuted. Those who had the courage, as almost all of them had, to refuse the odious Constitutional Oath were ruthlessly massacred or forced to fly for their lives. Father Flaget, acting under the advice of his superiors resolved to devote his life to the American Missions and embarked for America towards the close of the year 1791. In the fall of 1792 Father Flaget was sent by Bishop Carroll to Vincennes. There he labored with indefatigable zeal for more than two years. His zeal soon operated a thorough change in the religious aspect of the town. Toward the close of the year 1794, Father Flaget was recalled to the East by Bishop Carroll and placed on the staff of Georgetown College. His superiors, however, appointed him to the Island of Cuba with a view to establishing there a college and a seminary. About the year 1801, Father Flaget was recalled to Baltimore, to take a professorship in St. Mary's College. He continued in this situation for nine or ten years until he was elevated to the See of Bardstown. He arrived at Bardstown in June, 1811,

---

10. HERBERMANN, *The Sulpicians in the United States*, p. 157, New York 1916; Cf. BERTRAND, *Bibliothéque Sulpicienne*, p. 182, Paris.

remaining there until 1841, when the Holy See transferred his See to Louisville. There he remained until his death in 1850. For more than half a century the story of his life forms an integral and a very important part of that of the Catholic Church in the United States, of which he was so conspicuous an ornament. "His episcopacy stretches through a much larger period than that of any other American prelate; and he has justly merited the title awarded to him by general consent—of 'Patriarch of the American Hierarchy.' A prominent trait in the character of Bishop Flaget was his zeal for the salvation of souls. To secure this object, he spared no labor and was ready 'to spend and to be spent.' This was the subject upon which he most delighted to address his clergy, in his soul-stirring appeals replete with unction, which all well remember. This was the engrossing thought which supported him amongst the multiplied and protracted hardships of his episcopal career; which urged him on from one extremity to the other of his vast diocese; embracing for many years, the entire West and Northwest from the 34th degree of north latitude to the Lakes; a territory now comprising ten flourishing dioceses. To save a soul redeemed by Jesus Christ, or to prevent the commission of a single mortal sin, he deemed an object worthy of every privation and suffering, even unto the endangering sacrifice of life itself. The spiritual welfare and salvation of his flock engaged his anxious attention by day and often flitted across his mind in the visions of the night. This was a favorite subject of his conversation with his friends and it was that for which he prayed most frequently and most fervently, especially at the holy altar.'"[11]

To Bishop Flaget, therefore, goes the credit of having accomplished more than any single prelate for the growth and development of the Society for the Propagation of the Faith. His activity in its behalf in France, during that early epoch of its existence, when French prelates themselves failed

---

11. *The Metropolitan Catholic Almanac and Laity's Directory* 1851, pp. 50-61.

to realize the immense possibilities of such an organization with its universal appeal and its universal power for good, has placed him almost in the ranks of its founders.

After a century of existence the Society can boast of a development second to none among the Catholic institutions which make an appeal to the faithful of the world for the sake of the Gospel. France has always held the place of honor in the total contributions. Germany, Italy, Belgium, Great Britain, Switzerland and all the nations of Europe, even unfortunate Poland, are found on its lists. North and South America, Africa, the infant Churches of Asia and of Oceania also sent in their modest tribute of their neophytes. In a word, all the children of the Church are thus united in the Apostolate and cooperate by their offering in the propagation of the Gospel.[12]

We have now to see in a graphic way the scale of these contributions during the past century (1822-1918):

RECEIPTS OF THE SOCIETY FOR THE PROPAGATION OF THE FAITH

From Its Foundation until 1918, Inclusive

Total Receipts: 450,846,600 fr.

Of This Sum the Following Countries Have Contributed:

France	278,022,485 fr.
United States	32,305,473 "
Italy	30,783,713 "
Germany	25,487,346 "
Belgium	23,582,361 "
Great Britain	15,013,707 "
Holland	5,946,306 "
Spain	5,678,348 "
Switzerland	5,670,413 "
Argentine Republic	4,629,811 "
Mexico	3,653,795 "
Canada	3,074,654 "
Portugal	2,644,862 "
Austria	2,358,600 "
Africa	2,120,990 "
Chile	1,751,459 "
Malta and Gozzo	1,532,266 "
Luxemburg	1,336,510 "

12. LOUVET, *op. cit.*, p. 3a, 1894.

Central America	1,045,793 fr.
Oceania	855,379 "
Asia	759,412 "
Uruguay	526,566 "
Brazil	498,489 "
Peru	271,126 "
Turkey in Europe	261,060 "
Russia and Poland	204,905 "
Hungary	176,157 "
Scandinavian States	154,174 "
Greece	129,825 "
Colombia	80,181 "
Venezuela	68,371 "
Monaco	61,066 "
Guiana	52,034 "
Ecuador	48,660 "
Bolivia	32,181 "
Paraguay	12,461 "
Roumania	8,079 "
Bulgaria	3,540 "

Arranged by periods of ten years the figures of the receipts of the Society for the Propagation of the Faith, are indicative of the Society's growth. In the following table it will be seen that the Society has not ceased to progress although this rate of increase had diminished in a notable manner from 1872 to 1891:

From 1822 to	1831 S.P.F.	Recd.	1,807,091 fr.		
" 1832 "	1841	" "	11,732,983 "	Increase	9,925,791 fr.
" 1842 "	1851	" "	33,446,335 "	"	21,713,351 "
" 1852 "	1861	" "	45,516,139 "	"	12,069,803 "
" 1862 "	1871	" "	49,780,830 "	"	4,264,701 "
" 1872 "	1881	" "	60,033,164 "	"	10,252,333 "
" 1882 "	1891	" "	66,030,291 "	"	5,997,127 "
" 1892 "	1901	" "	66,832,650 "	"	802,359 "

The two periods from 1862 to 1871 and from 1882 to 1891 during which the growth of the Society slackened considerably, correspond to the creation of Peter's Pence and to the religious crises of the Church of France, during which time the charity of the faithful was solicited for the works of local interest. The practical disappearance of this increase during the period between 1892 and 1901 was due chiefly to the marked financial depression which affected Europe as well as America. In 1906 came the separation of the Church and State in France, and hence local charities made incessant demands upon the charity of the faithful. During the last period from 1912 to 1921 the World War could not fail to have a detrimental influence upon the offerings made to the Society.

It will not be without interest to see exactly what part each of the Catholic nations has taken in the contributions made to the total budget of the Apostolate. There are, in this detailed resumé of the Society, encouragements for some nations, regrets for others and lessons for all.

I.—FRANCE

(1822-1892)

From	1822	to	1831	France	Gave	1,764,696 fr.		
"	1832	"	1841	"	"	8,025,928 "	Increase	6,261,221 fr.
"	1842	"	1851	"	"	19,064,863 "	"	11,038,834 "
"	1852	"	1861	"	"	27,833,660 "	"	8,768,797 "
"	1862	"	1871	"	"	34,501,034 "	"	6,667,374 "
"	1872	"	1881	"	"	40,549,771 "	"	6,048,736 "
"	1882	"	1891	"	"	42,331,209 "	"	1,781,438 "

It is evident that Catholic France, the birthplace of the Society for the Propagation of the Faith, has made it a point of honor to guard her rank of eldest daughter of the Church since she alone has always furnished two-thirds of the budget of the Apostolate. Since 1822, the date of its foundation, the Society has not ceased to make progress in France, even after the loss of the two dioceses of Alsace and Lorraine, or even during the ten years between 1882 and 1891 when the Church in France was crippled.

II.—ITALY

(1827-1892)

From	1827	to	1831	Italy	Gave	1,128 fr.		
"	1832	"	1841	"	"	1,268,233 "	Increase	1,267,105 fr.
"	1842	"	1851	"	"	5,460,396 "	"	4,192,162 "
"	1852	"	1861	"	"	5,687,035 "	"	226,639 "
"	1862	"	1871	"	"	3,918,759 "	Decrease	1,768,276 "
"	1872	"	1881	"	"	3,227,920 "	"	690,388 "
"	1882	"	1891	"	"	3,912,589 "	Increase	684,669 "

Italy ranks second, after France; at the beginning, Italy made a splendid showing and seemed to promise much for the future. But since 1860, the political revolutions of which it has been the theatre have produced a decrease. After having attained in 1858 the figure of 844,447 francs, Italy fell in 1891 to about 350,000 francs. In 1891, there were about 150,000 Associates in Italy.

III.—GERMANY AND AUSTRIA-HUNGARY

(1827-1892)

From 1827 to 1831	Germany	Gave	5,125 fr.			
" 1832 " 1841	"	"	779,014	"	Increase	773,888	fr.
" 1842 " 1851	"	"	2,554,560	"	"	1,775,546	"
" 1852 " 1861	"	"	2,713,889	"	"	159,328	"
" 1862 " 1871	"	"	2,458,734	"	Decrease	255,155	"
" 1872 " 1881	"	"	6,153,431	"	Increase	3,694,697	"
" 1882 " 1891	"	"	7,472,606	"	"	1,319,174	"

The different states of Germany were backward in joining the work, but after 1870, the increase is apparent. In the beginning Austria wished to form a group apart, and on April 15, 1829, it instituted, as we have seen, the Leopoldine Society, organized, like the Society for the Propagation of the Faith, into groups of ten, the average of its annual receipt before 1890 amounted to about 40,000 florins (100,000 fr.), which were applied exclusively to the German Missions of the United States. A few years later Bavaria followed this example. It had, however, commenced well and from 1843 the receipts of the Propagation of the Faith reached 232,748 fr. That year, according to the order of its Prince, it retired from the Society so that it too might found its local Society.

For a long time Prussia and the Protestant States of Germany were the only ones to support the great French Society. There was even a slight decrease from 1862 to 1871; but after this period the receipts grew in rapid proportion and neither the violences of Kulturkampf nor the numerous societies in Germany which made demands upon the charity of Catholics, have been able to affect the movement in favor of the Society. It is but just to mention that the annexation of the two dioceses of Metz and of Strasbourg have been the means of including in the receipt of Germany up

to 1891 an annual average of 300,000 fr. In 1891 the subscriptions from Germany and Austria-Hungary represented
about 270,000 subscribers or Associates.

IV.—Belgium

(1825-1892)

From 1825 to 1831 Belgium Gave			32,042 fr.			
" 1832 " 1841	"	"	715,678	" Increase	638,636 fr.
" 1842 " 1851	"	"	1,751,426	" "	1,035,747 "
" 1852 " 1861	"	"	2,511,104	" "	759,678 "
" 1862 " 1871	"	"	3,007,008	" "	495,903 "
" 1872 " 1881	"	"	3,621,890	" "	614,881 "
" 1882 " 1891	"	"	3,640,949	" "	19,059 "

In proportion to the number of its inhabitants, Belgium
ranked immediately after France. In 1891, out of 35,000,000
Catholics, France gave 4,200,000 fr. or 0.12 centimes per
person. Belgium out of 5,500,000 Catholics, gave 330,000
fr. or 0.06 centimes per inhabitant. No other Catholic
State has so high a proportion. Since 1825, the Society for
the Propagation of the Faith has increased its progress in
Belgium, although the rate has been slow. From 1880 to
1890 this progress was almost stationary.

V.—Great Britain

(1833-1892)

From 1833 to 1841 G. B. Gave			562,885 fr.			
" 1842 " 1851	"	"	1,768,144	" Increase	1,205,259 fr.
" 1852 " 1861	"	"	2,420,456	" "	652,311 "
" 1862 " 1871	"	"	1,596,066	" Decrease	824,389 "
" 1872 " 1881	"	"	1,698,479	" Increase	102,413 "
" 1882 " 1891	"	"	1,722,905	" "	24,425 "

In 1833, Great Britain entered for the first time into the
receipts of the Propagation of the Faith with the modest
offering of 51 fr., but the movement rapidly took possession
and in 1858 Great Britain reached the figure of 545,923 fr.
This figure, however, it never again reached until 1891. After
the year 1860, a decrease continued to make itself felt and the
annual average was lowered 150,000 fr.

VI.—NORTH AMERICA

(1833-1892)

From	1833 to 1841	N. A. Gave		9,291 fr.			
"	1842 " 1851	"	"	573,115 "	Increase	563,823 fr.	
"	1852 " 1861	"	"	1,851,615 "	"	1,278,500 "	
"	1862 " 1871	"	"	1,451,713 "	Decrease	399,901 "	
"	1872 " 1881	"	"	1,253,791 "	"	197,922 "	
"	1882 " 1891	"	"	2,635,960 "	Increase	1,382,168 "	

North America includes the Dominion of Canada, the United States, Mexico and the Antilles. It was only after 1840 that Canada and the United States entered into the Propagation of the Faith. During a long time the largest offerings came from Canada. Mexico seemed to be ignorant of the existence of the Society and the United States was only acquainted with it through the abundant assistance which it received from the Society to organize its young churches. Nevertheless, the receipts showed a continuous and progressive increase until about 1860. Little by little Canada withdrew from the Society to devote itself exclusively to its own Missions. The United States remained stationary, reserving all of its resources for the development of local works. Mexico began to be seriously interested in the Society when delegates went there in 1889, to make it known and understood. It has been the same in Cuba and in the West Indies, and in all the Latin countries.

The contributions of North America in 1891 was as follows:

Dominion of Canada	....	21,457 fr.
United States	....	201,519 fr.
Mexico	....	334,880 fr.
Antilles	....	23,592 fr.
Total	....	581,499 fr.[13]

In the first seventy years, the United States received from the Society 28,364,725 fr., and in 1918, the contributions from the United States for the first time equalled the total it received from the Society.

_____

13. Ut supra, pp. 3a-8a, Louvet has compiled these statistics from the *Compte Rendu* in the *Annales.*

Of the total collections, $100,341,625.33, the United States contributed $10,983,452.06. In 1920, the total receipts were $3,414,647, of which $1,622,569 were offerings from American Catholics.[14]

For a long time the Central Councils of the Society sought to develop their work in the United States and many Archbishops and Bishops of America encouraged them to do so. On March 12, 1891, they asked the Very Rev. Father Chevalier, to take up the work. The real beginning of the growth of the Society in the United States came as a result of the action taken by the Fathers of the Third Plenary Council of Baltimore, in 1884. When the Council of Baltimore convened, the Society had given more than 22,000,000 fr. and had only received 3,000,000 fr., in return. At this Council the cause of the Society was upheld, and it was decided that a collection should be made each year in all the Churches in the United States, part of which would be reserved to the Negro and Indian Missions and part to the Propagation of the Faith. But progress was slow at first, and in 1891, Father Chevalier had to resign from the work of making the Society known in the United States.[15]

On October 20, 1891, the President of the Council of Paris, M. Hamel, wrote to Cardinal Gibbons, petitioning him to make an appeal to the Archbishops of the United States in favor of the Society. A few weeks later at an assembly of the Archbishops of the United States, Archbishop Chapelle received a letter from Cardinal Gibbons asking him to support the request of the Council before the Archbishops who met at St. Louis at the end of November. On April 13, 1892, Cardinal Gibbons informed the Council that he had spoken to the Archbishops of the United States assembled at St. Louis in the interest of the Society. His letter was full of sentiments of benevolence and sympathy for the Society.

---

14. Cf. Statistics of the total contributions in the *Appendix* of this work.

15. GUASCO, *Note sur les Origines de la Délégation de l'Oeuvre de la Propagation de la Foi*, specially compiled at my request; ANDRE, *Amérique (Etats Unis d')* Catholicisme, in VACANT, *Dictionnaire de Théologie Catholique*, p. 1073.

During the summer of 1892, Mgr. Ireland, while visiting Paris, was consulted by M. Guasco. The Archbishop of St. Paul immediately took an interest in the project and suggested that the Council address the Sulpicians of Baltimore to find a representative for the work. Meanwhile the World's Fair was about to open in Chicago, and the Council decided to participate in the exposition with its publications in different languages and its maps. Father Durin, of West de Pere, Wisconsin, was appointed to represent the Society at Chicago as a delegate of the Council during the time of the exposition. The President of the Council of Paris made a proposal to the Superior General of St. Sulpice on a subject of the action which the Society proposed to begin in the United States and received a favorable answer. In the meeting of May 8, 1896, the President announced to the Central Council of Paris that the Superior-General of the priests of St. Sulpice had left for the United States, provided with a letter signed by the President in the name of the Council, appointing him to come to an understanding with Cardinal Gibbons in order that the priests of St. Sulpice be empowered to promote the Society of the Propagation of the Faith in the United States, as delegates of the Council. On November 1, 1896, His Eminence Cardinal Gibbons addressed to the President of the Council a letter in which he evinced the favorable disposition which the American Archbishops had manifested in their annual meeting; they approved without reservation that a priest of St. Sulpice be the delegate of the Central Council. The Archbishops were all of the opinion that the Seminary of St. Sulpice, called St. Mary's, at Baltimore, should be the center of the Society in the United States. Father Magnien accepted, but being unable to devote himself to the details of the administration of the Society, took as an Associate, Father Granjon. When Father Granjon became Bishop of Tucson, Father Magnien appointed Mgr. Freri as a successor. At the end of 1903, on the proposal of Mgr. Freri and after the approval of His Eminence Cardinal Gibbons, the transfer of the center of the Society from Baltimore to New York was decided.

Cardinal Gibbons' letter of November 1, 1896, reads as follows:

I am quite late in replying to the letter which you have kindly sent me by the Superior General of St. Sulpice. I pray you to believe that it is due neither to forgetfulness nor negligence on my part. The Society for the Propagation of the Faith has shown itself in the past and still shows itself so generous with regard to the missions of the United States that it is for us not less a duty than a pleasure to endorse your noble designs to give to this admirable Society all the extension it can require. In the annual meeting of the American Archbishops which recently took place at Washington I submitted to my venerable colleagues your wishes and your proposals. I am happy to announce to you that they all accepted them with eagerness: they have approved without any restriction that a priest of St. Sulpice should here be the delegate of your Central Council. The members of this Society direct three very important seminaries and could have much influence over the clergy. We were all of the opinion that the Seminary of St. Sulpice, otherwise called St. Mary's, at Baltimore, should be the center of the Society in this country and we leave to the intelligence and to the zeal of him who shall be chosen by your delegate, the details of the organization and the determination of the means to be taken to develop the Society. The Superior General of St. Sulpice, during his visit at Baltimore, spoke to me of the Society in very sympathetic terms and said that he would do all in his power to give to that one of his confreres who shall be chosen the means to accomplish his work for the greater glory of God, and in relation to the needs of the missions. I am sure that the Bishops animated with the same dispositions as their Metropolitan will favor the extension of the Society in their dioceses.[16]

The Society was incorporated under the laws of the State of Maryland with the following directors:

His Eminence Cardinal Gibbons, *Archbishop of Baltimore.*
Most Reverend M. A. Corrigan, *Archbishop of New York.*
Most Reverend W. H. Elder, *Archbishop of Cincinnati.*
Most Reverend P. J. Ryan, *Archbishop of Philadelphia.*
Most Reverend J. Ireland, *Archbishop of St. Paul.*
Very Reverend A. Magnien, SS, D. D., President, St. Mary's Seminary.
Reverend G. W. Devine.
Reverend C. B. Corrigan.
Reverend T. J. Broderick.
Reverend C. F. Thomas.[17]

---

16. A copy of this letter was sent to me by M. Guasco.
17. FRERI, *op. cit.*, p. 13, 1900.

On July 13, 1900, the President of the Central Council of Paris, wrote to Father Magnien as follows:

I have the honor to acknowledge the reception of your letter of June 21 informing us that Mgr. Granjon, Bishop of Tucson, until this time charged with the Society of the Propagation of the Faith in the United States, has departed for his diocese. We have expressed to Mgr. Granjon all our gratitude for the zeal with which he was willing to work for the development of so important a Society and one now more useful than ever. The Council with all its heart reaffirms the praises which you have spoken of the truly admirable activity which he has directed with remarkable intelligence of the needs of the Society for the Propagation of the Faith, a perfect prudence, and a complete submission to our directions, conditions essential for the good functioning of a very complicated administration. We received with joy the successor of Mgr. Granjon, Dr. Freri, well persuaded that, chosen by you, and being presented to the Council under your patronage, he will fulfill all the desired conditions to continue to manage well the Apostolic campaign so happily commenced by the Respectable Superior of the Seminary of St. Mary of Baltimore and of the Bishop of Tucson.[18]

As detailed by Monsignor Freri, the funds contributed by the Catholics in the United States for the Society were as follows:

Year	Contributed	Year	Contributed	Year	Contributed
1822	$........	1846	886.40	1870	8,053.69
1823	....	1847	810.67	1871	13,265.43
1824	....	1848	807.00	1872	16,684.97
1825	....	1849	709.12	1873	9,713.53
1826	....	1850	765.00	1874	10,274.14
1827	....	1851	600.00	1875	9,477.22
1828	....	1852	16,026.41	1876	13,173.60
1829	....	1853	7,842.13	1877	11,459.14
1830	....	1854	11,337.32	1878	10,852.64
1831	....	1855	7,235.91	1879	7,128.66
1832	....	1856	10,328.65	1880	11,686.85
1833	6.00	1857	13,713.12	1881	20,845.67
1834	....	1858	30,612.18	1882	41,601.36
1835	....	1859	37,730.81	1883	26,731.69
1836	....	1860	12,303.68	1884	15,609.33
1837	....	1861	8,529.02	1885	17,456.84
1838	....	1862	8,644.31	1886	14,786.54
1839	....	1863	8,255.13	1887	42,964.18
1840	1,023.10	1864	8,291.22	1888	52,759.22
1841	824.00	1865	7,462.43	1889	41,687.82
1842	875.49	1866	10,361.17	1890	39,092.76
1843	816.99	1867	9,341.73	1891	40,303.85
1844	15.30	1868	10,209.52	1892	35,907.58
1845	1,655.30	1869	13,162.89	1893	44,753.58

18. A copy of this letter was also sent me by M. Guasco.

1894	25,065.68	1905	157,057.98	1916	500,223.27
1895	34,707.39	1906	185,287.71	1917	759,346.70
1896	32,855.54	1907	193,054.44	1918	971,888.48
1897	34,196.31	1908	193,122.36	1919	1,372,896.13
1898	55,511.79	1909	220,082.78	1920	1,315,752.62
1899	69,402.49	1910	268,314.08	1921	1,245,403.53
1900	71,229.35	1911	281,234.38		....
1901	77,000.00	1912	366,460.59		
1902	85,408.44	1913	440,004.31		$10,983,452.06
1903	92,503.48	1914	477,427.94		[19]
1904	156,942.92	1915	503,619.08		

VII.—Holland

(1837-1892)

From 1837 to 1841	Holland	Gave	25,367 fr.		
" 1842 " 1851	"	"	819,377 "	Increase	794,010 fr.
" 1852 " 1861	"	"	916,461 "	"	97,083 "
" 1862 " 1871	"	"	847,677 "	Decrease	68,784 "
" 1872 " 1881	"	"	1,052,259 "	Increase	204,582 "
" 1882 " 1891	"	"	1,122,767 "	"	70,502 "

Save for a slight downward trend from 1862 to 1871, Holland has progressed moderately and continually. Out of 1,647,000 Catholics in 1891, including Luxembourg, there were 38,460 Associates.

VIII.—Switzerland

(1827-1892)

From 1827 to 1831	Switzl'd	Gave	3,336 fr.		
" 1832 " 1841	"	"	163,636 "	Increase	160,000 fr.
" 1842 " 1851	"	"	446,821 "	"	283,185 "
" 1852 " 1861	"	"	476,909 "	"	29,987 "
" 1862 " 1871	"	"	484,056 "	"	7,247 "
" 1872 " 1881	"	"	593,307 "	"	109,250 "
" 1882 " 1891	"	"	810,365 "	"	217,058 "

Progress, in the work of the Society, while swift at the beginning, slowed down considerably in Switzerland from 1852 to 1870. The crisis of Swiss radicalism, and the interest taken in Peter's Pence, easily explain this decline. In the years between 1872 and 1891, the movement again quickened and the country approached the figure of 100,000 fr. a year.

---

19. Freri, *op. cit.*, in the *Annals*, vol. LXXXV, p. 68, 1922.

IX.—Portugal

(1837-1892)

From 1837 to 1841 Portugal Gave	93,573 fr.			
" 1842 " 1851	"	"	336,530 "	Increase	242,956 fr.
" 1852 " 1861	"	"	232,684 "	Decrease	103,845 "
" 1862 " 1871	"	"	336,434 "	Increase	103,749 "
" 1872 " 1881	"	"	493,848 "	"	157,414 "
" 1882 " 1891	"	"	482,908 "	Decrease	10,940 "

From 1872 to 1891, the receipts from Portugal varied between 40,000 and 50,000 fr. Of a total Catholic population of 4,300,000, there were about 18,000 Associates.

X.—South America

(1840-1892)

From 1840 to 1841 S. A. Gave	2,894 fr.			
" 1842 " 1851	"	"	153,138 "	Increase	150,244 fr.
" 1852 " 1861	"	"	261,306 "	"	108,167 "
" 1862 " 1871	"	"	384,692 "	"	123,386 "
" 1872 " 1881	"	"	447,195 "	"	62,502 "
" 1882 " 1891	"	"	334,942 "	Decrease	113,256 "

The republics of South America, a prey to the plague of secret societies and to the intrigues of politicians, scarcely permitted any stability to Catholic societies. Although the Catholic population surpassed 40,000,000 souls, the Society for the Propagation of the Faith has developed very slowly.

XI.—Spain

(1839-1892)

From 1839 to 1841 Spain Gave	33,274 fr.			
" 1842 " 1851	"	"	167,661 "	Increase	134,386 fr.
" 1852 " 1861	"	"	158,020 "	Decrease	9,641 "
" 1862 " 1871	"	"	110,142 "	"	47,787 "
" 1872 " 1881	"	"	178,198 "	Increase	68,056 "
" 1882 " 1891	"	"	706,039 "	"	527,840 "

If the noble and Catholic Spain, ranks in the eleventh place after all the Catholic States, the fault is not with her but with the policies of her Government, which proscribed the Society in its infancy (1840). Until the year 1880, the native land of St. Francis Xavier, the patron of the Society, was represented by an annual contribution of four or five thousand francs. In 1890, it had surpassed 100,000 fr.

XII—Levant

(1827-1892)

From 1827 to 1831	Levant	Gave	498 fr.		
" 1832 " 1841	"	"	47,102 "	Increase	46,674 fr.
" 1842 " 1851	"	"	188,894 "	"	141,492 "
" 1852 " 1861	"	"	266,494 "	"	77,599 "
" 1862 " 1871	"	"	210,088 "	Decrease	56,406 "
" 1872 " 1881	"	"	218,343 "	Increase	8,255 "
" 1882 " 1891	"	"	247,768 "	"	29,424 "

Under the name Levant are grouped in the Society's budget the contributions of the Island of Malta, of European Turkey, of Roumania, of Greece, of the Islands of the Archipelago. All these countries, with the exception of Malta, being still in the condition of Missions, the progress of the Society has been necessarily slight.

XIII.—Africa

(1857-1892)

From 1857 to 1861	Africa	Gave	30,399 fr.		
" 1862 " 1871	"	"	325,471 "	Increase	295,071 fr.
" 1872 " 1881	"	"	308,885 "	Decrease	16,585 "
" 1882 " 1891	"	"	326,374 "	Increase	17,489 "

Africa, the land of the Missions, could offer to the Apostolate little but its prayers and its sufferings.

XIV.—Oceania

(1843-1892)

From 1843 to 1851	Oceania	Gave	502 fr.		
" 1852 " 1861	"	"	31,189 "	Increase	30,687 fr.
" 1862 " 1871	"	"	50,311 "	"	19,121 "
" 1872 " 1881	"	"	104,170 "	"	53,858 "
" 1882 " 1891	"	"	152,639 "	"	48,469 "

The contributions of Oceania are furnished by Australia, by New Caledonia, by the Sandwich Islands and the Marquises Islands. It is to be regretted that the Philippines, with their 4,000,000 excellent Catholics, were not represented in 1891.

XV.—RUSSIA AND POLAND

(1837-1892)

From 1837 to 1841	Territory Gave		6,102 fr.			
" 1842 " 1851	"	"	129,757 "	Increase	123,654 fr.
" 1852 " 1861	"	"	124,539 "	Decrease	5,217 "
" 1862 " 1871	"	"	13,557 "	"	110,982 "
" 1872 " 1881	"	"	22,760 "	Increase	9,202 "
" 1882 " 1891	"	"	20,697 "	Decrease	2,062 "

Up to 1891 Poland had given 300,000 fr.

XVI.—ASIA

(1848-1892)

From 1848 to 1851	Asia Gave		1,035 fr.			
" 1852 " 1861	"	"	30,236 "	Increase	29,183 fr.
" 1862 " 1871	"	"	84,902 "	"	54,666 "
" 1872 " 1881	"	"	107,308 "	"	22,406 "
" 1882 " 1891	"	"	89,467 "	Decrease	17,841 "

In Asia are included Asiatic Turkey, India, Cochin-China and China. In 1891 their contributions were still small being the alms of the poor, it is particularly dear to the heart of God.[20]

Even missionary countries gave the Society a good number of Associates. To implant a fruitful missionary spirit in its beneficiaries, it has been the constant practice of the Society to ask help, even from those who are receiving it. Little by little, as the need for assistance diminishes, the country in which the Faith has been established and preserved increases its support to the continued extensions of the Missions of the Church. The readiness to train and send out missionaries so that others may enjoy they spiritual blessings, is perhaps the best guarantee of the genuine establishment of the Faith in any locality. How far the purpose of the Society in this direction is effective may be seen by the report published each year in the June number of the *Annales* of the help contributed even by countries in which the Church is as yet scarcely settled.[21]

---

20. LOUVET, *op. cit.*, pp. 3a-8a.
21. FRERI, *op. cit.*, p. 9, 1912.

CHAPTER VII

The Success of the Society

In a chapter devoted to the accomplishments of the Society for the Propagation of the Faith during the past one hundred years, the chief difficulty is to keep within the proportionate limits which this subject should be alloted in our work. Those accomplishments are of so universal a nature, touching as they do, the apostolate of our Holy Faith, Catholic education in its various branches, welfare work in pagan and civilized lands, and certain incidental fields of activity in which the Society takes its place as the promoter of scientific progress. To give the cumulative results of its century of success in Europe, in Asia, in Africa and in the Americas in anything like a worthy manner would take far more space than can be spared in this work, which is of a general historical character. Especially is this true for the history of the Society's activities in behalf of the Missions of the United States. A glance at the statistical tables at the end of this chapter will reveal the vastness of the subject, even for the United States. To some future occasion must be postponed the more detailed story of the Society's success in this country.

Brunetière has well summed up the accomplishments of the Society in the Conclusion which he wrote to the well-known work on the history of the Missions compiled by Piolet: *Les Missions Catholiques Françaises.* In whatever part of the world the missionary has gone to exercise his apostolate, he writes, he has labored for the growth and spread of civilization. Everywhere the light of the West penetrates the darksome shadowlands of the East, family life is bettered, savage customs are obliterated, slavery is driven out, and manners are softened and made more humane. Surely this, he adds, can never be considered a heavy burden to the West, and especially to Western Catholics, who have so admirably aided in the propagation of the Gospel.' It is quite natural

---

1. Piolet, *La France au Dehors, Les Missions Catholiques Françaises au XIX Siècle.*

that Brunetière would see in these accomplishments a great
boon to the French nation; since France, the home of refine-
ment, thus carries to the world, sitting in darkness, the light
of our modern progress. The "Vocation of the Gentiles," as
Fénelon has described the work of aiding the missionaries,
has been one that has always appealed to the Christian heart;
and so it is that the great French Society has accomplished
things for God and for humanity which far surpass in number
and in quality those of any similar organization in the world.

It must be also be remembered that the Society for the
Propagation of the Faith does not exercise any jurisdiction
in the training and placing of missionaries, still less with
the internal administration of the Missions. Its only aim
is to invite the prayers of the faithful for the extension of
the Church and to create a fund out of which all the Missions
may receive an annual subsidy in porportion to the number
of workers and their relative needs.[2] Ever since those eloquent words of M. Benoît Coste at the foundation of the
Society: "We are Catholics and we must form a 'catholic'
society," that is, one which assists the Missions of the whole
world, the Society has always made it a principle to assist
all Catholic Missions. The spirit of charity which animates it
knows no limit, neither does it exclude any people, any
country, any language, from its assistance; so-called Catholic
Nations, such as France, Italy, Austria and Spain, are however excluded from these allocations.[3] After the example of
the early faithful, the Society makes collections the product of
which it divides according as it seems most useful for the
good of the souls. Such is the Society for the Propagation
of the Faith; such its spirit and its acts.

Its first collection in 1822 was distributed as follows:
one-third went to New Orleans, one-third to Bardstown, and
one-third to the *Société des Missions Étrangères* for the

---

2. FRERI, *Propagation of the Faith*, in the *Catholic Encyclopedia*,
vol. XII, p. 461.

3. *Annales*, t. XLIX, pp. 157-160.

Orient. In 1827 we find Africa and Oceania (represented by the Sandwich Islands) included in the apportionment of the missionary funds. Only five years after its beginning the Society had fulfilled the "catholic" character its founders had given it.[4]

To speak of what the Society for the Propagation of the Faith has accomplished is to speak of our Missions and their results. These results are of a moral and religious nature and can neither be counted nor measured. By this very fact, they are very difficult to appreciate. What can be said of these results, however, will give at least a partial satisfaction to those interested in the disbursements of the Society, and will give a sufficient reply to a query which one often meets namely, whether our foreign missionaries lose their time, their efforts and the funds of which they dispose.[5]

The Society for the Propagation of the Faith, whose activities so powerfully aid in the diffusion of the Gospel, produces first of all results of *evangelization,* properly so called, of *education* and of *charity* and renders valuable services to *science* and to *civilization.*[6] "Since the beginning of the 19th century what is the progress that Catholicism has made? There is the numeric progress; the hierarchical progress; progress in works of benevolence and of civilization; in influences and in hopes, often bold, which at times the facts themselves surpass in the most extraordinary manner. But what strikes us most here is the weakness, and the unlikeliness of the means by which this progress has been obtained. Often the means appeared so opposed to their ends, according to human wisdom, that one ought rather to call them obstacles: their triumph has shown us visibly the finger and the action of God. Let us cite the facts."[7]

---

4. FRERI, *op. cit.,* p. 10, 1912.
5. PIOLET, *Nos Missions et Nos Missionnaires,* p. 27, Paris.
6. GASPARRI, *Letter to M. Delmas, Supérieur du Séminaire des Missions Étrangères,* in *La Société des Missions Étrangères,* Paris, 1919.
7. MIGNE, *Encyclopedia Théologique, Dictionnaire des Missions,* p. VIII, Paris, 1863.

In the 300 Missions of Asia, Africa and Oceania, supported by the Society there are about 15,000 missionary priests. In seminaries all over the world, laborers eager, ardent and numerous, are being prepared for the apostolate. How to provide for the expense, of their ecclesiastical formation, of their voyages, of their modest support on the Missions—these are the main problems of the Society. In the course of the nineteenth century, a number of Societies, responding to this necessity, have assisted in the budget of the apostolate. The principal Society of this nature is of course, the Society for the Propagation of the Faith. The progress of this Society up to the present has been phenomenal; but few persons, perhaps, even among the Society's most fervent associates have an exact idea of these needs; that is why it will not be inappropriate to present a rapid sketch of them.

A good index of the growth of the Apostolate may be found in the remarkable increase in the personnel during the last century. In 1822, the harvest was great, but the laborers were few, being scarcely 1,000 in all. Today the missionary army is made up of some 60,000 persons, 15,000 of whom are priests and religious, 4,000 teaching brothers and 40,000 sisters, not to speak of the priests, brothers and sisters native to the regions where they work, catechists and others who make up the personnel of the Mission, and the laborers among the Oriental Rites.[8] The missionary establishments essential for the activity of this army of missionaries have also shown a proportionate increase. From 1822 to 1922 the Society for the Propagation of the Faith received from all sources and from all parts of the world a total of $100,341,625, the total for the first year being but $4,000. Just as in the time of Christ, ''faith cometh by hearing,'' and ''how can they hear without a preacher,'' so the missionaries are the principal human cause of conversions. The Society has made it possible for missionary orders to accept all those candidates who appear fitted for the life of

---

8. FRERI, *op. cit.*, in *Annals*, vol. LXXXV, p. 19, 1922.

an evangelist. To the gift from the Society which assures the personal existence of numerous apostles it added annual allocation for the Missions themselves which vary according to the resources and according to the importance of these Missions.

Besides what is indispensable for the life of the missionary in a country occasionally deprived of resources, which they evangelize, the Society must support, in addition, the expense of the voyage of those who go into these distant regions to aid in the work, to replace those who have died, to supply the insufficiency of others whose health these rude labors or an unhealthy climate have badly undermined. For these new auxiliaries it is necessary, as for the first, that the Society furnish subsidies with the aid of which they procure clothing, books, the necessary objects of worship, and utensils of all kinds even including agricultural implements which they do not find in these countries.[9]

The funds which it provides, employed with wisdom and economy, permit missionaries to create and sustain these religious activities and works of general interest, either educational or charitable. A recent writer, in analyzing the nature of missionary work, emphasized the point that, in addition to the spiritual end, the Society had its educational, philanthropic, social, medical and economic ends or purposes. ''The problem,'' he continues, ''of the missionary is to bring civilization to the native. The next problem is to protect the native against the civilization which has been brought. The missionary must also be an educator. He must labor to develop the character, the intelligence and the opportunity of the native.''[10]

The. alms of the Society enable the missionary to open chapels, seminaries, schools, orphanages and hospitals and to sustain all these works which constitute and assure the development of the Mission.

---

9. *L'Oeuvre de la Propagation de la Foi,* in the *Annales,* t. XLIX, p. 157.

10. MOORE, *The Expansion of Christendom and the Naturalization of Christianity in the Orient in the XIX Century,* London, 1920.

The funds of the Society for the Propagation of the Faith are employed: 1, for the support of the missionaries; 2, to bring up young men for the priesthood; 3, to establish schools; 4, to print books of religion; 5, to build and support churches in the Missions; 6, to baptize infidel infants; 7, to buy back Christian children fallen into the hands of the pagans. The Superior of the *Séminaire de Missions Étrangères*, M. l'Abbé Langlois, at the beginning of the Society, expressed this thought as follows: "The missionaries . . . and native priests, the catechists, the students of seminaries and of the colleges, the neophytes, in one word all those who participate in the fruits of your charity, share in the sentiments of our gratitude and force themselves to attract by their vows and their prayers the benedictions of heaven on all the members of the Association."[11]

In the century that is passed the Society has brought each year new proofs of the solidity of its organization, of the zeal and ability of its councils and of its marvelous utility. It is assuredly one of the most efficacious means, of which Providence has made use, for the development of the Missions in our time. It has founded hundreds of new churches, has sent to every part of the world thousands of priests, to establish seminaries, colleges, schools, hospitals, orphanages and multiply the number of neophytes. What it began in 1822, it has continued to maintain and develop. The assistance which the Society has accorded to the Catholic missionaries is, however, far below that which the Protestant Church gives to its Bible Societies; but the Catholic missionary lives in poverty and very little is necessary for his personal needs.

In the strictly religious work of the Missions, the personnel generally consists of a bishop or head of the Mission, of a diocesan and religious clergy. The necessary expenses involved in training and supporting this personnel in the whole world are met by the alms provided by the Society. Following the example of his Master, the missionary must learn to live amid privations. Nevertheless, it is necessary to finance his

---

11. LAUNAY, *op. cit.*, t. II, p. 516.

education, the long voyages which he must make to reach his destination, to assure him his daily sustenance.[12] At certain points it is seminaries which are lacking; however, it is very necessary to provide for the perpetuation of the priesthood wherever a native clergy is possible; and the Society gives its assistance to this sacred need. If persecution should break out in some of the Foreign Missions, the Society must make exceptional allocations to that place.

The establishments which are indispensable for the work of the Apostolate are churches, chapels, stations for public worship and instruction and presbyteries, all of which must be built, furnished and maintained.

Education constitutes a very important activity, and the missionaries have everywhere done much for education. It is by education, indeed, by the formation of new generations, that a country is transformed, elevated and civilized and changed from a pagan land into a truly Christian people.[13]

The schools and educational establishments possess a particular importance since in many lands the task of reclaiming adults of a low cultural level, whose minds are obsessed with superstitions and brutalized by crime, is a well-nigh impossible one.[14] The personnel, which is consecrated to this educational work, consists of priests who devote themselves to education, and of teaching communities of brothers and sisters. Funds must be provided for the expense of this personnel, as well as for that of its education and this is in large part provided for by the Society. There are besides many native Sisterhoods who teach Christian doctrine and inspire an affection for the Faith in the people. These pious women need convents to shelter them and subsidies for their works.

This assistance is also given to the colleges and boarding schools. Colleges and schools of all kinds must be erected and maintained and monasteries and convents must be provided, as well as novitiates. Three-fourths or four-

---

12. LOUVET, *op. cit.*, p. 1a.
13. PIOLET, *Nos Missions et Nos Missionnaires*, pp. 31-32.
14. KENNEDY, *Missions, Catholic,* in the *Catholic Encyclopedia*, vol. X, p. 376.

fifths of the whole personnel of the Missions labor in the field of education. Thirty thousand teachers are engaged in the work of education, in the following schools:

Universities	2
Colleges	125
Seminaries	87
Orphanages	304
Schools	9,428
Total	9,946

The number of students in 1900 was as follows:

Europe, Missionary Countries	10,927	Children
Asia	272,544	"
Africa	165,291	"
America	52,615	"
Oceania	16,900	"
Total	518,277	Children[15]

From the material point of view, the following facts for 1900 are significant: In Africa there were over 58 agricultural schools, and over 200 in Asia, where children were taught to work in the gardens and the fields. When they were grown up, they possessed sufficient instruction to know how to handle tools. Others were trained in the workshops generally next to the Mission, and became carpenters, joiners, farmers, bricklayers, bakers, shoemakers and tailors.

In similar establishments, girls were trained by the Sisters for the work and the professions suitable for their sex. Being at once, teachers and artisans, catechists and cultivators, the Sisters and Brothers rapidly raised the level and the material situation of the peoples to whom they ministered.[16]

In addition to the ordinary means of instruction, a press destined to provide books and newspapers were necessary here or there, for they were indispensable arms with which to defend religion against the attacks of inimical persons.

There was hardly a Mission in which it was not necessary to raise and instruct the children of idolatrous parents, to

---

15. PIOLET, *ut supra*, pp. 32-33.
16. PIOLET, *ut supra*, pp. 28-29.

redeem slaves, to found Christian villages in these infidel
lands. This welfare work so vitally linked with missionary
activity demanded a personnel similar to that engaged in educational activity.

In many places hospitals, leprosaria, homes of refuge,
orphanages, asylums in which to instruct catechumens, or
agricultural schools or other kinds of establishments were
erected. There was scarcely a Mission which was without dis-
pensary to which the natives came in large numbers every day
to ask for consultation and to procure remedies. Orphanages
were built in which to receive abandoned infants, to give them
an education appropriate to their future needs and to protect
them until they were definitely established in life. The number
of these different works of charity was very large, there were
655 such institutions in Asia, 323 in Africa, 13 in Oceania,
47 in the Missions of America; in all 1,038.[17] A large amount
of money was required to finance these institutions and the
greater share of this money was provided by the Society for
the Propagation of the Faith. At times, unforeseen accidents
occurred such as fires, floods, extraordinary famines, wars and
their disastrous consequences, periods of unemployment which
reduced the local resources of the Missions and for the moment
compromised their existence.[18] Far from being able to support
the missionary at these periods, the missionary on the contrary, had to look elsewhere for aid, and it was chiefly through
the assistance of the Society for the Propagation of the Faith
that he was able to obtain it.

Apart from all this ecclesiastical and social activity, the
Society aids the missionary in the important work of civilizing
the people to whom he is sent. Local superstition and traditional prejudices against Christianity have to be driven out of
the hearts of these pagans. The missionaries give to their catechumens a consciousness of their dignity. They put them in a
position to know themselves, to discipline themselves and to
govern themselves. In rendering them participants in the life

17. Piolet, *ut supra,* p. 31.
18. *L'Oeuvre,* etc., in the *Annales,* t. XLIX, p. 159.

of the Gospel they introduce them to a new and superior life; they make of them Christians. They deliver the oppressed; they liberate prisoners and thus the interests of civilization are served. In whatever part of the world they exercise their Apostolate, the progress of civilization is assured. One can find more than one proof of it in the history of the Missions, but in return wherever the missionaries establish their peaceful empire the arts of the West follow them; everyday life improves, family relations are more firmly established or are purified.[19]

For example, the natives of Oceania, once inveterate cannibals, have today become peaceful and inoffensive farmers. The negroes of Africa, among whom there existed neither marriage nor family, nor any reverence for woman, among whom were committed unspeakable cruelties as a consequence of superstition or of passion, are now united in marriage and set themselves to live civilized lives in established villages, with order and tranquillity. Infanticide has rapidly diminished in proportion as the Society of the Holy Childhood developed. Slavery has diminished and rapidly disappeared. The law of property, public morality, Christian decency, the flower and safeguard of virtue, respect for women, for children, for the aged, have developed and multiplied under the influence of the missionaries whose work was made possible by the funds of the Society.[20]

In addition to these three main divisions of missionary activities: Religion, Education and Charity, other incidental results have been attained through the coöperation of the Society. The spiritual reaction upon the donors themselves is one very important incidental result. The charity and zeal which they practice in behalf of their less fortunate brothers has no little influence upon their own spiritual life. An instance of this is found in the revival of zeal in France after the apostolic tour of Bishop Flaget in 1838. The layman who

---

19. BRUNETIERE, in PIOLET, *Les Missions Catholiques Françaises au XIX Siècle*, t. VI, pp. 496-497; Cf. *La Propagation de la Foi*, in the *Annales*, t. LXXVIII, pp. 429-430.
20. PIOLET, *ut supra*, pp. 28-29.

thus participates in Apostolic work inevitably becomes a better Catholic. Through its publications, the Society, has been productive of much good. One can readily imagine the number of persons whose eyes have been opened and whose souls have been comforted by a description of the trials and sufferings willingly supported for the glory of God, contained in these works. Indirectly too, it wins apostles, who upon reading it become inflamed with zeal for the kingdom of God; both men and women are moved to go forward to carry the good tidings of salvation to distant lands. Undoubtedly, no one becomes an apostle without a divine call; but that call is manifested by exterior signs of which the most usual is example in the first place, seconded by a knowledge of the need of souls. Example awakens generous emulation. How many levites, how many priests and how many virgins have felt their souls moved at the recital of the work of missionaries, and abasing themselves in humility and prayer have arisen, saying: *I, too, wish to be an Apostle!* Nowhere are the needs of souls portrayed in livelier and more pleasing colors than in the letters which fill the *Annales.* As an eloquent orator has said: ''An astonishing and glorious fact marks the close of the century. Speculators and economists laud the resources, salubrity and charms of a country; and they do not always succeed. The publications of the Propagation of the Faith speak of nothing but privations, perils and struggles; the more they darken the picture, the more they kindle the zeal for Missions, especially if they open the sombre perspective of martyrdom.''[21]

The Blessed Chanel, ordained priest the 15th of July, 1827, named assistant at Amberieux, then pastor of Crozot, was ceaselessly pursued by the thought of the Missions. ''I read one day a number of the *Annales* which upset my soul. I seemed to see the poor islanders, these idolators, these cannibals, whom the demon held under his empire. They held out their arms to us,—I seemed to hear their piercing cries: 'Who will dissipate our darkness? Who will break our chains of

---

21. FRERI, *op. cit.,* p. 16, 1912.

slavery? Come to our aid'.'' There is no doubt but that the reading of the *Annales* was influential in the development of the vocation of Blessed Perboyre. Theophane Venard, put to death for the Faith in Tonkin on February 2, 1861, felt that the desire to be a missionary was born within him while perusing the *Annales de la Propagation de la Foi;* it was also the same with Mgr. Ridel who died in Korea: ''It was in a humble Breton college that a child was playing by his mother's side when he beheld in her hand a copy of the *Annales.* 'Mother, are there stories in that book?' 'Yes, my child, stories of missionaries.' 'But what are missionaries?' 'They are the priests who go far away among the savages to teach them to know and love God, to save their souls and to go to Heaven.' 'Well, then, I want to go and tell them myself so that they will come with us to Paradise.' The valiant mother embraced her child: 'Poor little one,' she said, 'may thy life be God's.' Some years later the son of the Breton woman entered Korea. In 1870 he was consecrated Bishop and on June 28, 1884, after a long captivity, the confessor of the Faith died with regret that he had not been able to shed his blood for Jesus Christ. It is quite possible that nearly all those who have been put to death for the Faith since 1822 had in some way or another received aid from the Society, and insofar as it has aided them it has to that extent partici-pated in the supreme sacrifice which they gladly offered.''[22]

The labor of the missionary also has its patriotic, economic, and scientific sides, which must not be overlooked.

The patriotic or national side of missionary activity is a delicate subject to discuss. The motto of the American College of the Immaculate Conception at Louvain: *Missionarii Patria Sancta Mater Ecclesia,* is the ideal of the true missionary. As Bishop Le Roy has written: ''Let us not deceive our-selves, God is neither French, Russian nor Spanish, nor Portu-gese nor English nor German nor Italian, but He makes use of that nation which He finds to be best equipped to carry out

---

22. GUASCO, *op. cit.,* pp. 30-31, 1904; TISSOT, *L'Oeuvre de la Prop-agation de la Foi et ses Publications, Discours prononcé dans l'Eglise Primatiale de Lyon le 23 Mai, 1894,* p. 25, Lyon, 1894.

His work." [23]   Many French writers who discuss the Missions have indulged in a certain amount of boasting regarding the national propaganda carried on by their missionaries.   It would be hard to separate the missionary from his nationality and to prevent his fatherland from profiting from his labors.[24]

But other great services are those which the missionaries have rendered to science, to literature, to linguistics, to cartography, to geography, ethnography, natural history.   An enumeration of the scientific works of the missionaries, the discoveries which we owe to them, the books which they have published, the services which they have rendered to our voyagers and explorers, the lands which they have made known, the observatories, etc., which they have founded, the maps which they have prepared, leave one literally astonished at the catalogue of progress accomplished by the missionaries.

That incomparable collection, the *Lettres Edifiantes,* contains a description of places and an enumeration of natural curiosities with notices of botany, zoology, ethnography, linguistics, historic information, analyses of local superstition, traits and customs, characteristic anecdotes: in truth, nothing is lacking which could contribute to the more precise knowledge of the earth or of man.[25]

From the $100,000,000 which this Society has distributed to the Missions throughout the world, an immense good therefore has resulted.

For all these indispensable works the missionaries receive an annual income from 500 to 600 francs together with some assistance, more or less uncertain, which is sent by their families or by their friends in Europe.[26]   In

23. LE ROY, *A La Fin D'Un Siècle* in the *Annales*, t. LXXI, p. 427.
24. BAUDRILLART, *Le Pape et les Interêts Françaises dans le Monde*, in *L'Écho de Paris*, Feb. 14, 1921.
25. BRUNETIERE, in PIOLET, *Les Missions Catholiques*, etc., t. VI, p. 491, Paris, 1900.
26. Kennedy in his article on the Catholic Missions in the *Catholic Encyclopedia* discredits all estimates of the total financial contributions for the support of the missionaries and particularly comparisons between the total budget for Catholic missions and that of Protestant missions. Even a hazardous estimate may, however, enable us to form a fair idea of the poverty of our missionaries, and for this reason, is useful.

order to show more in detail the income of each missionary and the establishments which he must support by means of it a few quotations will be given from authorities on this question: Mgr. Le Roy estimated that a budget of 7,000,000 fr. was to be divided among 70,000 missionaries throughout the world, which would average 100 francs per year to each. These revenues, he says, must suffice for the support, the lodging, the voyages, the personnel, church construction, expenses of all kinds, including expenses for pleasure.[27] Louvet in 1891 estimated the budget at 6,779,363 fr. which total was divided among 277 missions, allowing on an average 24,474 fr. to each mission. From this must be taken the living expenses of the Superior of the Mission and the missionaries and the same for native priests if there are any, also the support of the seminary and the schools of the Mission. The expense of the catechumenate, the salary of the catechists, etc., the support of churches, chapels and other establishments of the Mission, the support of hospitals, refuges and other establishments of charity, varying according to the place, the assistance from poor, persecuted Christians, must likewise be provided. These are the indispensable works of each mission. Without these works, more or less developed according to the locality, it is impossible to do good or to found anything permanent. Louvet summarizes the material needs of the Missions in these words: "One must feed the apostolic laborers, build churches in which to celebrate worship, open schools for the instruction of the children, found and support thousands of works of the apostolate and of charity." For example the following is the table of the obligatory expenses of the mission of Saigon in Western Cochin China in 1891:

1) Traveling Expense of the Vicar Apostolic and 49 Missionaries .... 33,660 fr.
2) Ecclesiastical Retreats, Time in Hospital and Voyages of Missionaries .... 3,000 "
3) Traveling Expenses of 44 Native Priests .... 14,520 "
4) Expense of Ordination, Chapels for Native Priests and Supply of Vestments .... 2,000 "
5) 120 Scholarships at the Seminary .... 18,000 "

27. LE ROY, *Discours, etc.*, in the *Missions Catholiques*, No. 1544, p. 1a.

6) Maintenance of the Seminary Buildings .... 4,000 "
7) 120 Parish Schools .... 24,000 "
8) Construction of New Schools and Support of Others .... 6,000 "
9) 40 Catechists, Including Voyages .... 10,000 "
10) Support of Churches, New Construction, Assistance to
    Catechumens .... 35,000 "

$$\text{Total.......................150,180 fr.}$$

The sum of 150,000 fr. is strictly necessary in order to assure the functioning of the present work without founding any new works.[28]

The author of *La Société des Missions Étrangères* designates the establishments which were supported by the Propagation of the Faith and the Holy Childhood as works of general interest, either charitable or educational; hospitals, homes for foundlings, orphanages, work rooms, schools; the construction of churches, oratories and presbyteries. "Thanks to their labors," he says, "the favorable events of which we have spoken, the results in conversion, in works of zeal, of education and of charity were considerable." Some general statistics will throw additional light on the disbursements of the Society:

Personnel and Establishments.	1822	1860	1917
Missions	5	22	35
Bishops	6	21	40 and 2 Archbishops
Missionaries	27	230	1,234
Native Priests	135	300	1,043
Seminaries	9	11	50
Seminarians	250	400	
Christians	300,000	550,000	1,639,853

For 1917 the additional statistics were 3,268 catechists, 6,839 European and foreign sisters, 5,322 colleges, boarding-schools and schools with 2,594 children, 388 orphan asylums with 16,598 children, 476 dispensaries and pharmacies, and 114 hospitals, homes and leprosaries. The number of conversions obtained in 1913 was 31,903; in 1914, 32,839; in 1916, 36,434; in 1917, 29,331.[29]

---

28. LOUVET, *op. cit.*, pp. 8a-9a.
29. *La Société des Missions Étrangères*, pp. 32-34, Paris, 1919.

In order to enable one to appreciate the happy influence this Society has exercised, a comparative planisphere of the missions in 1822 and in 1885 has been prepared by the directors. The distribution of Catholics over the earth is also shown by another map for the year 1885, but the meagre statistics, especially for the year 1822, do not permit a satisfactory comparison.[30]

How many churches, schools and hospitals have been built, how many new Missions have been made possible by the generous budget provided?

The success realized in the Missions has gone hand-in-hand with the progress of the Church in these nations, and has been described in the official *Notices sur l'Oeuvre*, etc., as follows:[31]

---

30. WERNER-GROFFIER, *Atlas des Missions Catholiques*, Fribourg, 1886.

31. *L'Oeuvre de la Propagation de la Foi, Notice Publiée par Les Conseils Centraux de Lyon et de Paris*, 1898, in the *Appendice, Histoire Succinte des Missions Au Dix-Neuvième Siècle*, pp. 39-54; *L'Oeuvre de la Propagation de la Foi, Dix Années d'Apostolat dans les Missions*, 1898-1907, pp. 39-110. The results of the Catholic missions, produced by means of the funds which the Society has distributed, have been continually chronicled in various forms in the *Annales:* for example, the *Nouvelles des Missions, L'Année Apostolique, La Situation des Missions en 1822, en 1840, en 1844, en 1849, en 1878*, etc., the histories of the missionary societies: *Les Pères du Saint Esprit, La Société des Missions Étrangères de Paris, La Congrégation Belge du Coeur Immaculé de Marie, La Société des Missions Africaines de Lyon, La Congrégation des Lazaristes, La Société du Verbe Divin, La Société de Marie, Les Pères Capucins, Les Frères Mineurs, Les Oblats de Marie Immaculée, La Société Saint Joseph de Mill Hill, L'Institut Lombard de Milan, Les Missionnaires de Saint François de Sales, Les Pères Dominicains, La Compagnie de Jésus, Les Pères des Sacrés-Coeurs, Les Silésiens de Don Bosco, Les Missionnaires du Sacré-Coeur, Les Prêtres de Saint Sulpice, Les Oblats de Saint François de Sales, Les Prêtres du Sacré-Coeur de Jésus, La Congrégation des Passionistes.* The monumental work of Louvet gives a splendid survey of the progress of the missions in the last century and a good exposition of what money the Society has placed at the disposal of the missions in the different countries and continents. Only a laborious study of many years would reveal what an important role this Society has played in the success of Catholic missionary endeavor. And this study could only be made from the letters from the chiefs of the missions in the archives of the Society in Paris, Lyons and Fribourg.

EUROPE

Due to the Greek schism and Protestantism, which in the course of ages have come to shatter the unity of the Church, and to tear the seamless cloak of Christ, a large part of Europe remained to be reconquered by Catholicism. The hierarchy having been destroyed wherever heresy was dominant, these unfortunate people were reduced to the state of Missions and the Catholics there were directed by Vicars Apostolic who were dependant upon Propaganda.[32]

ENGLAND AND SCOTLAND

Three great facts dominate and explain the marvelous progress of Catholicism in Great Britain during ninety years of the nineteenth century: the emancipation of Catholics, the ritualist and Pusey movement, and the reestablishment of the hierarchy, first in England, then in Scotland. At the beginning of the last century oppressive laws weighed heavily upon the Catholics of Great Britain: political events and the strength of truth which imposed itself on many elevated minds favored their abrogation.[33] The Catholic religion had no need of the protection of governments for its life and prosperity; on the contrary, this protection is often fatal to it; liberty and opportunity alone are necessary. In 1800 there were in England and Scotland together only 120,000 Catholics. In 1890, 1,690,000 Catholics. In 1800 there were 6 Vicars Apostolic and 55 priests, in 1890, 18 Bishops, and 2,795 priests. The Catholics in England and Scotland in 1897 numbered 1,865,000 distributed in 3 archdioceses and 18 dioceses. In 1800 there were only two or three educational establishments on the Continent which the French Revolution suppressed. In 1840 there were 9 Catholic colleges in Great Britain. In 1880 there were in England 23 Catholic colleges and 4 in Scotland in addition to 600 parish schools having 118,000 children. In 1890 England had 11 seminaries and 800 stu-

---

32. LOUVET, *op. cit.*, p. 3.
33. Ut supra, p. 25; Cf. WERNER-GROFFIER, *Atlas, etc.*, p. 14, 1886; MIGNE, *Encyclopedie*, etc., *Dictionnaire des Missions*, pp. viii-ix.

dents, 29 colleges with 3,000 students, Scotland had 3 seminaries with 84 students, 4 colleges with 400 students.[34] All the works of Catholic charity also developed in like proportions. The Society for the Propagation of the Faith greatly aided the Missions in England and Scotland up to 1860. After that period it continued to aid them though in more restricted amounts. In 1898 one Vicariate Apostolic in Wales alone received aid. Ireland has also enjoyed a favorable place in the distribution of the Society during long years, but in 1898 only one station in the diocese of Ross received aid.[35]

NORWAY, SWEDEN AND DENMARK

It was only in 1868 that the laws which oppressed the Catholics in Sweden were in part done away with and in 1873 these laws were again modified in favor of tolerance. However, from 1833 there was a Vicariate Apostolic in Norway and Sweden composed of 300 Catholics, all foreigners in the realm. In 1869 the two Missions in Norway and Sweden were separated, they formed in 1898 two Vicarites Apostolic. The Vicariate of Sweden numbered nearly 1,300 Catholics and that of Norway 1400. From the year 1869 to 1897 Sweden received from the Society for the Propagation of the Faith nearly 470,000 fr. and Norway, during the same period, nearly 830,000 fr. Prior to 1869 these countries received substantial assistance for different uses. Up to June 9, 1847, harsh laws were enforced in Denmark against the Catholics. After this date the Church of Denmark could hope to revive. In 1898 Denmark constituted a Vicariate Apostolic with several thousand Catholics. The Society for the Propagation of the Faith from 1869, the time of the erection of the Prefecture Apostolic, to 1897, the Society gave it more than a million francs.[36]

---

34. LOUVET, *ut supra*, pp. 31-33; Cf. GUASCO, *op. cit.*, p. 62; GUASCO, *Cent Ans d'Apostolat Catholique dans les Missions.*
35. *L'Oeuvre*, etc., p. 40, 1898.
36. Ut supra, p. 41, 1898.

GERMANY

Louvet says that in the North of Germany at the beginning of the 19th century there were about 6,000,000 Catholics. In 1890 their number was 12,767,000. If Germany has showed herself generous towards the Society the latter, on its part, has also been generous with its subsidies. In 1898 the Missions of Germany still received important subsidies from the Society. In 1897 it received over 140,000 fr.[37]

SWITZERLAND

Persecutions have not been wanting to the Catholic Church in Switzerland during the 19th century and in spite of this number of the faithful had continually increased. The Catholics formed scarcely a third of the population in 1800, but composed two-fifths of it in 1890. In 1894 there were 1,169,000 Catholics in Switzerland. In the distribution of funds the Central Councils gave the missions of Switzerland 47,000 fr. in 1897.[38]

EASTERN EUROPE AND THE BALKAN PENINSULA

For seventy years the Popes have maintained diplomatic relations with the Sultans, and the Catholics have been submissive subjects of the Porte. There are numerous dioceses and establishments in these countries aided by the Society for the Propagation of the Faith. In 1897, 300,000 fr. were distributed to these dioceses by the Society.[39]

ASIA

In the Extreme Orient in 1822 the Episcopate was composed of 12 Pontiffs assisted by one or two missionaries; two Bishops for India, 6 for China and 4 for Indo-China. The following is a list of the number of Catholics in Asia in 1800:

---

37. Ut supra, p. 41, 1898.
38. Ut supra, p. 42, 1898.
39. Ut supra, p. 42, 1898.

Asia Minor	381,000	Catholics
Arabia	......	"
India	475,000	"
Indo-China	320,000	"
Japan	......	"
Corea	6,000	"

Total for All Asia....... 1,369,000 Catholics[40]

There were about this time 54,000 Catholics in Japan, 720,000 in China, 827,000 in Indo-China, 1,628,000 in India, 3,419,000 in all Asia. The Hindu peninsula and the Island of Ceylon possess 26 Archbishops or bishops, 1200 priests, and Indo-China, China and Japan possess 50 Vicars or Prefects Apostolic, 1400 priests. The Latin Patriarchate of Jerusalem was reestablished in 1848. There were only two priests in the Holy Land. Today there are large numbers of secular and religious priests. The Society has sent the Patriarchate more than 2,000,000 fr. from 1848 to 1898 exclusive of what was given directly to the Island of Cyprus and to the Seminary of St. Anne of Jerusalem for the Greek "Melchites." This seminary has received 318,000 fr. from the Society from time of its foundation up to 1898. More than 1,200,000 fr. was given to Archepiscopal See of Smyrna; the Lazarists and the Sisters of Charity received approximately the same amount up to the year 1898. The Apostolic Delegation of Mesopotamia received more than 1,500,000 fr. from the Society; the Dominicans have received 1,300,000 fr., the Capuchins have received 900,000 fr. and the Carmelites 390,000 fr. It was with very great difficulty that Arabia could be evangelized due to Mohammedan fanaticism. The Society has given the mission of Aden, confided to the Capuchins, over 300,000 fr. At the beginning of the last century there were in India 2 Archbishops, 2 Bishops, 2 Vicars Apostolic. The Missions of India received in 1897, 572,446 fr. from the Society. Indo-China received in 1897 about the same amount as India received. In "Birmania," Siam, Malacca there were in 1800, 1 Vicariate Apostolic, 9 priests and 9,800 Catholics. In 1898 there were 5 Vicariates Apostolic, 188 priests and 94,000

---

40. LOUVET, *op. cit.*, p. 16.

Catholics.   In 1800 there were 3 Vicariates Apostolic, in
Annam and 300,000 Catholics.   In 1897 there were 8 Vicars
Apostolic, 261 missionaries, 481 native priests and 726,000
Christians.   In 1898 Cambodge had 1 Vicariate Apostolic, 32
missionaries, 19 native priests and 27,000 Catholics.   In the
middle of the century the Mission of Borneo was reopened and
since then has received about 250,000 fr. from the Society.
The Dutch East Indies, after having been sustained by the
Society for many years, in 1898 received only small subsidies.
In 1800 the number of Catholics in China was 202,000 divided
in 5 Missions.   In 1897 there were 40 Missions with 40 Bishops,
697 missionary priests, 394 native priests and 649,000 Catholics.   The Society for the Propagation of the Faith distributed
in 1897 to the Missions of China 885,000 fr.   In 1846 Gregory
XVI reestablished the Vicariate Apostolic of Japan, but the
missionaries could only be restored after the treaties of commerce concluded with European nations in 1861.   The Church
of Japan was divided in 1898 into 4 Vicariates with 4 Bishops,
109 missionaries, 37 natives priests, more than 52,000 Catholics.   It received in 1897 143,000 fr. from the Society.   Korea,
for such a long time persecuted with violence, in 1898 had
1 Bishop, 31 missionaries, 3 native priests and 32,000 Catholics.
The Society for the Propagation of the Faith from 1832 to
1898 has distributed to it about 13,000,000 fr.

Leo XIII in the Encyclical *Christi Nomen* which is quoted
in Chapter V appealed to this Society and the Schools of the
Orient for funds to promote the work of uniting with Rome
the Greek and Oriental Churches.

The Society for the Propagation of the Faith has always
come to the aid of the Apostolate among the schismatic
churches of the Oriental Rite to such an extent as its resources
will permit. Leo XIII asked the Central Councils to cooperate
in aiding him to realize the union of the schismatic Oriental
churches to the Roman Church and for the Latin establishments in the Levant it put at the disposition of the Pope in
1895, 300,000 fr., in 1896, 200,000, in 1897, 200,000 fr.   About
1,000,000 fr. is each year given by the Society to aid toward

union with schismatic rites and for the prosperity of the Oriental Churches of the Uniate Rite."

AFRICA

In 1800 there were 1,500 Catholics in Northern Africa and 500,000 in 1898. The total sum sent by the Central Councils to the different Missions of Northern Africa is over 7,000,000 fr. In 1840 on the West Coast of Africa in the diocese of St. Paul de Loanda there were 8 or 10 priests and 700,000 Catholics. The Society for the Propagation of the Faith has given several million francs to this part of Africa. The Vicariate of Senegambia alone received over 1,300,000 fr. The allocations made by the Society to the Missions of South Africa have been very liberal. The Vicariate of Cape Occidental with the Prefecture Centrale has received about 1,000,000 fr. since its foundation and that of Cap Est more than 800,000 fr. The sums accorded by the Society to South Africa have amounted to many millions of francs. Eastern Africa received in 1897 over 130,000 fr. from the Society. Central Africa was receiving on an average 250,000 fr. per year in 1898. Madagascar in 1897 received 139,980 fr. and Port Victoria received a regular allocation from the Society; other Missions received aid irregularly.[42]

OCEANIA

In 1800 Australia, Tasmania and New Zealand did not have a single Catholic priest. In 1898 the Catholics formed a third of the total population. In 1898 the Cardinal Archbishop of Sydney was at the head of 20 dioceses. The Church of Australia with the diocese of Hobart in Tasmania received more than 3,000,000 fr. from the Society. In 1898 only rarely were establishments in Oceania supported by the Society, but subsidies destined for the voyages of missionaries or sisters were provided by the Society. New Zealand received the first

41. *L'Oeuvre*, etc., pp. 42-48, 1898.
42. Ut supra, pp. 48-50, 1898.

Catholic missionaries in 1838. In 1898 the Ecclesiastical Province of Wellington had three suffragan dioceses and a Catholic population of about 90,000. New Zealand has received about 3,000,000 fr. since its separation from the rest of Oceania, but previously it had been the principal point of Western Oceania to which the Society had given about 800,000 fr. The other islands of Oceania had received more than 21,500,000 fr. from the Society up to 1898.[43]

North America: Canada

In 1820 the Dominion of Canada had 1 Archbishop, 5 Vicars Apostolic, 302 priests and 540,000 Catholics. In 1898 there were 2,107,000 Catholics distributed among 7 archdioceses and 23 dioceses, with 2,720 priests. The Society for the Propagation of the Faith has liberally assisted all this region of America; but for a number of years before 1898 it had suppressed its assistance to the eastern part of Canada which was very rich and very prosperous. It continued to come to the aid in a large way of the Vicariates Apostolic of Athabaska-Mackenzie, of Saskatchewan, of the dioceses of St. Boniface, of St. Albert, of New Westminister confided to the Oblate Fathers of Mary Immaculate, of the Indian Missions of the Society of Jesus in Canada, in Alaska and in the Rocky Mountains.[44]

Central America and the Antilles

In Central America and the Islands of the Gulf of Mexico the Society has also distributed its benefits. In 1898 San Domingo, Jamaica, Trinidad, Curacao and British Honduras received allocations from the Society.[45]

South America

In South America the Vicariate Apostolic of Surinam, the Prefecture Apostolic of Ayapock and Patagonia confided to the zeal of the sons of Don Bosco received allocations. The

43. Ut supra, p. 52, 1898.
44. Ut supra, p. 50, 1898.
45. Ut supra, p. 51, 1898.

Dominican Mission among the Canelos Indians also received subsidies during some years, and the Central Councils accorded at different times important sums for the voyages of different missionaries.[46]

THE UNITED STATES

It is not practical to give here more than a brief summary of the work done by the Society for the Church in the United States.

The funds received by the dioceses of the United States each year from the Society for the Propagation of the Faith, as given by Mgr. Freri, are as follows:

Year	Received	Year	Received	Year	Received
1822	$2,757.00	1857	$99,404.60	1892	$23,000.00
1823	5,200.00	1858	115,288.20	1893	16,700.00
1824	6,940.00	1859	173,623.80	1894	13,300.00
1825	10,340.00	1860	152,342.20	1895	10,800.00
1826	8,740.00	1861	118,014.00	1896	8,500.00
1827	20,700.00	1862	130,802.00	1897	11,312.50
1828	22,000.00	1863	119,800.00	1898	10,900.00
1829	24,268.00	1864	117,600.00	1899	10,292.86
1830	23,394.00	1865	124,450.00	1900	11,022.00
1831	25,294.00	1866	115,660.00	1901	28,226.00
1832	22,960.00	1867	97,260.00	1902	27,649.00
1833	19,604.00	1868	100,290.00	1903	26,524.00
1834	20,564.00	1869	99,975.00	1904	32,909.00
1835	29,053.60	1870	41,000.00	1905	41,571.82
1836	44,133.60	1871	87,200.00	1906	46,228.96
1837	37,916.20	1872	98,200.00	1907	51,645.42
1838	53,501.60	1873	75,600.00	1908	47,226.51
1839	68,025.00	1874	74,000.00	1909	55,830.18
1840	125,572.80	1875	73,040.00	1910	70,493.84
1841	122,261.00	1876	82,200.00	1911	73,716.27
1842	127,360.40	1877	67,440.00	1912	61,086.27
1843	126,259.60	1878	60,600.00	1913	87,765.47
1844	131,432.80	1879	57,080.00	1914	51,467.19
1845	107,400.00	1880	52,200.00	1915	45,613.16
1846	116,328.20	1881	56,600.00	1916	29,671.74
1847	87,980.00	1882	51,600.00	1917	81,363.54
1848	72,762.00	1883	59,360.00	1918	80,121.32
1849	95,316.00	1884	66,000.00	1919	76,992.94
1850	80,735.00	1885	60,840.00	1920	96,570.39
1851	78,287.00	1886	56,000.00	1921	101,098.85
1852	103,101.00	1887	51,400.00		516,592.04
1853	126,452.00	1888	42,440.00		
1854	127,439.20	1889	40,080.00		$7,020,974.27
1855	101,084.60	1890	42,740.00		[47]
1856	105,761.40	1891	33,920.00		

46. Ut supra, pp. 51-52, 1898.
47. FRERI, *op cit.*, in the *Annals*, vol. LXXXV, p. 68, 1922.

CHAPTER VIII

ALLIED AND SUBORDINATE ACTIVITIES

The methods of administration used by the Society and the remarkable growth in its collections, together with its accomplishments, have been treated. There are other activities, which are subordinate to the main work of this Society, and these must be briefly described.

One of the auxiliary functions which has largely contributed to the success of the Society is its official organ, the *Annales de la Propagation de la Foi*. The natural process by which this publication evolved can be traced back to the *Lettres Edifiantes et Curieuses* which had been written in order to place missionaries in direct contact with their benefactors during the preceding century. The first number of this valuable collection appeared in 1702, and the last issues were printed in the reign of Louis XV. Later, in 1780, Father Querboeuf issued an edition of the *Lettres*, but with a stricter attention to classification and method. The edition was in 26 volumes.[1] Since that date, the *Lettres* have often been reprinted, and in 1809-14 there appeared a choice selection of the documents. The last edition is that of Paris (1875).

As the natural center of the Missions of the world it appeared logical that the Society for the Propagation of the Faith, destined to receive alms and to distribute them according to the needs of the Missions, should create an organ which would be a sort of continuation of the *Lettres Edifiantes*. It was at first decided by the Society to publish its organ under the title *Nouvelles des Missions;* then, *Annales de l'Association de la Propagation de la Foi*, with the sub-title *Collection faisant suite à toutes éditions des Lettres Edifiantes*. The first volume is especially valuable to the American historian, since

---

1. *Lettres Edifiantes et Curieuses*, p. x, 1875; GUASCO, *Les Missionnaires et la Science*, p. 23, 1908.

it contains a letter on the Missions of Louisiana and Badin's valuable sketch of the Kentucky Missions.

This publication has spread throughout the world a knowledge of the work, the fatigues, the perils and the success of the Apostolic laborers, and has made known to the learned as well as to the unlearned the habits and the customs of missionary countries which were at this epoch entirely unknown; it has established a correspondence between the missionaries and the whole Catholic world, and thus it has interested even the least of the faithful and enabled them in some way to cooperate in the accomplishment of the Divine Plan. The Catholic press gave a hearty reception to this new periodical. The *Quotidienne* wrote: "Independently of the great interest of the propagation of the Faith in the world, they offer a wealth of ideas concerning geography, interior administration, habits and customs, the political and commercial resources of the different regions which here pass in review."[2] The utility of publication to the Society and to the Missions results from the zeal and charity of the faithful and the clergy, which it awakens and sustains. Without it, it would have been difficult, if not impossible, to attract the attention, to keep alive the interest, to stimulate the desire to aid and to encourage the perseverance of the contributors. It accomplishes this result by emphasizing, in the words of the missionaries themselves, the sad conditions of the peoples living in the darkness of paganism, the possibilities of their conversion, their absolute poverty which makes it impossible for them to support the Missions and by demonstrating the results already attained.

Another important service which this publication has performed, through the Society's annual financial statement which it contains, is that it has thus forestalled much hostile criticism of the Society's administration which otherwise would have been aroused. By this publicity public powers,

---

2. LAUNAY, *Histoire Générale de la Société des Missions Étrangères*, t. II, pp. 519, et seq. Cf. *La Propagation de la Foi* in the *Missions Catholiques*, t. XXVI, pp. 518, 519; *ibid.*, t. I, p. 1, 1868; GUASCO, *op. cit.*, p. 29, 1911.

foreign governments, missionaries and the faithful were all able to ascertain the exact amount of money received, the expenses incurred and the Missions and religious orders supported by the Society. Thus suspicions and charges of partiality in favoring the Missions of any particular country or the missionaries of any particular nationality have been avoided and disproved.[3]

The *Annales* was at first annual; two issues were published in 1824; three in 1826; four in 1830; and after 1835, six issues a year. The *Annales* is sent free to the chief of each group of ten who circulates it among each of the group after which it is returned to him and becomes his property as a recompense for his care in encouraging its reading. It was soon translated into many languages: English, Italian, Spanish, Portugese, Dutch, Polish, Flemish, Basque, Maltese, German and Breton. The first English edition was published in Paris in the year 1838. In May, 1839, or earlier a Dublin edition was begun. The American edition, published by the national office of the Society in New York, dates from the year 1903. In 1922, 375,000 copies of this publication were printed bi-monthly in various languages.[4]

It was soon found necessary to supplement the *Annales* by the publication of a weekly periodical in order to discuss many subjects which could not find a place in the *Annales*. *Les Missions Catholiques* made its appearance in the year 1868. This weekly review is sold by yearly subscription, and it soon acquired an important place among contemporary publications, a place merited by the importance of its object and the sublimity of its end. In it is recorded each week the correspondence exchanged between apostolic men in all parts of the globe concerning religion, history, geography, science and industry of the most important missionary countries. A quantity of the documents emanating from the Missions concern voyages, statistics, scientific subjects, obituary notices and bibliography. The text offers an interest, a variety, a

---

3. *L'Œuvre de la Propagation de la Foi*, p. 9, 1898.
4. Freri, *op. cit.*, in the *Annals*, t. LXXXV, p. 58, 1922.

charm and a picturesqueness which are admirable. It is well printed and richly illustrated with numerous maps and pictures, and including photographs sent in by missionaries.[5]

Among other publications of this Society must be mentioned the *Almanach des Missions* and the *Petit Almanach de la Propagation de la Foi*, both of which are sold for the profit of the Missions. The same can be said of the *Album des Missions*.[6]

Three very interesting and important brochures have been published under the auspices of the Society which treat of its origins, of its foundation, of its organization, of its history, of the spiritual favors accorded, of the pontifical and episcopal testimonials and of the history of the Missions. The first of these entitled *L'Œuvre de la Propagation de la Foi*, published in 1898 by the Central Councils of Lyons and Paris; the second with the same title, published in 1908, and the third also with the same title, published by M. Alexandre Guasco, the General Secretary of the Central Council of Paris, which has gone through several editions, the first of which appeared in 1904, the second in 1904, and the third in 1911, published in conjunction with a brochure by Monsignor Freri, *The Society for the Propagation of the Faith and the Catholic Missions*, give the official history of the Society.

The brochures, in which are printed the annual sermons delivered by the foremost pulpit orators of France in the primatial church of Lyons are published by the Society and receive wide circulation and have considerable influence in making the Society known and loved by the people. *L'Année Apostolique* gives a summary of the progress of the Catholic Missions each year. A summary of the progress of the Missions during the 19th century is found in M. Alexandre Guasco, *Cent Ans d'Apostolat Catholique dans les Missions*. The Society renders invaluable service to the missions by publishing such works as that by Louis-Eugène Louvet, *Les*

---

5. *Missions Catholiques*, t I, p. 1, 1868.
6. *L'Œuvre*, etc., p. 10, 1898.

Missions Catholiques au XIXᵉ Siècle. The Society also makes a practice of distributing such special works as the *Petit Manuel de Piété à l'Usage des Membres de l'Œuvre de la Propagation de la Foi,* by Mgr. André Saint-Clair.

The American Branch of the Society for the Propagation of the Faith has published two brochures by Mgr. Joseph Freri, *Native Clergy for Mission Countries,* and *The National Religion of Japan.*

The maps which the Society has published form a collection of considerable importance. In the *Annales* itself have appeared at different periods maps of the *Missions du Levant, des Etats-Unis et du Canada, Missions de la Chine, l'Inde, Tong-King, la Cochinchine, Siam et Birmanie.*[7]

The *Missions Catholiques* has made it a practice of giving premiums to their subscribers of maps of different missionary countries which today are sufficiently numerous to form an important collection. These are also on sale in Lyons. This collection includes the following:

LAUNAY, *Planisphère de la Hiérarche catholique à travers le monde.*[8]

Carte de l'Eglise catholique dans les Iles Britanniques, 1910.

Carte de l'Eglise catholique dans les Balkans, 1911.

Carte des Missions catholiques des Pays Scandinaves, 1909.

Carte de la Terre Sainte, 1914.

Carte de la Syrie septentrionale, 1915.

Carte des Missions catholiques du Siam, de la Birmanie et du Laos, 1904.

Carte de l'Inde ecclésiastique, 1907.

Carte des Missions catholiques dans l'Indo-Chine française, 1888.

L'Eglise catholique en Chine Orientale, 1912.

---

7. *Carte des Missions du Levant,* in the *Annales,* t. VIII, p. 409; *Carte des États-Unis et du Canada,* in the *Annales,* t. IX, p. 337; *Carte des Missions de la Chine,* in the *Annales,* t. X, p. 80; *Carte de l'Inde,* in the *Annales,* t. XI, p. 576; *Carte du Tong-King, de la Cochinchine, de Siam et de la Birmanie,* in the *Annales,* t. XII, p. 112.

8. This work is on sale at the office of the Society in Lyons but was not given out as a premium.

L'Eglise catholique en Chine Occidentale, 1913.
Carte des Missions catholiques au Japon, 1898.
Carte du Sahara et du nord-ouest de l'Afrique, 1895.
Carte des Missions du Soudan français et de la Côte occidentale d'Afrique, 1897.
Carte des Missions de Madagascar, 1903.
Carte du Nord-Est Africain et du Soudan Egyptien, 1899.
Carte des Missions du Centre Africain, 1901.
Carte des Missions du Sud Africain, 1902.
Carte des Missions catholiques en Afrique, 1905.
Carte du Canada catholique, 1893.
Carte des Missions catholiques aux États-Unis, 1900.
Carte de l'Amérique du Sud ecclésiastique, 1908.
Carte des Missions catholiques de la Mélanésie, Micronésie et Polynésie, 1896.
Carte des Missions catholiques en Australie, 1906.

M. Valérien Groffier has rendered a signal service to Christian history by translating and enlarging Werner's *Katholischer Missions-Atlas* which traces the ecclesiastical organization of the missionary countries under the jurisdiction of the Sacred Congregation de Propaganda Fide. By indicating the precise geographical situation of hundreds of Missions the name of which is familiar, but the location of which on the globe more or less vaguely known, this work enables us to follow the progress of the Missions.

The libraries of the Society for the Propagation of the Faith, which are established in connection with the offices of their two Central Councils in Lyons and in Paris, contain a fairly good collection of publications of missionary societies, of a large variety of books devoted to particular missionary countries, of ecclesiastical directories, and of all the works published by the Society. The library in Paris is well arranged and well catalogued, but there is no provision made for those who are not connected with the Society to make use of it.

In Lyons there was a much larger collection of books, but they are neither well-arranged nor well catalogued. It was quite evident that no provision had been made for permitting outsiders to make use of the books in their possession.

Another valuable record of the progress of the Missions may be found at the headquarters of the Society in Lyons; not in their books, but in the thousands of mementos of missionary activity gathered from every quarter of the globe. Instruments of war and peace, instruments of torture and relics of martyrs make a collection that represents heroic achievements worthy to rank with the first ages of Christianity.[9] This well arranged museum is laid out in two rooms, one of which contains objects of general interest, whereas the other is devoted exclusively to relics of confessors or martyrs. The whole collection is thoroughly catalogued so that the visitor can easily learn the interesting points about each object. No study is more interesting for those who have at heart the progress of religion and civilization; nothing better shows the benevolent influence exercised by the missionaries of the world than the Museum of the Propagation of the Faith. A few words concerning the origin of this museum and the riches which it contains will not be out of place. From the first years of the Society the missionaries have wished to testify their gratitude toward their benefactors by sending either relics or souvenirs of the apostolic laborers who have died for the Faith, or of interesting and precious objects which are specimens of primitive art in the countries being evangelized. The Religious Congregations have added other objects to this collection, and these have been admirably arranged and catalogued, so that the visitor can now follow step-by-step and, as it were, day by day, the progress of the apostolate through the different countries.[10]

Another means of publicity employed by the Society is afforded by the expositions or World's Fairs to which it sends an exhibit. At Chicago its publications and its maps were displayed. The exposition of Lyons in 1894, that of Paris in 1900, endeavored to translate the action of missionaries, which

9. FRERI, *op. cit.*, p. 10, 1912.
10. *Missions Catholiques*, t. XXII, p. viii, 1890; *ibid.*, t. XXV, p. 347, 1893.

for the most part is moral, into a material exhibition by showing the statistics, the maps and other exhibits which strike
the eye.   The exhibits were of interest for the study of comparative religions as well as for geography, history, ethnography, natural history, teaching, questions of interest to hospitals and the fine arts.   The publications of the Society
and its maps were given a prominent place.[11]   These expositions
led Piolet to suggest that they should be transformed into a
museum and thus acquire a permanent character.[12]

Two reasons are urged by Piolet in favor of a permanent
museum for all Catholic Missions: Many people are ignorant
of the very existence of our Missions; even among those who
know of them few understood their importance.   It was
therefore urgent, to awaken public attention, that a museum
of the Missions be created; to inform the public curiosity
more abundantly, that a large central library of the Missions
be organized.   What value would attach to such a central
museum which would unite all these riches, Chinese vases, the
collection of all the woods of the country, of Punic and
Roman antiques, inscriptions, monuments, clothes, arms, utensils of a savage people which have disappeared or is about
to disappear, ancient books, ancient manuscripts, codices,
inscriptions which at times have an inestimable value; all
that is related to the local worship or superstition or customs
and the objects made under the direction of the missionaries.
Such a museum would attract visitors and awaken attention;
but the curiosity aroused would demand a more ample and
more precise information.   A library would respond to this
new need: it would constitute the central archives of the
Missions.   It should be extended, like the museum to all the
Catholic Missions of every nationality, to those who desire to
study the most abundant and the most certain information.
To be such, in a word, that, without having consulted it, it
would not be permissible for any one to speak of the Missions.

---

11. Ut supra, t. XXVI, p. 463, et seq., 1894; *ibid.*, t. XXXII, p.
97, 1900.
12. Piolet, *Rapport sur les Missions Catholiques Françaises*, p. 123,
Paris, 1900.

It should therefore contain : all the books written or published by the missionaries; all the books translated or printed or illustrated by them in their printing establishments; all the text books, those used for teaching and for religion, employed by missionaries; all books written concerning the history or the present condition of the Missions, be they favorable or not; all the reviews published by the Missions, or speaking of them; all the archives of all the Missions or at least a copy of these archives. To unite them, it is true, would be long and costly, but though it only succeeded partially and for the ancient Missions, it would already be a great attainment. The simple index of the archives of the *Société des Missions Étrangères* fills 12 folio volumes. Such a collection of documents exists nowhere, but they are disseminated throughout the entire universe, divided among some fifty Societies. He who desires to write the history of our Missions is truly at a loss to find his information. This library would furnish him complete information at first hand.

Leo XIII was complimented on having opened the Vatican Archives, says Piolet, and thus rendered less difficult the task of writing the history of the Church. To give the same facility to the historian of our Missions, this vital part of the Church would be the completion of the work of Leo XIII, but in the reorganization of the Society for the Propagation of the Faith which apparently is under consideration, it would be of untold value to the world of science, of letters, and to the study of history, if the Society were to devote part of its enormous funds to the creation of a Library of Books on the Missions, a central Archives for all missionary societies, where original and duplicate copies of documents might be housed, and a museum on the scale of that at Kensington (London) where under one direction all the objects of interest in the field of primitive civilization might be found.[13]

13. PIOLET, *Nos Missions et Nos Missionaires,* pp. 55-62, Paris.

CHAPTER IX

Critical Essay on the Sources

The sources for the study of the Society for the Propagation of the Faith consist mainly of unpublished and published materials. The unpublished documents are to be found in the archives of the dioceses, archdioceses, Missions and religious orders throughout the world. Copies of the correspondence which the Society carried on with the Missions are in the registers of the offices of the two Councils, at Lyons and Paris. The more important part of the correspondence is that which has been received from the Missions themselves. This explains their status, their poverty, the good that could be accomplished but for lack of funds, and the plans and hopes for the future. These documents were sent either to the Superior Council, which existed from 1822-1830 when it disappeared in the Revolution, or to the Central Council of Lyons or to that of Paris, or indirectly to one of these Councils through the intermediary of some influential person whose interest was felt to be advantageous to the Missions. I referred the question of the American correspondence (1822-1830) sent to Monseigneur le Prince de Croy, President of the Superior Council of Paris, Grand Aumonier de France, to M. Guasco, the present General Secretary. who replied as follows: "There are no letters in the Oeuvre (Society) concerning the Conseil Superieur or Monseigneur de Croy, except those that were published in the *Annales*. As regards the *Archives Nationales,* should there have been any documents concerning the Society for the Propagation of the Faith in the Tuileries at the time of the Revolution, they would have been given up to the *Archévêché* preferably to the *Archives Nationales,* and the *Archévêché* in its turn, would have given them to the Society for the Propagation of the Faith—such has not been the case, one can presume, therefore, that there are no documents or that they have been destroyed during that troubled period.''

The correspondence for 1822-1830 sent to the Superior Council of Paris has not yet been located. If it is extant, it may have been intermingled with the documents received by the Central Council of Lyons; but a search for it in the *Archives Nationales* was not successful. The unpublished documents for the United States are for the most part in the Archives of the Central Council of Paris, where they have been carefully sorted by dioceses in separate *dossiers* and are arranged chronologically. An accurate idea of the contents of this depot can be judged from the appendix which shows the American dioceses which have received money from the Society. It was the custom of the Society to require a report from the diocese or Mission or religious community each year that financial aid was given. These letters are written generally by the Bishop, as the Society preferred to deal with the hierarchal head of each ecclesiastical territory. At times these letters were written by the Chancellor or Secretary of the Bishop or by one of the priests or superiors of some religious community within the diocese and were at times endorsed and recommended by the ordinary. The earliest documents relating to the Church of the United States, i. e., from 1822 to about 1838, were not to be found in Paris, nor were these duplicate copies. It was necessary, therefore, to go to Lyons for the material relating to these years. But another difficulty presented itself at Lyons. The troublesome period of the separation in 1906 caused the Central Council of that city to take the precautionary measure of boxing up their material and shipping it into Switzerland. It was found necessary to take a trip to Fribourg in the hope of finding these papers. M. Groffier, the General Secretary of the Central Council of Lyons, generously offered to do this for me. His plan was to go to Fribourg and to select the material which I might then consult in the Lyons office. The amount of important historical material to be found in these archival depots may be judged from the time spent in translating and copying the interesting parts of these letters.

Although I began the study in the library of the Society for the Propagation of the Faith in October, 1920, it was soon discovered that the published sources were incomplete and hence unsatisfactory, and great difficulty was experienced in gaining access to these archives. In January, 1921, the Central Council of Paris granted me this permission and I was given the *dossiers* of the American dioceses in alphabetical order. It soon became evident that it would take many years to translate and transcribe all this American material. Some selection was forced upon me. I decided to consult first the archdioceses and then those dioceses particularly associated with the Society for the Propagation of the Faith either on account of the amount of money given to them by the Society, or on account of the prominence of the Ordinary whose letters were contained therein. Much more material of interest to American scholars still remains in Fribourg and there is a large quantity of documents from America, which have not yet been consulted, in the Paris archives. It is quite possible, also, that considerable material relating to the American participation in the foundation of the Society for the Propagation of the Faith may be found in the archives of the Grand Seminary of St. Irenaeus, Lyons, France: Fr. Cholleton, the superior of the institution, knew personally several American Bishops and missionaries. Monseigneur Béchetoille, President of the Central Council of Lyons and Vicar-General of Lyons, has in his possession a note book of authentic copies of documents relating to the Missions Étrangères, and to Mlle. Jaricot's participation in the foundation, the originals of which have been sent to Rome to be used in the cause of her beatification.

In Rome, in the Archives of the Sacred Congregation de Propaganda Fide there are many interesting documents concerning the Society for the Propagation of the Faith. Many of these have special reference to the struggle of the Society to maintain unity and universality so constantly threatened by tentatives of independent national missionary societies in almost every country in Europe. The documents in Propaganda referring to the relations between the American dioceses and the Society for the Propagation of the Faith could only be located by searching through all the material concerning each diocese or each Bishop. The frequent references to M. l'Abbé Carrière, Superior of Seminary St. Sulpice, in the letters from American Bishops indicated that he had exerted considerable influence with the Central Council of Paris and this led me to believe that in all probability many interesting letters would be found in the archives of Saint-Sulpice. M. l'Abbé Levêsque, the librarian and archivist, searched out all the material relating to the Church of the United States, but, unfortunately, there were no documents which threw any light on the foundation of the Society and very few which concerned the assistance rendered by the Society to the Church of the United States.   Letters from Bishop Flaget of Bardstown, from Father Richard of Detroit, and an unpublished manuscript of the history of Saint Mary's Seminary, Baltimore, were the most interesting materials located.   Although the Sulpicians showed considerable interest in the United States and aided it with their good offices before the Central Council of Paris, they never received any material aid from the Society, unless it was through the Ordinary of the diocese in which they were established.

The delegates of the Society for the Propagation of the Faith in America after 1897 had their office at the St. Mary's Seminary, Baltimore, and it was thought that some unpublished documents of importance to my study would be found there, but these materials were transferred when the delegate moved his office to New York in 1903. In the Mother House of the Congregation of the Mission at Paris it was believed there would be many letters from the American seminaries and missions which this Congregation established, but at the time of the separation in 1906 their archives were also shipped out of Paris so it was not possible to consult them. Concerning the archives of the *Séminaire des Missions Étrangères*, the

Superieur informed me that there was no material relative
to the Church of the United States, but that there were
letters from missionaries in Canada. In Vienna is the headquarters of the Leopoldine Association, another Foreign Mission association that has given much money to the Church
of the United States. When Dr. Guilday and I were at
Vienna together we procured the collection of the *Berichte*,
but the Vicar-General assured us that the original documents relating to the Church of the United States had
not been preserved. A third possible source was the archives
of the Ludwig-Missionsverein at Munich. At the request of
Dr. Guilday, Rev. Dr. Joseph Schabert went to Munich to
obtain a set of the published documents and to investigate
the contents of their archives. Since that date the collection
of documents of the Ludwig-Missionsverein has been procured
for the Catholic University of America, but they contain nothing cognate to my study. Nothing of importance for my subject was found in the American College at Rome, or the
American College at Louvain.

In the archives of the Central Council of Lyons
and of Paris the greatest collection of the original
material for this work was found. Its historical value for
the American Church is great because the bishops wished to
prove that their dioceses deserved financial assistance from
the Society, and hence arose the necessity of presenting facts
about the religious situation of their dioceses, its size, its
population, its Catholic population, the racial and national
divisions of the population, the number of priests, both foreign
and native, the number of churches, chapels and Mission
stations, the number of baptisms, infant and adult, the number of Easter Communions, the information regarding the
Seminary, Colleges, boarding schools, and day schools, and the
religious conducting the same, with similar data for the hospitals, orphan asylums and other charitable institutions.
These letters also included the plans for the succeeding year
and the financial expenditures involved in obtaining more
priests and more seminarians and providing for their support,

for new or enlarged buildings such as churches, seminaries, noviciates, presbyteries and monasteries, and for similar requirements for educational and charitable activities. The Society also desired to know the financial situation of the diocese; and the bishop was asked what was the certain income for the next year, what could be expected from pew rents, the sale of lands in possession of the diocese, from the voluntary contributions of the faithful or from the stole fees. In a word, what was the probable amount of the accounts receivable for the ensuing year? On the credit side of the questionnaire was to be entered the bills and accounts payable item, including the debt of the diocese or of the parishes for which the bishop was held responsible, both the total amount and the amount due or payable during the coming year. Then a statement of the expenditures required for establishments already founded and the portion due during the following year together with the same details for establishments to be founded during the coming year. Thus it was possible to construct in advance an income sheet for the ensuing year and the Society then planned to assist the diocese by providing a portion of the anticipated deficit. There was generally an explanation of one or many of the items on this questionnaire, either in the columns provided for remarks or in the letter which accompanied the report. All this data was not given for every diocese each year but the Central Council expressed its desire to have all this information in its hands before allocating the collections to the different Missions. This material was too bulky to be submitted to the Directors themselves, of the Central Councils, so that in each case an analysis of the report was made and entered in a book provided for that purpose, while a duplicate copy of the report was sent to the other Central Council.

Such is the nature of this original unpublished material, and there is scarcely a question concerning the history of the Church in the United States which does not have new light thrown upon it by these documents. Being private reports from American prelates or superiors of a religious community to a foreign office which, it was understood, would not publish them without the consent of the author and which had no jurisdiction in the administration of the diocese, the author might readily express his sincere conviction about many subjects which he might not be able to state openly in America.

Certainly he was able to speak frankly of the difficulties and dangers, the loss and the gain, his plans and his hopes. There are letters from about eighty American dioceses covering an average period of about thirty years. In addition to the diocesan letters there are letters from some religious orders which received money directly from the Society independent of or in addition to what they may have obtained from the Ordinary in whose diocese they were established, e. g. Jesuits, Vincentians, Oblates, etc.

The published sources for the study of the Society for the Propagation of the Faith consist chiefly of the collection of the *Annales de la Propagation de la Foi.*[1] The first number appeared in 1822 in the form of a modest pamphlet circulated among the members of the newly founded Association. It contained a long letter about the missions of Louisiana (Diocese of New Orleans) and another about those of Kentucky (Diocese of Bardstown). Since then the *Annales* have appeared regularly and have preserved the same character and almost the same modest form without any pretense to literary or scientific achievement. Nevertheless the humble publication contains invaluable information for the religious history of the countries whose evangelization it narrates.[2] In the beginning it contained the correspondence between missionaries (including bishops and religious superiors), and the Society for the Propagation of the Faith, or their superiors, relatives, friends or benefactors, giving an account of their situation, their labors, their success and whatever they considered worthy of attention. In this regard it would be well to quote a word from the preface of the monumental

---

1. *Encyclopédie des Sciences Religieuses,* p. 207, Paris.
2. FRERI, *op. cit.*

work of L. E. Louvet *Les Missions Catholiques au XIXe Siècle*: "I do not pretend to be believed on my own word. I advance nothing which I have not found in the official collections, the *Annales* of the Propagation of the Faith and those of the Sainte-Enfance, the *Bulletin des Ecoles d'Orient*, the *Missions Catholiques*, the letters and reports of missionaries, all the venerable documents which inform us day by day of the labors, the sufferings and the victories of the Apostolate. One who disdainfully rejected such evidence would not be free from malice; several have come to us sealed with the blood of martyrs. According to the word of Pascal 'one ought to believe witnesses who have suffered death.'"

Although many of these letters are of the same high standard as the unpublished letters described above, at times the names and dates are missing. The letters may have been "edited." It may have been found necessary to suppress portions of them, and the questionnaire itself with all the precise information it contains is not published. The letters or articles were, moreover, written or selected at times not with the intention of showing precisely and in detail the full extent of the needs of the Mission or the diocese and all the data concerning the employment of the funds distributed and thus enabling one to gain an insight into the exact service rendered by the society to that diocese or Mission. At least this information was not continuously shown for every year, as can be seen in the unpublished letters which were used for determining the allocations. But often the published letters were selected because they were *édifiantes et curieuses* —edifying and interesting, with the aim of increasing donations, advertising the Society, glorifying the missionaries and stimulating vocations. To quote from the *Annales* themselves: "There is no need of mentioning that news is taken from the most authentic sources and that it is only published with the special approbation of the bishops or chiefs of missions."[3] At times the editors of the *Annales* and even the Central Council complained about the scarcity of information

---

3. *Annales*, t. I, fasc. i, p. 5.

and the infrequency of letters from the United States. Bishop Rosati, in a letter, August 3, 1828, explains: "The reason of the silence of most of our priests is, I believe, the persuasion which they have of the little interest which an account of their labors, could excite in the faithful of Europe, who generally expect to find something very extraordinary in the occupation of a missionary living at the extremity of the civilized world.''[4] The editor of the *Annales* asserted in 1830 that "our modest Catholic missionaries furnish us scarcely sufficient material to publish, four times a year, a little pamphlet of a hundred pages for the edification of the pious persons who cooperate in their support.''[5] In the *Missions Catholiques* the nature of the material published in the *Annales* is described as "the most important, it is that which constitutes, properly speaking, the materials for the history of the church in the countries of the Missions. They will continue to justify their title in editing the acts of martyrs and of confessors and in ascertaining the general progress of the Apostolate.''[6]

In order to estimate the services rendered by the *Annales*, one must not lose sight even of the points of view, ethnographic, geographic and historical of distant countries, that were not available at the moment of their publication. The *Annales* remain no less, a most precious collection, containing details which often afford great interest; details which were observed by the very men who were not content to live in the maritime or commercial cities, but who penetrated as far as the smallest settlements. Being a popular publication, circulating among all classes, its appeal was however popular.

Like the first Apostles who wrote to the different churches, the missionaries were always very careful to keep the Christion people informed concerning their works, by narrating, either to their superiors, to princes or to important personages who were their benefactors, the different episodes of their

---

4. Ut supra, t. III, p. 545.
5. Ut supra, t. IV, p. 185.
6. *Missions Catholiques*, t. I, p. 1, 1868.

diversified life, their fatigues, their labors, their successes. They found in this custom the means of instruction, of sustaining vocations, and of engaging pious souls to aid them, with their prayers and their generosities.[7] A need was felt for uniting the letters of all the missionaries into one collection which became the *Lettres Edifiantes*. These letters, at first given without order, were later the object of a new edition divided into four parts. The first was consecrated to the Levant, the second to America, the third to the Indies, the fourth to China, to Cochinchina and to Tonkin. The *Lettres Edifiantes* soon formed such an important collection that there were editions composed of a choice of the most interesting Lettres. Thus the first collection of this nature, published in 1809, through the care of a canon of Notre Dame of Paris, was re-edited and enlarged in 1824. A new series of the *Lettres Edifiantes* entitled *Nouvelles Lettres Edifiantes* appeared in volumes by Adrien le Clère in the years 1818, 1820, 1821, 1823.

There is no justification for the harsh criticism of the *Annales* by the *Encyclopédie des Sciences Religieuses* to the effect that the news which this collection (*Lettres Edifiantes* and the *Annales*) is not always accurate: "But the inexactitude of many of their affirmations has been so peremptorily demonstrated that one hesitates very much before according his confidence to the other accounts of such suspected witnesses. The other Catholic documents do not appear in general to merit much more confidence and impartial information to control their affirmations is very often lacking us."[8]

In the first issue of the *Missions Catholiques* the editor, in describing the scope of this weekly journal, spoke of the number of readers who were desirous of following, with their mind as well as with their heart, the advance of the missionaries in distant continents or in unknown islands, who are interested in the least details of these long and perilous voyages. They wish to know day by day, so to speak, the

---

7. GUASCO, *op. cit.*, p. 27.
8. *Encyclopédie des Sciences Religieuses*, p. 207.

works of these Apostolic laborers. They esteem that even
to only consider the human side of these things, of such
voyages, of such labors, merits the attention of the educated
world. Are not the missionaries the most serious of observers?
The knowledge of the language and the customs of the peoples
whom they evangelize naturally places them in a position to
gain exact notions concerning history, geography and the
arts and sciences." Much of the historical material is found
in articles written by missionaries which often are in serial
form running through several issues. In it are reproduced
the interesting historical occurrences under the heading
Ephémérides which are at times closely associated with the
history of the Church in the United States. The official letters of the bishops or religious superiors do not very often
find their way into this publication, but it contains the
Pontifical encyclicals and briefs, the *acta* of national and
provincial councils and the sermons of celebrated orators.
Some of this material is usually found in both the *Annales*
and the *Missions Catholiques*.

Other material for the study of the Missions in general
as well as for the Missions in the United States in particular
is to be found in the contemporary literary sources published
by the different religious orders. The *Annales de la Congrégation de la Mission* contains biographical sketches of all the
members of that congregation shortly after their death.
Besides the general information concerning their activity in
the United States there is found much material relating to
Baltimore, the Barrens, Mo., Cape Girardeau, Mo., Donaldson-
ville, La., Emmitsburg, Md., Galveston, Texas, Germantown,
Pa., La Salle, Ill., Los Angeles, Calif., Niagara, N. Y., New
Orleans, La., Sante Genevieve, Mo., St. Louis, Mo., and San
Francisco, Calif. The index to the *Annales de la Congrégation
de la Mission* is well arranged and is of great aid to the
scholar.

The *Woodstock Letters* is a private publication of the
Fathers of the Society of Jesus and, although of an entirely

---

9. *Missions Catholiques*, t. I, p. 1, 1868.

different nature from the famous *Jesuit Relations*, it is nevertheless of considerable interest as a contemporary literary source. The index to this publication, covering the years from 1872 to 1896, is divided into three parts, first, a general list of the articles, second, an index of the authors, third, sketches and obituary notices. The index was published in 1898. The Society of Jesus received $263,000 to be used in the United States, directly from the Society for the Propagation of the Faith, in addition to what their various establishments may have received from the Ordinaries of the dioceses in which they were located. Consequently, the *Woodstock Letters* are of considerable interest to one who desires to trace the results of these alms from the Society of the Propagation of the Faith.

The printed sources for the study of the results of the activity of the Society for the Propagation of the Faith in the United States are partly to be found in the publications of the American Catholic historical societies. The work of Martin I. J. Griffin, who was an indefatigable delver into the by-ways of the past and who published a large amount of original data which is of much value and assistance to the historian of the development of the Church in the United States, is found in the two quarterly publications, the *American Catholic Historical Researches* and the *Records* of the American Catholic Historical Society of Philadelphia. The *Historical Records and Studies* of the United States Catholic Historical Society in New York is also a valuable source publication. Among the more recent historical publications the *Catholic Historical Review* is found by scholars to be indispensable for the history of any place or any period of the Church in the United States. The other local publications such as the *Illinois Catholic Historical Review*, the *St. Louis Catholic Historical Review*, and the *Acta and Dicta* of St. Paul, are each of value for the history of their locality. In the *Catholic Encyclopedia* there is an article by Monsignor Joseph Freri on the Society for the Propagation of the Faith. There are also many articles on the different dioceses, bishops and nationalities. In the *Dictionnaire de Théologie Catholique,* Father G. André has an excellent article upon *Catholicism in America.* The splendid map of the ecclesiastical provinces and another showing the former location of the Indian tribes in this work are of considerable aid to the reader. Among all the works treating of the history of the Missions in general that which is preeminent is the monumental work by M. l'Abbe L. E. Louvet, *Les Missions Catholiques au XIXe Siècle.* Without it the author of this work would have been at a loss to find data upon many subjects which he has treated. Father J. B. Piolet, both in the great work *Les Missions Catholiques Françaises au XIXe Siècle,* as well as his brochure *Nos Missions et Nos Missionaires* and in others which he published with the collaboration of Ch. Vadot upon the missions of China, India and Africa, are very useful. Adrien Launay, in his *L'Histoire Générale de la Société des Missions Étrangères,* provides the student in search of the antecedents of the Society for the Propagation of the Faith much important material which is ordinarily overlooked. For the history of the Church in the United States, John Gilmary Shea, especially in his first two volumes, has treated his subject in a masterly way, and although the two latter volumes are inferior still they are very useful to the student. Shorter works on the history of the Church in America are provided in O'Gorman's *History of the Roman Catholic Church in the United States* and in the work of Father A. André, *Le Catholicisme aux Etats-Unis.* Father Thomas Hughes, in his *History of the Society of Jesus in North America,* provides a wealth of material which is not to be found elsewhere. The biographical sketches in the *Metropolitan Catholic Almanac* and *Laity's Directory* as well as the concise information in this directory concerning the different dioceses and ecclesiastical institutions contain much useful material. For the educational work of the Church, which was made possible in part by the financial assistance obtained from the Society for the Propagation of the Faith, the works by Father Burns are invaluable. For a study of the movements which cul-

minated in the foundation of the Society for the Propagation of the Faith, the biography of Miss Jaricot by M. J.
Maurin, although inclining more towards hagiography than
to impartial history, is nevertheless of distinct value.   The
two notices published by the Central Councils on *L'Oeuvre
de la Propagation de la Foi* in 1898 and 1908, together with
the brochure of the same title by M. Alexandre Guasco, the
General Secretary of the Central Council of Paris, and that
by Mgr. Joseph Freri, the delegate of the Society in the
United States, are all official, thoroughly reliable, and sincere
treatments of the foundation, organization, progress and
results of the Society for the Propagation of the Faith.   Rev.
F. Demartino's work, *Sinossi delle più interessanti notizie,*
etc., was found to be rather popular in its treatment of this
subject.

A graphic classification of this material, including only the
main sources and books used in the composition of this work,
may be given as follows:

I—SOURCES

A—Still in Manuscript

These have already been described above.   The main archival depots are those of the Propaganda, in Rome, the general
archives of the Society at Paris, and the other archival source-
material, either at Lyons or in Fribourg. There is no necessity
of giving a tabulated text of diocesan or corporative centres.

B—Printed

The most interesting general account of the printed publi-
cations concerning the Society is that contained in the
Discours by the celebrated Father Joseph Tissot, at Lyons,
May 23, 1894.

1—Publications of the Society

Annales de la Propagation de la Foi, Vol. 1, contains the
Annales for the first four years; after 1840 there is one
volume a year, and the 1922 volume is the ninety-fifth.

2—Publications of Missionary Orders

Annales de la Congrégation de la Mission.   (Lazarists or
Vincentians.)
Woodstock Letters.   (American Jesuits.)
*Missions de la Congrégation des Missionaires Oblats de Marie
Immaculée.*
Annales des Sacrés-Cœurs.   (Picpus Fathers.)
Bulletin des Ecoles Chrétiennes.   (Christian Brothers.)
Année Dominicaine.
Bulletin Trimestriel des Anciens Elèves de Saint Sulpice.

3—American Catholic Historical Publications

American Catholic Historical Researches.
Records of American Catholic Historical Society (Philadel-
phia).
Historical Records and Studies of the United States Catholic
Historical Society (New York).
Catholic Historical Review (Washington, D. C.).
Illinois Catholic Historical Review (Chicago).
St. Louis Catholic Historical Review (St. Louis, Mo.).
Acta and Dicta (St. Paul).

II—BOOKS

I—Repertories

The Catholic Encyclopedia (New York).
Encyclopedia Brittanica.
Encyclopedia of Religion and Ethics (Hastings).
La Grande Encyclopédie (Paris).
Encyclopédie des Sciences Religieuses (Paris).
Encyclopédie Théologique (Paris) 1863.
Realencyklopodie für protestantische Theologie und Kirche.
Dictionnaire de Théologie Catholique (Vacant) Paris, 1900.
Dictionnaire d'Histoire et de Géographie Ecclesiastiques
(Paris, 1913).
Kirchenlexicon.

I—DIDACTIC WORKS

I. General Works

A. Missions

1. In General

The Catholic Foreign Mission Field and the Society of the Propagation of the Faith. Two papers read at the Missionary Conference held at Washington, D. C. (April 6-12, 1904), by the Rev. J. Freri, D. C. L., National Director and the Rev. Jas. A. Walsh, Boston Diocesan Director of the Propagation of the Faith.

Henrion, *Histoire Générale des Missions* (1219-1844) Paris, 1850.

Louvet, *Les Missions Catholiques au XIXe Siècle* (Paris, 1894).

Piolet, *Les Missions Catholiques Françaises au XIXe Siècle,* (Paris, 1903).

Piolet, *Les Missions Catholiques Françaises* (Paris, 1900).

Piolet, *La France Hors de France* (Paris, 1900).

Piolet, *Nos Missions et Nos Missionnaires* (Paris, 1904).

Groffier, *Héros Trop Oubliés de Notre Epopée Coloniale* (Paris, 1906).

Leroy-Beaulieu, *Les Congrégations Religieuses et L'Expansion de la France* (Paris, 1904).

Guasco, *Cent ans d'Apostolat Catholique dans les Missions* (1800-1900) Paris, 1900.

Werner, *Atlas des Missions Catholiques* (Fribourg, 1886).

Marshall, *Christian Missions, Their Agents and Their Results* (London, 1863).

Moore, *The Expansion of Christendom and the Naturalization of Christianity in the Orient in the XIX Century* (London, 1920).

2. In Particular Countries

Piolet-Vadot, *La Religion Catholique en Chine.*

Piolet-Vadot, *L'Eglise Catholique en Indo-Chine.*

PIOLET-VADOT, *L'Eglise Catholique dans le Continent Noir.*
PIOLET-VADOT, *L'Eglise Catholique aux Indes.*

3. MISSIONS OF PARTICULAR ORDERS

HEIMBUCHER, *Die Orden und Kongregationen der Katholischen Kirche*, 3 volumes—Paderborn, 1907.
Mémoire Historique sur les Constitutions de la Congrégation des Missions Etrangères.
LAUNAY, *L'Histoire Générale de la Société des Missions Etrangères.*
La Société des Missions Etrangères (Paris, 1919).

4. PROTESTANT MISSIONS

The most important organization, whose history parallels that of the Society the first hundred years is the Society for Promoting Christian Knowledge, which was founded in 1698 at London. The Society for the Propagation of the Gospel was founded in 1701, at London, for special missionary work in the United States, Cf. SEWALL, *The Society for Promoting Christian Knowledge* (London, 1885) and *An Important Chapter in English Church History, the S. P. C. K.* (London, 1900).
PISANI, *Les Missions Protestantes à la Fin du XIXe Siècle* (Paris, 1903).
BALDWIN, *Foreign Missions of the Protestant Churches* (Chicago, 1900).
MONDAIN, *Un Siècle de Mission Protestante à Madagascar* (Paris, 1920).
DIETERLEN, *Pourquoi les Missions?* (Paris, 1920).
Almanach des Missions (Montpelier, 1921).

B—CHURCH HISTORIES

Apart from the general Church histories of Hergenröther, Kraus, Funk and others, the work which gave special direction to this volume is:
MOURRET, *Histoire Générale de l'Eglise* (Paris, 1920).

Other works of value are:

PECHENARD, *Un Siècle de Mouvement du Monde* 1800-1900 (Paris, 1899).

FORBES, *L'Eglise Catholique au Dix-Neuvième Siècle* (1800-1900) (Paris, 1903).

LORETTO, *Petite Histoire de L'Eglise Catholique au XIXe Siècle* (Paris, 1909).

BAUNARD, *Un Siècle de L'Eglise de France,* 1800-1900 (Paris, 1919).

C—CHURCH HISTORY OF THE UNITED STATES

BAIRD, *La Religion aux Etats-Unis D'Amérique* (Paris, 1844).

VICOMTE DE MEAUX, *L'Eglise Catholique et la Liberté aux Etats-Unis* (Paris, 1893).

JANNET, *Les Etats-Unis Contemporains* (Paris, 1876).

CHEVALIER, *Lettres sur L'Amérique du Nord* (Paris, 1837).

DETOCQUEVILLE, *The Republic of the United States of America.*

SHEA, JOHN GILMARY, *The Catholic Church in the United States.*

   The Catholic Church in Colonial Days, Volume 1, 1521-1763.

   The Life and Times of Archbishop Carroll, Volume 2, 1763-1815.

   History of the Catholic Church in the United States, Volume 3, 1808-15 to 1843, Volume 4, 1843-1866.

O'GORMAN, *A History of the Roman Catholic Church in the United States* (New York, 1895).

ANDRE, *Le Catholicisme aux Etats-Unis de L'Amérique du Nord* (Paris, 1910).

ANDRE, *Une Page D'Histoire sur les Associations Cultuelles* (Paris, 1907).

ANDRE, *Luttes pour la Liberté de L'Eglise Catholique aux Etats-Unis* (Paris, 1907).

HUGHES, THOMAS, S. J., *History of the Society of Jesus in North America,* 4 vols. (London, 1910-17).

SHEA, JOHN GILMARY, *History of the Catholic Missions Among* the *Indian Tribes of the United States,* 1529-1854, New York, 1855.

The Laity's Directory to the Church Service, for the Year of Our Lord, 1822.

The Metropolitan Catholic Almanack and Laity's Directory, 1833.

The Catholic Directory.

SPALDING, M. J., *Sketches of the Early Catholic Missions of Kentucky* (Louisville, 1844).

TIMON, *Missions in Western New York and Church History of the Diocese of Buffalo* (Buffalo, 1862).

II. SPECIAL WORKS

BURNS, *Catholic Education* (New York, 1917).

BURNS, *The Principles, Origin and Establishment of the Catholic School System in the United States* (New York, 1912).

BURNS, *The Growth and Development of the Catholic School System in the United States* (New York, 1912).

L'Œuvre de la Propagation de la Foi (Paris, 1898).

L'Œuvre de la Propagation de la Foi, Dix Années D'Apostolat Catholique dans les Missions, 1898-1907 (Lyons, 1908).

GUASCO, *L'Œuvre de la Propagation de la Foi* (Paris, 1911).

FRERI, *The Society for the Propagation of the Faith and the Catholic Missions* (New York, 1922).

DEMARTINO, *Sinossi delle più interessanti notizie sull 'Opera della Propagazione della Fede* (Sorrento, 1893).

STEINER, *History of Education* (Washington, 1894).

III

BIOGRAPHIES

MAURIN, *Vie Nouvelle de Pauline-Marie Jaricot* (Paris, 1892).

MASSON, *Pauline-Marie Jaricot* (Lyons, 1899).

HUEN-DU BOURG, *Vie du Cardinal de Cheverus* (Paris, 1841).

O'DANIEL, *The Right Rev. Edward Dominic Fenwick, O. P.* (Washington, 1921).

Laveille, *Le Père De Smet* (Liège, 1907).

Desgeorge, *Mgr. Flaget, Evêque de Bardstown et Louisville* (Paris, 1855).

IV
Periodicals

Le Correspondent, Tome 284 (Nouv. Serie: 248e) (September 25, 1921).

Etudes, Tome 167e May 5, 1921 (Paris).

L'Echo de Paris, February 14, 1921.

L'Action Catholique, October 19, 1921 (Montreal).

L'Osservatore Romano, 27 Gennalo, 1921 (Rome).

The Western Tablet, March 27, 1852 (Chicago).

CONCLUSION

At the conclusion of this general survey of the foundation, organization, administration and success of the Society for the Propagation of the Faith during the first hundred years of its existence, it is fitting that the reader's attention should be drawn expressly to the fact that the great Church of the United States which has benefited so much from the generous funds of the Society has a history special to itself and deserves a separate volume of its own. The phenomenal growth of the Catholic Faith in this country since the consecration of John Carroll as its first bishop in 1790, has no parallel in history. From every part of Europe immigrants came, and with the many unforeseen difficulties they met here in their new homes, they looked to their native lands for help and for encouragement. The Societies of Vienna and of Munich did splendid work in supporting the people of Germany and Austria in the development of their religious life in this country; but over and above their assistance, the Society of Lyons and Paris came to the aid of the bishops, priests and people, without distinction, in the colossal task which faced them. Consequently the Society for the Propagation of the Faith has interwoven its own story into the story of Catholicism's advance in the New World, and every advance it made in science, in literature, in the apostolate, of the Gospel, of education and of social welfare, has its corresponding effect upon the inner life of the Church in this country.

During the past few years, especially since the time that the Church in the United States was removed from the jurisdiction of the Sacred Congregation de Propaganda Fide (1908), a movement has been supported by members of the American Hierarchy for the purpose of bringing within the control of the American Episcopate the disbursement of all funds gathered in this country for the upkeep of the Missions.

This sentiment was expressed in the Pastoral Letter of the American Hierarchy in 1919, and has since been under consideration by the authorities at Rome.

Recently (Dec. 16, 1921), Cardinal Van Rossum, Prefect of the Sacred Congregation of Propaganda wrote to Archbishop Moeller, former Chairman of the Department of Missions, Home and Foreign, of the National Catholic Welfare Council, and now one of the Board of Governors of the American Board of Catholic Missions, to the effect that his Holiness, Benedict XV, in an audience granted December 12, had ratified and confirmed the American plan for promoting missionary activity. The letter is as follows:

Roma, 16 Dicembre, 1921.

Illme. ac Revme. Domine.

Cum amplitudo tua Episcoporum Comitatus pro Missionibus catholicis adiuvandis vota ac desideria in congressu hierarchiae Americae Septentrionalis superiore septembri habito manifestatâ SSmo. Dno. Nostro retulerit Consociationis illius ad probationen necnon spirituales favores enixe expostulans, benigne voluit Summus idem Pontifex ut res, duabus iam vicibus ab hac S. C. Christiano Nomini Propagando perpensa, tertio tandem ab eadem examinaretur.

Porro Emi Patres in consessu diei 5 Decembris, disaptato denuo integro negotio, in hoc demum convenerunt ut S. C. paratam se ac propensam declararet ad annuendum desideriis saepius ab Episcopis Americae Septentrionalis expressis.

Simul tamen voluerunt ut antequam gratia concedatur et super hac re rescriptum detur S. Congregationi manifestaretur quota pars totius collectae pro Missionibus exteris reservetur arbitrio S. Sedis distribuenda.

Quam Emorum, Patrum sententiam SSmus., Dnus., Noster Benedictus Div. Prov. P. P. XV, in audientia diei 12 Decembris Sacrae huius Congregationis Secretario concessa ratam habuit ac confirmavit.

Quae omnia libenter Tecum eiusdem Summi Pontificis iussu, communico ut Episcopis omnibus Comitatu adherentibus referas, eam spem nutriens fore ut brevi, clarum responsam ab A. T. excipiam quo aequivocatione omni sublata, negotium hoc, magni momenti rite citoque expediatur.

Interim vero precor Deum ut Amplitudini Tuae donis cumulatissimus faveat.

Addmus Servus

G. M. Van Rossum

Praef.

More recent decisions of the Congregation of Rites provide for the insertion of an invocation in the Litany of the Saints and for a Votive Mass of the Propagation of the Faith. These decisions are as follows:

Rescripta Ad Augendam Celebritatem Sollemnium Tertio Exeunte Saeculo Ab Instituta Sacra Congregatione De Propaganda Fidei Indictorum.

I

De Additione Opportunae Invocationis Litaniis Sanctorum

Beatissimo Padre,

La Commissione per i festeggiamenti del centenario della S. Congregazione di Propaganda, presieduta sall'Emo Cardinale Prefetto della medesima, supplica instantemente la Santita Vostra perche voglia benignamente degnarsi di approvare la seguente invocazione e di dare ordine che venga inserita nelle Litanie dei Santi:

Ut omnes errantes ad unitatem Ecclesiae revocare, et infideles universos ad Evangelii lumen perducere digneris: Te rogamus, audi nos.

ROMANA

Sanctissimus Dominus Noster Pius Papa XI, referente infrascripto Cardinali Sacrae Rituum Congregationi Praefecto, suprascriptam invocationem pro privata et publica recitatione, necnon pro additione Litaniis Sanctorum post invocationem *Ut cuncto populo christiano*, etc., approbare et ad universam Ecclesiam extendere dignatus est. Contrariis non obstantibus quibuscumque. Die 22 martii, 1922.

A. Card. Vico, Ep. Portuen. et S. Rufinae,
S. R. C. Praefectus.

L. S.   Alexander Verde, *Secretarius.*

II.

De Celebratione Missae Votivae Pro Fidei Propagatione Semel in Anno in Qualibet Dioecesi.

Beatissimo Padre,

La Commissione per i festeggiamenti del terzo centenario della S. Congregazione di Propaganda, presieduta dall'Emo Cardinale Prefetto della medesima, supplica umilmente la Santita Vostra perche voglia benignamente disporre che in ogni diocesi sia celebrata una volta l'anno, in giorno da stabilirsi dai rispettivi Ordinari, la Messa votiva *de Fidei Propagatione*, nell'intento di eccitare cosi maggiormente il clero a favore delle sacre missioni ed ottenere dal Signore gli aiuti necessari per il maggior sviluppo delle medesime.

ROMANA

Sanctiisimus Dominus Noster Pius Papa XI, his precibus ab infrascripto Cardinali Sacrae Rituum Congregationi Praefecto relatis, benigne annuit pro gratia iuxta petita, ita tamen, ut praedicta Missa votiva *de Propagatione Fidei* cum *Gloria* et *Credo* celebrari possit semel in anno diebus ab Ordinario cuiusque loci designandis, exceptis tamen Festis duplicibus I et II classis, Dominicis maioribus, necnon Octavis I et II ordinis, Feriis et Vigiliis quae sint ex privilegiatis: servatis Rubricis. Contrariis non obstantibus quibuscumque. Die 22 martii, 1922.

A. Card. Vico, Ep. Pottuen. et S. Rufinae,
S. R. C. Praefectus.
Alexander Verde, *Secretarius*

L. S.

(*Acta Apostolicae Sedis* Vol. XIV. No. 7,
3 April, 1922, pp. 200-201).

No tribute need be paid to those who have done noble service in Paris and in Lyons, in directing the work of cooperating with the Catholic hierarchy of the United States in their devotion to the Church of Christ. From the very origin of the Society, its leaders have desired to remain unknown, and, in fact, unseen. Theirs has been the greater plan of working in the quiet for the spread of the Faith, and the rounding-out of the first hundred years of the activities of the Society they have strengthened and solidified with their unstinted effort is the best tribute that might be offered in this centenary year.

APPENDIX

TOTAL RECEIPTS OF THE SOCIETY FOR THE PROPAGATION OF THE FAITH

	frs.		frs.		frs.
1822	22,915	1866	5,145,558	1910	7,088,690
1823	49,487	1867	5,149,918	1911	7,382,319
1824	82,259	1868	5,308,867	1912	8,178,902
1825	122,598	1869	5,217,092	1913	8,114,983
1826	104,888	1870	4,198,867	1914	5,592,642
1827	254,993	1871	5,020,897	1915	6,275,987
1828	267,269	1872	5,602,645	1916	6,334,565
1829	300,659	1873	5,524,175	1917	6,778,816
1830	293,082	1874	5,485,515	1918	8,005,704
1831	308,936	1875	5,797,463	1919	17,929,292
1832	309,947	1876	5,930,950	1920	
1833	354,345	1877	6,142,926	1921	
1834	404,727	1878	6,591,741		
1835	541,675	1879	6,031,648		
1836	729,867	1880	6,020,039		
1837	927,304	1881	6,906,058		
1838	1,343,640	1882	6,414,438		
1839	1,895,682	1883	6,370,516		
1840	2,473,578	1884	6,832,518		
1841	2,752,214	1885	6,629,258		
1842	3,233,486	1886	6,649,952		
1843	3,562,088	1887	6,462,276		
1844	3,540,903	1888	6,362,142		
1845	3,707,561	1889	6,541,918		
1846	3,575,775	1890	7,072,811		
1847	3,513,687	1891	6,694,457		
1848	2,845,691	1892	6,621,674		
1849	3,060,516	1893	6,599,622		
1850	3,082,729	1894	6,820,164		
1851	3,323,893	1895	6,587,049		
1852	4,790,468	1896	6,332,686		
1853	3,935,149	1897	6,772,879		
1854	3,722,766	1898	6,700,921		
1855	3,778,180	1899	6,820,273		
1856	3,905,067	1900	6,848,700		
1857	4,191,716	1901	6,728,666		
1858	6,684,567	1902	6,598,044		
1859	5,260,595	1903*	6,375,241		
1860	4,547,399	1904	6,907,694		
1861	4,700,227	1905	6,626,734		
1862	4,721,194	1906	6,522,922		
1863	4,788,496	1907	6,695,553		
1864	5,090,041	1908	6,472,437		
1865	5,139,895	1909	6,786,088		

(*Totals from 1903 to 1913 are for disbursements and differ from receipts of the year because of reserve fund from previous year.)

MONEY RECEIVED BY THE AMERICAN DIOCESES

FROM

THE SOCIETY FOR THE PROPAGATION OF THE FAITH

Alaska	$88,726	From	1893	to	1912
Albany	43,844	''	1847	''	1866
Alexandria	175,069	''	1854	''	1918
Alton	41,600	''	1857	''	1869
Baker City	24,722	''	1905	''	1922
Baltimore	56,757	''	1823	''	1865
Boise	38,454	''	1870	''	1922
Boston	52,839	''	1829	''	1864
Brooklyn	4,800	''	1856	''	1867
Buffalo	110,214	''	1847	''	1866
Burlington	40,200	''	1853	''	1884
Charleston	220,360	''	1828	''	1922
Cheyenne	9,514	''	1897	''	1918
Chicago	99,655	''	1844	''	1866
Cincinnati	118,569	''	1823	''	1869
Cleveland	62,644	''	1847	''	1876
Columbus	3,200	''	1868	''	1869
Concordia	37,160	''	1887	''	1901
Corpus Christi	75,866	''	1874	''	1922
Covington	37,000	''	1854	''	1887
Crookston	16,604	''	1911	''	1922
Dallas	4,050	''	1891	''	1902
Denver	47,477	''	1868	''	1918
Detroit	113,453	''	1828	''	1887
Dubuque	119,398	''	1838	''	1866
Duluth	16,814	''	1890	''	1918
El Paso	200	''	1912	''	1920
Erie	30,600	''	1854	''	1869
Fargo	15,949	''	1890	''	1920
Fort Wayne	34,400	''	1858	''	1869
Galveston	249,370	''	1846	''	1901
Great Falls	15,793	''	1909	''	1922
Green Bay	25,650	''	1868	''	1888
Hartford	51,028	''	1845	''	1866
Helena	19,678	''	1882	''	1918
Indianapolis	237,978	''	1834	''	1869
Kansas City	2,000	''	1880	''	1881
La Crosse	15,720	''	1868	''	1887
Lead	26,396	''	1904	''	1922
Leavenworth	118,490	''	1856	''	1883
Lincoln	1,005	''	1889	''	1918
Little Rock	105,120	''	1844	''	1892
Los Angeles	99,800	''	1849	''	1877
Louisville	159,816	''	1822	''	1867
Marquette	61,380	''	1854	''	1885
Milwaukee	56,432	''	1844	''	1866
Mobile	109,918	''	1828	''	1918
Nashville	100,767	''	1839	''	1887
Natchez	197,701	''	1839	''	1922

Newark	23,600	From	1854	to	1866
New Orleans	124,160	"	1822	"	1872
New York	112,160	"	1827	"	1866
North Carolina	70,559	"	1868	"	1918
Oklahoma	100,073	"	1876	"	1918
Omaha	60,360	"	1859	"	1883
Oregon City	171,294	"	1844	"	1891
Peoria	1,000	"	1877		
Philadelphia	51,161	"	1829	"	1859
Pittsburgh	85,600	"	1843	"	1868
Portland	18,190	"	1856	"	1867
Richmond	128,125	"	1841	"	1922
Rochester	4,000	"	1868	"	1869
Sacramento	36,200	"	1860	"	1876
St. Augustine	118,347	"	1836	"	1908
St. Cloud	13,140	"	1889	"	1890
St. Joseph	6,600	"	1868	"	1872
St. Louis	196,155	"	1827	"	1872
St. Paul	95,785	"	1850	"	1872
Salt Lake	16,400	"	1872	"	1887
San Antonio	34,209	"	1874	"	1918
San Francisco	45,600	"	1853	"	1884
Santa Fe	206,114	"	1851	"	1918
Savannah	146,465	"	1850	"	1922
Seattle	120,842	"	1847	"	1892
Sioux Falls	13,900	"	1889	"	1894
Tucson	136,148	"	1869	"	1922
Wheeling	58,205	"	1850	"	1879
Wichita	7,640	"	1887	"	1895
Wilmington	16,920	"	1868	"	1892
Porto Rico	61,702	"	1906	"	1921
Philippine Islands	331,024	"	1905	"	1921
Hawaii	162,058	"	1899	"	1921
Guam	2,400	....			1921
*Miscellaneous	849,702				
Total	$7,020,974	"	1822	"	1922

*Of this amount $516,592 was given to some Religious Orders in addition to what they may have received from the Ordinary in whose diocese they were established.

The following sums were given to Religious Societies for use in the United States:

Jesuits	$263,089
Lazarists	158,800
Oblates	45,657
Congregation of the Holy Cross	18,657
Redemptorists	11,088
Fathers of Mercy	7,980
Benedictines	6,000
Dominicans	5,320
Total	$516,592

II. PERSONNEL OF THE MISSIONS ASSISTED BY THE PROPAGATION OF THE FAITH IN 1921

Augustinians (O. S. A.)	1256	Rome.	Vic.: Cookstown, Hunan, N. Pref.: Amazon.
Augustinians of the Assumption (A. A.)	1851	Rome.	Dio.: Athens. Vic.: Constantinople.
Augustinian Recollets (A. R.)	1438	Spain.	Vic.: Casanare. Pref.: Palawan.
Benedictines (O. S. B.)	529	Mt. Cassin.	Vic.: Katanga, Kimberley (Australia), Wonsan. Pref.: Lindi, Transvaal, No. Zululand.
Canons of the Holy Cross (Croisiers) (O. S. C.)	1211	Holland.	Mis.: Uelle, N.
Carmelites (Discalced) (O. C. D.)	1528	Rome.	Dio.: Quilon, Verapoly. Pref.: Bagdad.
Children of the Immaculate Heart of Mary (C. I. H. M.)	1849	Spain.	Vic.: Fernando Poo. Pref.: Choco.
Chinese Mission Society	1916	Omaha, Nebr.	Mis.: Hupeh, E.
Cistercians (Trappists) (O. C. R.)	1098	Rome.	Dio.: Hakodate. Mis.: Chili, N.
Congregation of the Holy Cross (C. S. C.)	1821	Rome.	Dio.: Dacca.
Congregation of the Holy Ghost (C. S. Sp.)	1848	Paris.	Dio.: Port Louis. Vic.: Bagamoyo; Diego Suarez; Gaboon; Guinea (Fr.); Kilima Ndjaro; Loango; Senegambia; Sierra Leone; Ubanghi; Ubanghi-chari; Zanzibar No. Pref.:Cameroon; Congo, Lower; Cubango; Katanga, No.; Mayotta (Nossi Be); Niger, Lower; St. Peter and Miquelon; Teffé.
Congregation of Jesus and Mary (Eudists) (C. J. M.)	1643	Rome.	Vic.: Gulf of St. Lawrence.
Congregation of the Missions (Lazarists) (C. M.)	1632	Paris.	Dio.: Ispahan. Vic.: Abyssinia; Chekiang, East; Chekiang, West; Chili, Central; Chili, East; Chili, Maritime; Chili, North; Chili, Southwest; Ft. Dauphin; Kanchow; Ki-han-fou; Kioukiang; San Pedro de Sulam; You-kiang. Pref.: Arauca.
Congregation of the Passion (Passionists) (C. P.)	1737	Rome.	Dio.: Nicopolis. Mis.: Hunan, N.

Congregation of the Sacred Hearts of Jesus and Mary (Pic-pusians) (S. H. Pic.)	1817	Braine, Belgium.	Vic.: Hawaii; Marquesas; Tahiti. Pref.: New Guinea, West.
Company of Mary (M. C.)	1705	St. Laurent sur Sevres, France.	Vic.: Llanos de San Martin; Shiré.
Dominicans (O. P.)	1215	Rome.	Vic.: Amoy; Canelos e Macas; Curacao; Fokien; Tonkin, Central; Tonkin, East; Tonkin, North; Uellé, East; Urubamba. Pref.: Formosa; Langson; Shikoku.
Foreign Missions (American) (A.F.M.)	1910	Maryknoll, New York,	Mis.: Canton.
Foreign Missions (Belgian) (B. F. M.)	1865	Scheut-lez-Bruxelles, Belgium.	Vic.: Free State (Leopoldville); Kansu, North; Kassai; Mongolia, Central; Mongolia, East; Mongolia, South; New Antwerp. Pref.: Ili; Kansu, South.
Foreign Missions (England) (E. F. M.)	1866	Mill Hill, England.	Dio.: Madras. Vic.: Upper Nile. Pref.: Borneo, North; Kafiristan.
Foreign Missions (Milan) (M. F. M.)	1850	Milan, Italy.	Dio.: Hyderabad; Krishnagar. Vic.: Burma, East; Honan, East; Honan, North; Honan, South; Hongkong.
Foreign Missions of Paris (P. F. M.)	1663	Paris.	Dio.: Coimbatore; Hakodate; Kumbakonam; Malacca; Mysore; Nagasaki; Osaka; Pondicherry; Tokyo. Vic.: Burma, North; Burma, South; Cambodia; Canton; Cochin China, East; Cochin China, North; Cochin China, West; Hainan; Kien-tchang; Kui-chow; Kwangsi; Laos; Manchuria, North; Manchuria, South; Seoul; Siam; Si-chuan, East; Si-chuan, South; Si-chuan, West; Swatow; Taikou; Thibet; Tonkin, Maritime; Tonkin, South; Tonkin, Upper; Tonkin, West; Yun-nan.
Foreign Missions of Parma (F. M. P.)		Parma, Italy.	Vic.: Honan, West.
Foreign Missions of (Rome (R. F. M.)	1874	Rome.	Vic.: Shensi, South. Mis.: Lower California.
Foreign Missions of Turin (Consolata) (T. F. M.)	1900	Turin, Italy.	Vic.: Kenia. Pref.: Kaffa.

Franciscan Minors (O. F. M.)	1209	Rome.	Vic.: Alep; Beni; Chaco; Egypt; Hunan, South; Hupeh, East; Hupeh, Northwest; Hupeh, South; Lybia; Morocco; Shansi, North; Shansi, South; Shantung, East; Shantung, North; Shensi, Central; Shensi, North; Zamora. Pref.: Rhodes; Sapporo; Ucayali. Mis.: Assiout; Constantinople; Putumayo.
Franciscan Capuchins (O. M. Cap.)	1858	Rome.	Dio.: Agra, Ajmere; Allahabad; Candia; Lahore; Port Victoria; Simla. Vic.: Arabia; Bluefields; Borneo, South; Caroline and Marianne Islands; Dar-es-Salaam; Eritrea; Gallas; Goajira; Guam; Sofia. Pref.: Araucania; Belgian Oubanghi; Caqueta; Djibouti; Misox and Calanca; Rhetia; Sumatra; Upper Solimoes. Mis.: Mardin; Syria; Trebizonde.
Missionaries of Africa (White Fathers)	1868	Algiers, Africa.	Vic.: Bamoko; Bangueolo; Congo, Upper; Kivu; Nyassa; Ougadougou; Tanganyika; Uganda; Unyanyembe; Victoria Nyanza. Pref.: Ghardaia.
Missionaries of La Salette (M. S.)	1852	Susa, Italy.	Vic.: Antsirabe.
Missionaries of St. Francis de Sales (Annecy) (M. S. F. S.)	1833	Annecy, France.	Dio.: Nagpur; Vizagapatam.
Missionaries of the Sacred Heart (Issoudun) (M. S. H.)	1854	Rome.	Dio.: Port Victoria. Vic.: Gilbert and Ellis Is; Marshall Is; New Britain; New Guinea (British); New Guinea (Dutch).
Oblates of Mary Immaculate (O. M. I.)	1826	Rome.	Dio.: Colombo; Jaffna. Vic.: Athabaska; Basutoland; Keewatin; Kimberley (Africa); Mackenzie; Natal; Transvaal; Yukon. Pref., Cimbebasia Lower.
Oblates of St. Francis de Sales (Troyes) (O. S. F. S.)	1871	Rome.	Vic.: Orange River. Pref.: Grand Namaqualand.
Premonstratensians (Norbertins) (O. Praem)	1119	Rome.	Pref.: Uellé West.

Priests of the Sacred Heart (St. Quentin) (S. H. Q.)	1877	Rome.	Vic.: Stanley Falls. Pref.: Adamaua; Celebes Is.
Redemptorists (C. SS. R.)	1732	Rome.	Dio.: Perth; Roseau. Vic.: Dutch Guiana. Pref.: Matadi.
Religious Missionaries of Marianhill (R. M. M.)	1913	S. Africa.	Mis: Mariannhill (Natal).
Secular Priests			Vic.: Antofagasta; Cape, East; Cape, West; Denmark; Norway; Sweden; Tarapaca. Pref.: Cape, Central; French Guiana.
Society of the African Missions of Lyons (L. Af. M.)	1856	Lyons.	Vic.: Benin; Dahomey; Delta of Nile; Gold Coast; Ivory Coast; Niger, West; Togo. Pref.: Koroko; Liberia; Niger, East.
Society of the Divine Saviour (S. D. S.)	1881	Rome.	Pref.: Assam.
Society of the Divine Word (S. V. D.)	1875	Steyl, Holland.	Vic.: Shantung, South. Pref.: New Guinea, East; Nygata; Sunda Islands.
Society of Jesus (Jesuits) (S. J.)	1540	Rome.	Dio.: Bombay; Calcutta; Galle; Mangalore; Patna; Poona; Trichinopoly; Trincomali. Vic.: Alaska; Batavia; British Guiana; British Honduras; Chili, Southeast; Fianarantsoa; Jamaica; Nankin (Kiangnan); Napo; Tananarive. Pref.: Kwango; Zambezi.
Society of Mary (Marists) (S. M.)	1836	Rome.	Dio: Wellington Vic.: Central Oceanica; Fiji; Navigators Islands (Samoa); New Caledonia; New Hebrides; Solomon Islands, South. Pref.: Solomon Islands, North.
Society of St. Francis de Sales (Salesians) (S. S. F. S.)	1855	Turin, Italy.	Vic.: Magellan; Mendez et Gualaquiza; Patagonia, North; Shiu-chow. Pref.: Rio Negro.
Sons of the Sacred Heart of Jesus of Verona (V. A. M.)	1867	Verona, Italy.	Vic.: Bhar-el-Gazal; Khartoum.
Sylvestrin Benedictines (S. O. S. B.)	1231	Rome.	Dio.: Kandy.
Syro Malabar Rite....			Vic.: Changanacherry; Ernakulam; Kottayam; Trichur.
Trinitarians (O. SS. T.)	1198	Rome.	Pref.: Benadir.

Exercise 1918

REPARTITION

Somme disponible de ....

Somme disponible de ....

Difference ed ....

M ....

MISSIONS	1re Décision LYON	1re Décision PARIS	2e Décision LYON	2e Décision PARIS	3e Décision LYON	3e Décision PARIS	1917	OBSERVATIONS
EUROPE								
1 Essex							"	
2 Lausanne & Genève	10,000						10,000	
3 Coire	"						"	
4 Bâle	5,000						5,000	
5 Cologne	"						"	
6 Trèves	"						"	
7 Munster	"						"	
8 Paderborn	"						"	
9 Allemagne du Nord	"						"	
10 Limbourg	"						"	
A REPORTER	15,000						15,000	

RÉCAPITULATION

Année Précédente	CHAPITRES	1re Décision LYON	1re Décision PARIS	2e Décision LYON	2e Décision PARIS	3e Décision LYON	3e Décision PARIS
194,500	Europe	222,300					
750,500	Asie	785,500					
813,274 £6	Afrique	856,000					
184,000	Amérique	174,000					
185,500	Océanie	190,000					
2,555,000	Gdes Congrégations	3,350,000					
4,682,774 £6	Total	5,577,800					

VITA

Edward J. Hickey was born at Detroit, Mich., December 13, 1893. He attended the Cathedral School of that city, and then entered the University of Detroit, where he graduated in 1914 with the degree of Bachelor of Arts. He then entered the Graduate School of Business Administration of Harvard University, and completed this course with the degree Master in Business Administration, in 1916. Later, he submitted a thesis to the University of Detroit, for which he received the degree A. M. His theological course was made at St. Paul Seminary, St. Paul, Minn., and he was ordained to the priesthood in Detroit by Right Rev. Michael James Gallagher, D. D., on June 15, 1919. He then entered the School of Philosophy of the Catholic University of America, as a graduate student. In 1920, he received the degrees S. T. B. and J. C. B. from the University. In company with his major professor Dr. Guilday, he went to Europe, and during the academic year 1920-1921, he attended the Institut Catholique de Paris, where he followed a course in the French Revolution under Professor Gautherot; the Sorbonne, where he studied the History of Modern Europe, and the History of Contemporary Europe, under Prof. Seignobos; and the École des Chartes, where he studied Latin Paleography under Prof. Berger. During the Scholastic year 1921-1922 he was a member of the American Church History Seminar, under Rev. Dr. Peter Guilday. He followed the course in American Political History under Professor Charles H. McCarthy, Ph. D. To all his professors, the writer expresses his sincere gratitude and appreciation.